Militarism in India

For Veronica and Violetta
My loves, my life

Militarism in India

The Army and Civil Society in Consensus

Apurba Kundu

TAURIS ACADEMIC STUDIES
London • New York

Published in 1998 by Tauris Academic Studies
an imprint of I.B.Tauris & Co Ltd
Victoria House, Bloomsbury Square, London WC1B 4DZ
175 Fifth Avenue, New York NY 10010

In the United States and Canada distributed by St. Martin's Press
175 Fifth Avenue, New York NY 10010

ISBN 1 86064 318 3

A full CIP record for this book is available from the British Library
A full CIP record for this book is available from the Library of Congress

Library of Congress catalog card: available

Printed and bound in Great Britain (from
camera-ready copy supplied by the author)
by WBC Ltd, Bridgend

CONTENTS

TABLES, MAPS AND ILLUSTRATIONS

Tables

Maps

Illustrations

PREFACE

The study of any country's civil-military relations is a sensitive issue at the best of times. This is even more applicable in the case of India for, despite its unarguable democratic nature, successive governments have taken inherited British ideas of government secrecy to new heights. Not that I was hindered in any way from conducting my research, far from it: government officials more than once visited my family home in Calcutta to inquire after my work! However, India's remarkable record of never having experienced a military coup d'état made my examination all the more politically sensitive and open to misunderstanding. I was not surprised to learn that my research was being portrayed by certain circles in the Indian parliament and Indian (and US) press as 'a thinly disguised suggestion' that the military consider a coup d'état'.[1] In fact, the opposite is true. From the outset, my research was an attempt to understand the factors which have made a military takeover of government in India extraordinarily unlikely.

In order to examine the 'non-event' of an Indian coup, I turned first and foremost to those who bear most responsibility for this enviable state of affairs; that is, senior retired Indian armed forces' officers themselves. Although there remains no systematic way of seeking them out (the Indian government publishes no such list of names and addresses), once found, I discovered these men forthright, open and keen to share their experiences and opinions on a variety of sensitive topics. I salute their unfailing kindness and generosity of time and energy for, without their cooperation, this book would not have been possible nor my research so enjoyable. Frustratingly, due to their position and/or the sensitive nature of my research, I cannot mention them by name here. However, my thanks are sincere and heartfelt.

Happily, I can acknowledge the deep debt of gratitude owed to Thomas J. Nossiter, Professor Emeritus of Government at the London School of Economics and Political Science and Visiting Professor at the University of Leeds. His guidance and encouragement have been infinite and inspirational. I also am indebted to Lieut.-General Dr. M.L. Chibber for allowing me access to his unpublished list of Indian officers compiled in the course of his own research. I wish, too, to thank Professors David Palmer and Thomas Thornton of the Johns Hopkins University School of Advanced International Studies for having set me on my way to discovering the rich and barely tapped vein of Indian civil-military relations. My colleagues at the University of Bradford Department of Social and Economic Studies (SES) deserve a mention for their support and understanding, as do the librarians of the British Library of Political and Economic Science, Nehru Memorial Museum and Library, and School of Oriental and African Studies (SOAS) for their invaluable help and assistance.

As my research progressed, I had the opportunity to present my findings at a variety of conferences and seminars. For their encouragement as well as their searching questions, I wish to thank the various audiences of the British Association for South Asian Studies, Institute for Commonwealth Studies, King's College Department of War Studies, Political Studies Association (PSA) of the United Kingdom, Punjab Research Group (PRG), Ruprecht-Karls-Universität Südasien-Institut, SOAS Centre of South Asian Studies, University of Hull Centre for Indian Studies, and Wolfson College, Cambridge. Some of the material presented in this book has appeared in one form or another in a variety of journals and, as such, I wish to acknowledge the respective editors and referees of *Asian Affairs, Defence Today, Indian Defence Review* and *Pacific Affairs* for their valuable comments and constructive criticism. My research findings also have appeared in the conference and/or working papers of the PRG, PSA and SES.

Non-academics I must thank figure highly; none more so than Dr. Shubendu Kundu for his unflagging assistance at the initial stages of this work. Without the gracious hospitality of Ashutosh and Grace Majumdar in New Delhi and the Sett extended family in Bangalore and Goa, my research may have been possible but not nearly so enjoyable. My heartfelt thanks also go to Noma for her exemplary kindness always. Finally, a thought for my parents, Arabinda and Alessandra, who helped support my studies over all too many years: *grazie mille!*

Unless otherwise noted, all views and conclusions expressed herein are my own.

---

[1] 'London School's Survey Stirs Ire of Left', *The Washington Times Insight* section, 24 August 1987, p. 37.

INTRODUCTION

The crucial issue in any country's civil-military relations is not whether the armed forces will influence political decision-making—the state is ultimately a body of armed men—but to what degree and in what ways. A normal civil-military relationship has formal and informal boundaries between political and military roles accepted by both civilians and armed forces' officers. Officers are free to lobby their political masters over such items as the military's budget allocation, recruitment, pay rates, perquisites, weapons procurement and the like, so long as this pressure is carried out within regular channels, using mutually accepted codes-of-conduct. Where such boundaries are disdained or ignored, the civil-military relationship is ruptured, and with it the acceptance of civilian control over the military. In the worst-case scenario familiar in developing countries, officers' dissatisfaction moves them forcibly to overthrow the government.

Despite hopes that the fall of the Berlin Wall signalled the global ascendancy of democracy, the military coup d'état—the sudden and illegal replacement of a country's legitimate government through the use or threat of violence by a small group of conspirators drawn from within the armed forces—remains a real threat throughout the developing world. Estimates vary, but since India's independence in 1947, there have been well over 100 successful military coups throughout the world with perhaps an equal number of failures.[1] Armed forces have removed regimes in geographically large and populous nations and in geographically small and under-populated ones; in multi-ethnic, seemingly sophisticated and modernized countries as well as their opposite; in ex-British, French, Belgian, Dutch and Spanish colonies, and in nations with no colonial past; soon after independence yet also after years of civilian self-rule. In justification of their actions, coup executors have promised all manner of change, from sweeping socioeconomic reforms to radical retrenchment of conservative rule, but almost always promising to end the 'corruption' of the previous regime.

Upon removing a government, officers have installed regimes which include only themselves as the new rulers, a mix of themselves, other military personnel and/or civilians drawn from outside and/or inside the previous regime, or have refused to assume office.

The proliferation and diversity of military coups, and the unpredictability of their subsequent regimes' programmes has led some scholars to call for an end to attempts to systemise—and thus predict—instances of armed forces' intervention. Faced with the apparent inevitability of armed forces' coups occurring and recurring without predictable causes, many academics choose to study the more concrete manifestations of a military regime's performance rather than the factors which led officers to assume power. This work, however, concerns India, a country which has experienced neither a military regime nor an unsuccessful coup attempt. Given the global proliferation of forcible armed forces' interventions against governments, what factors have contributed to this remarkable state of affairs? Moreover, how does one structure an examination of what is, in effect, a non-event?

In almost any analysis of national civil-military relations and the factors influencing the (im)probability of a coup, much depends on understanding the country's military officers. In all of the competing and often contradictory coup prediction theories—which may be summarised into four, almost exclusive groups according to their respective views that a government is overthrown because officers are: ideally qualified citizens altruistically motivated to help their country's floundering attempts at modernisation; political actors seeking to maximize their power in fluid polities; reacting to threats to their perceived corporate self-interest; or fulfilling their personal and/or clientelist ambitions with little regard for the consequences[2]—it is the officers' perception of their role in society and their view of national events which ultimately decides whether or not the armed forces will remain in their barracks or move to overthrow the government.

Therefore, in the search for an explanation as to why India has never experienced a military coup, this work focusses on the views and opinions of senior Indian armed forces' officers for they were, and are the potential executors of any such action. One group, numbering almost 20, consists of illustrious 'king's commissioned officers' having published an (auto)biographical work, and includes General K.S. Thimayya, Admiral K.D. Katari and Air Chief Marshal P.C. Lal. The other comprises 108 senior retired 'Indian commissioned officers' from all three defence services, including 24 Lieut.-Generals, two Admirals and three Air Chief Marshals whose identities must remain confidential due to the sensitive nature of this work. These officers' respective views on a wide variety of issues concerning Indian civil-military relations are taken from one of two very similar versions of a detailed questionnaire distributed in 1988 and 1989, and/or comprehensive personal interviews conducted by myself from 1987-89, primarily in India but also in the UK and USA. Opinions expressed in complementary interviews of a number of Indian civilians with experience in, or expertise at the highest level of the country's civil-military relations as expressed in personal interviews are also employed. Throughout, the names are used only of those officers and civilians who have published their record of events; otherwise only the rank/title and key number of individuals appear (see **Appendix A**).

This reliance on written records and oral interviews has both drawbacks and advantages. As Major-General D.K. Palit, author of the recent *War in High Himalaya: The Indian Army in Crisis, 1962*, perhaps the definitive chronicle of the country's top civil-military decision-makers during the Sino-Indian War,[3] acknowledges that a

> memoir is a subjective record, a mix of fact and opinion, and time can play tricks with opinions. It is one thing to form an objective judgment with the advantage of hindsight; it is quite another to allow the years to blur the difference between opinion and held then and opinions held now.[4]

In the introduction to his *India's Political Administrators 1919-1983*, David Potter recognizes further disadvantages of works written after the fact:

> Powers of memory decline as one gets older...There is a tendency to exaggerate the importance of one's own career, to emphasize successes and play down or bury failures. In addition, certain types of people are far less likely to write reminiscences, the disreputable, for example.[5]

While the above criticisms of relying on records written after the fact also may be applied to oral interviews undertaken subsequent to events, there are undoubted advantages to using such materials. For Palit,

> Distance in time has the virtue that viewpoint distortions of contemporary events can be straightened out as they acquire perspective, and as emotion and prejudice recede. The

passage of years also makes available others' views and opinions which help to modulate subjective judgments formed under the stress of immediate reactions.[6]

Potter, too, argues that 'autobiographical materials, if used with care, do provide a most useful supplement to other forms of evidence'.[7]

Bearing in mind the advantages and disadvantages stated above, this work justifies its heavy reliance on (auto)biographical works, questionnaire responses and oral interviews written and/or undertaken after the events in question in a number of ways. Firstly, 'obvious whitewashes are not difficult to spot';[8] especially when, as in this case, a large number of contemporary accounts including (auto)biographies, questionnaire responses and oral interviews are available for cross-checking opinions and events described. (Of course, full use is also made of second-hand works by political scientists and historians to lend perspective to the above accounts.) Secondly, these records are very detailed: the officers' (auto)biographical books are works of some substance; the two versions of the questionnaire are very detailed, having 57 and 55 questions, respectively; and the oral interviews lasted well over two hours on average. Thirdly, officers answering the questionnaires and/or interviewed were chosen randomly from various official and unofficial sources[9] as the government of India does not release a systematic list of the names and addresses of armed forces officers, serving or retired. Fourthly, the high response rate of 96 completed questionnaires out of 412 mailed out is a statistically significant 23.3 per cent; especially given the officers' random selection, their having received a questionnaire with no prior solicitation, and their profession's usual reluctance to discuss sensitive civil-military topics.

Finally, and perhaps most importantly, the opinions expressed in the (auto)biographical works, questionnaire responses and interviews come from a wide mix of senior Indian military officers. Although it may be argued that, given the sensitive nature of my research, officers willing to answer a questionnaire and/or submit to interview may form a non-representative, liberal wing of the Indian armed forces may have some basis, I remain confident that the above sample accurately represents their peers: retired officers are both more able and likely to speak candidly of their attitudes to civil-military issues than are serving officers; a number of interviewees were selected because their questionnaire replies notably differed from those of their comrades; the respondents' religious mix was shown to reflect the variety found in the military as a whole; and the officers of the Indian armed forces always have been trained to display the professional attributes of the British ideal of an 'officer and gentleman', chief among which is just the respectful, non-political, liberal attitude towards civil supremacy-of-rule consistently displayed by the sample of questionnaire respondents and/or interviewees. Finally, and perhaps most importantly, the over 20 (auto)biographical books, 96 questionnaire responses, and 44 interviewees (officers and civilians) form a unique insight into Indian civil-military relations. These men were either the ultimate guarantors or executioners of civil supremacy-of-rule in India. Until now, no work has been able to tap the opinions of usually extremely reticent sources on such a sensitive topic as to why India has never suffered a military coup d'état (see **Table 1**).

While commissioned officers of independent India's armed forces have had to overcome challenges uniquely their own, their professional standards and understanding of their personal and institutional role *vis-à-vis* the civilian government has most directly been shaped by British military traditions. Chapter one examines the history and development of commissioned Indian officers from the 1918 admission of Indian cadets to the Royal Military College, Sandhurst, through the 1932 opening of the Indian Military Academy, Dehra Dun, to the eve of the Second World War. It reveals that Indian officers mastered their professional expertise in 'the management of violence'[10] and sense of organisational corporateness despite a multitude of formal and informal challenges including the trials of Sandhurst, the racist 'Indianisation' experiment, the prejudice of British officers and polite society, and even the discrimination visited by Indian Sandhurst graduates upon their Dehra Dun comrades. What remained to be seen was whether these officers, chosen for their loyalty to the Raj and trained to be full members of the ruling elite, would be able to transfer their professional sense of responsibility to the nationalist rulers of an independent India.[11]

A strong indication of commissioned Indian officers' future sense of professional responsibility may be seen from their pre-independence views of, and relationship with the Indian nationalist movement and its leaders. Would the Indian armed forces' special *esprit de corps* continue to shield officers from the greater political landscape of the subcontinent, but perhaps poisoning civil-military relations in a future independent India? Or would the struggle for independence cause Indian officers' professional responsibility to shift from the king-emperor to nationalist politicians, with potentially disastrous results for immediate military discipline and effectiveness? Chapter two shows the nationalist movement had little effect on the loyalty and discipline of commissioned Indian officers, despite some having had first-hand experience in nationalist activities before joining the armed forces. The almost total exclusion of the military in the nationalist struggle meant there was no mystification of the soldier as hero. When independence came, no military man would be in a position to challenge the right-to-rule of those nationalist leaders who became India's democratically elected representatives.

TABLE 1: Factors which have contributed to India never having experienced a military coup.*

1st	• *Professionalism of the armed forces.*
2nd	• *Diversity of peoples, cultures, languages.*
3rd	• *Initial political stability, quality, and/or democratic rule.*
4th	• *Nationally representative military personnel.*
5th	• *Sheer size of India.*
6th	• *Dominant Hindu culture.*
7th	• *Widely held belief in democracy.*
Joint 8th	• *Administrative efficiency.*
	• *Political awareness of the masses.*
	• *Wisdom and stature of national leaders.*
Joint 11th	• *Institutionalisation of diverse centres of power.*
	• *Decades-old habit of democracy.*
	• *Logistics unfavourable: five regional army commands, troops dispersed nationally, etc.*
Joint 14th	• *Independence struggle's non-violent nature.*
	• *Example of ineffectiveness of military rule in Pakistan and Bangladesh.*
16th	• *Other.*
17th	• *Political unawareness of the masses.*

* Ranked in order of importance by the 69 respondents of Questionnaire II.

Chapter three explores a potentially explosive exception to commissioned Indian officers' non-involvement in the independence movement. During the Second World War, various 'national' armies drawn from Indian prisoners-of-war (POWs) and civilians were formed with the express purpose of combating the Raj. Although these forces proved no match for the Allies in combat, their mere existence and *raison d'être* gave rise to fears for the loyalty of the British-led Indian armed forces' overwhelmingly Indian personnel. Such concerns were misplaced. Although some tens of thousands of Indian POWs did switch their allegiance, including a significant number of Japanese-held commissioned Indian officers, almost as many chose to endure the harsh regime of Axis prison camps. More importantly, those Indian soldiers and commissioned officers on active duty remained loyal to the Raj, believing their wartime allegiance and efforts would be rewarded by independence. This belief also quieted post-war qualms about what to do with those who had joined the various Indian national armies. So long as this 'clique' of ostensibly politicized men were not allowed back into the armed forces—and they were not—even commissioned Indian officers could agree with the public and nationalist politicians that such men had been true, if misguided, Indian patriots.

After the test of the Indian national armies came the challenges of the transfer of power from the British to the nationalist politicians and bureaucrats of an independent India (and Pakistan). Chapter four shows how commissioned Indian officers' constant belief in the quality of their professional expertise and corporateness enabled them successfully to meet the tests of immediate post-war strikes and mutinies, the division of the armed forces between India and Pakistan, the departure of British military personnel, and immediate actions in Punjab, Junagadh, Hyderabad, and Jammu & Kashmir. Although many officers feel that their efforts went unappreciated by the Indian political and administrative elite, they remained confident in the latters' ability to manage the difficult transition to independence and to govern effectively. This faith allowed commissioned Indian officers to transfer their professional responsibility smoothly from the British Raj to the new government of independent India.

What if the political leadership failed to live up to commissioned Indian officers' high expectations? Chapter five shows officers to have perceived the first decade of independence as one of governmental neglect of the military. Might they copy the example of their former comrade, General Ayub Khan, who justified his leading the Pakistan Army in a 1958 takeover of the country's government by saying that civilian politicians had proved incapable of managing the challenges of independence effectively? No. In just ten short years, any number of military, political, societal, international and even religious factors separated and differentiated Indian commissioned officers from their Pakistani counterpart in terms of their personal and professional understanding of their role in society. For the time being, at least, the former were content to remain in their barracks.

This contentment was steadily eroded by the rise in the late-1950s of Defence Minister Krishna Menon and Lieut.-General B.M. Kaul to the top rank of the civil-military establishment. Chapter six examines how these supremely ambitious individuals, alone and in tandem, used their administrative skills and close personal relationship with Prime Minister Jawaharlal Nehru to bypass the established civil-military decision-making hierarchy, play favourites and upset colleagues to the point of being openly charged with politicising the armed forces. The development of a Menon-Kaul nexus appeared to split the officer corps into two opposing camps, raising the possibility that either faction might intervene against the civilian government to ensure the furtherance of its respective interests. Yet, despite undoubted rancor in the armed forces, Sandhurst and Dehra Dun graduates continued to adhere to the notion of a professionalism based on perfecting management of violence skills at the expense of political awareness and/or activity. Most importantly, Nehru and his party continued to demonstrate their overwhelming popularity at the polls.

Civil supremacy-of-rule in India came under its gravest threat when defeat in the 1962 Sino-Indian War for the first time called into question the competence of the civilian government. Chapter seven exposes the shambolic nature of Indian civil-military decision-making before and during the war. It reveals how the army's field officers, that strata of any officer corps most likely to instigate a coup, held highly negative post-war attitudes towards both the political and military leadership, and perceived the public to be sympathetic towards the military and resentful of the political leadership. Despite this confluence of attitudes, there was remarkably little discussion of the possibility of the armed forces moving against the government, mainly because the Nehru administration took pains to address field officers' grievances with the country's top civil-military personnel, decision-making procedures and resource allocation.

After a period of relative success, civil-military relations were again tested in 1975 when Indira Gandhi appeared to end Indian democracy by imposing a draconian period of rule. With civil liberties under grave attack and the very legitimacy of the government being questioned, the behaviour of the country's armed forces was closely watched. Would officers support or oppose the ruling regime? Chapter eight examines officers' attitudes to the imposition and duration of Emergency rule, as well as their reactions to its sudden end 19 months later and the subsequent electoral defeat of Gandhi and the Congress party. Throughout this period, officers remained constant in their determination to keep their views of Emergency rule private and to respect the supremacy-of-rule due any legally constituted national government.

Chapter nine highlights the worst case scenario to date of the latest and perhaps most difficult challenge facing Indian civil-military relations; that is, the potential politicisation of armed forces' personnel when used to quell internal disturbances. In the 1984, the government ordered the army to flush out Sikh militants ensconced in their religion's most holy Golden Temple complex in Amritsar, Punjab. Although successful in its immediate aims, 'Operation Blue Star' caused thousands of Sikh military personnel to mutiny, thus calling into question the loyalty of Sikh men and officers posted throughout the armed forces in numbers disproportionate to their small share of the national population, as well as the army's continued preferential recruitment of this and other communities. Sikh and non-Sikh officers are sharply divided in their opinion of governmental responsibility for the deterioration of law-and-order in Punjab which led to Operation Blue Star, and the necessity of the action itself. Nonetheless, most officers agree that the subsequent indiscipline was an isolated reaction by poorly led and inexperienced troops. Since then, the armed forces have had no need to question the loyalty or efficacy of Sikh men and officers, nor the government to worry that sending the military on difficult internal policing duties endangers civil supremacy-of-rule.

That the armed forces and civil society always have agreed on civil supremacy-of-rule in India does not make the country unique among developing countries. If, as is obvious, negative instances shed light on positive ones, then this examination of the non-event of a coup may serve as a guide, not only to the working relationships between officer, politician and administrator in India, but also to a general theory of the conditions which preclude military intervention in politics.

---

[1] The most recent instances of alleged coup plans by military officers in South Asia include the September 1995 'Islamic' coup plot in Pakistan and the May 1996 high-level civil-military machinations and unauthorised mobilisation of men in Bangladesh.

[2] For a detailed explanation of the history and evolution of competing coup prediction theory, see A. Kundu, *Civil-Military Relations in British and Independent India, 1918-1962, and Coup Prediction Theory* (University of London PhD dissertation, 1996), pp. 23-49.

[3] See my review of D.K. Palit, *War in High Himalaya: The Indian Army in Crisis, 1962* (London: C. Hurst, 1991) in *Journal of Asian Studies* (Ann Arbor) February 1994, pp. 261-263.

[4] Palit, *War in High Himalaya*, p. ix.

[5] D.C. Potter, *India's Political Administrators 1919-1983* (Oxford: Clarendon Press, 1986), p. 16.

[6] Palit, *War in High Himalaya*, p. ix.

[7] Potter, *India's Political Administrators*, p. 16.

[8] Potter, *India's Political Administrators*, p. 16.

[9] See S.P. Baranwal, ed. and comp., *Military Yearbook* (New Delhi: Guide Publications, 1965-); *India and Pakistan Year Book Including Who's Who, 1948-1953* (Bombay: Times of India, 1948-1953); *India Who's Who* (New Delhi: Infa Publications, 1969-); *Indian Year Book And Who's Who, 1931-1947* (Bombay: Times of India, 1931-1947); S. Sarkar, ed., *Hindustan Year Book and Who's Who, 1992* (Calcutta: M.C. Sarkar & Sons Private Ltd., 1992); Jaswant Singh, ed. and comp., *Indian Armed Forces Yearbook* (Bombay: n.p., 1964-); *Times of India Directory and Year Book Including Who's Who, 1954-* (Bombay: Times of India, 1954-); *The Military Year Book, 1974-* (Government of India Ministry of Information and Broadcasting, 1974-). As noted in the preface to this work, Lieut.-General Dr. M.L. Chibber also allowed me access to his unpublished list of officers' names and addresses.

[10] H. Lasswell, 'The Garrison-State Hypothesis Today', as used in S. Huntington, *Changing Patterns of Military Politics* (New York: The Free Press of Glencoe, Inc., 1962), p. 51. See also Lasswell, 'The Garrison State', *American Journal of Sociology*, 46:4, January 1941, pp. 455-458.

[11] The three characteristics of expertise, corporateness and responsibility common to the military officer (and professionals in other fields such as law and medicine) are described by Samuel Huntington in his seminal work, *The Soldier and the State: The Theory and Politics of Civil-Military Relations* (Cambridge: Harvard University Press, 1957), pp. 7-18.

1. THE PROFESSIONAL INDIAN OFFICER

Commissioned military officers are the embodiment of that most traditional of all government institutions, the armed forces. As such, their organisational decisions—including whether or not to instigate a coup—are disproportionately affected by the weight of historical experience and precedent. The officers of independent India are no exception. While they have had to meet and overcome challenges uniquely their own, their professional standards and personal and institutional understanding of their role *vis-à-vis* the civilian government have been shaped most directly by British military traditions imported to the subcontinent over 300 years ago.

The British conquest of the subcontinent would have been impossible without the Indian soldiers, or jawans,[1] who constituted the rank-and-file of the Honourable East India Company's three presidency armies of Bengal, Bombay and Madras, respectively, and the subsequent Indian Army (unified in 1893). Yet, on the eve of the First World War, not one Indian was serving as a full king's commissioned officer (KCO) in the Indian Army. Instead, jawans were led by a unique combination of Indian non-commissioned officers (NCOs), Indian viceroy's commissioned officers (VCOs) and British KCOs. While Indian Army NCOs filled positions comparable to their counterparts in the British Army, VCOs held all the commissioned officer places normally taken by KCOs in a British Army regiment.[2] Only the commander of an Indian Army unit, a British lieutenant or second-lieutenant, was a KCO. The socioeconomic, ethnic, cultural, and language gulf between a regiment's British commanding officer (CO) and its jawans was bridged by VCOs who could attain great respect and responsibilities. Yet their career opportunities were limited; none were promoted beyond the regimental level and at no time could a VCO command British Army troops in joint operations.

The Indian Army's heroic performance during the First World War[3] and the need to secure the continued participation of the subcontinent at its height finally led the British authorities to open up command positions. Although almost invariably too uneducated or too old to rise far, nine serving VCOs and holders of temporary commissions won king's commissions before the Armistice, as did a few NCOs. Six of the 39 Indians in the sole graduating class of the Cadet College, Indore, opened in 1918 to give preliminary military training to 'a few carefully screened Indian boys',[4] were later granted regular king's commissions (including the first Indian to head the Indian Army, General, later Field Marshal, K.M. Cariappa). Nearly 700 Indian doctors serving in the military's auxiliary Indian Medical Service (IMS) also became KCOs during the First World War.

From King's to Indian Commission Officers

The First World War also saw the first permanent step in the creation of the modern Indian commissioned officer corps when the authorities opened the Royal Military College (RMC), Sandhurst, to Indians. Up to ten Indian 'gentleman cadets' (GCs) per year would be trained to be KCOs. The initial batch of were examined in 1918, attended from January 1919, and were variously commissioned from July 1920 to August 1921. Although, as full second-lieutenants of the British armed services, they were entitled to command any of his majesty's forces throughout the world, Indian KCOs (henceforth referred to as king's commissioned Indian officers, or KCIOs) had to make their careers in the Indian Army after spending their initial year with a British Army unit on a tour of duty in the subcontinent.

Entrance to the RMC for prospective Indian candidates was not easy. One had to have access to considerable funds, and the examination procedure varied tremendously. As a student at Highgate School, London, General J.N. Chaudhuri answered a newspaper notice inviting applications for a king's Indian cadetship to Sandhurst, then sat before just one interview board (which included Field Marshal Sir Claud Jacob) in the India Office.[5] Lieut.-General S.P.P. Thorat describes the more common and harrowing experience faced by Indian candidates on the subcontinent:

All applicants were first interviewed by the provincial Governors who submitted the names of deserving candidates to the Government of India. This initial screening was very selective and in 1924 only ten candidates from the whole of India and Burma were chosen to take the entrance examination. This small batch of raw sixteen-year old boys gathered in Simla...and was given a written test of the under-graduate level. Then followed a series of interviews. The first was by the Selection Board and I was overawed by the array of Army officers who constituted it. They asked me a few simple questions but followed each with exhaustive supplementaries to ascertain the depth of my knowledge. After this ordeal came the interview with the Commander-in-Chief, Field Marshal Sir William Birdwood...The next [and final] face I saw was His Excellency Lord Reading, Viceroy of India.[6]

Graduates of the Prince of Wales Royal Indian Military College (PWRIMC), established at Dehra Dun in 1922 (its initial batch of 32 cadets included future Indian Army Chief General K.S. Thimayya) to prepare Indian boys for the rigours of Sandhurst, bypassed preliminary selection rounds and advanced straight to Simla.

Throughout the selection process, preference was given first to sons of military officers and then those from conservative, 'politically inert'[7] families which had for generations constituted the Indian princely, landed and military elite. Belonging to one of the 'martial races' from which British commanders had preferentially recruited troops since the mid-eighteenth century also made a candidate that much more admissible.[8] A random sample of seven illustrious Indian graduates— Generals Thimayya, Chaudhuri and M. Ayub Khan (who reached this rank in the Pakistan Army and later become the country's President), Lieut.-Generals Thorat, S.D. Verma and B.M. Kaul, and Adjutant (later Ambassador) M.R.A. Baig—of the RMC reveals these preferences. Thimayya (a cousin of Field Marshal Cariappa who himself came from a westernized family with a tradition of government service) and Thorat came from wealthy and westernized families of traditional, martial race communities. Chaudhuri was raised in a rich and virtually bi-cultural though non-martial Bengali family. Khan's father was a land-owning, martial races' *risaldar-major* of the Indian Army's famous Hodson's Horse, while Verma's was an England-trained barrister-at-law. Baig's grandfather was a *risaldar* in a unit which later formed the nucleus of the elite Royal Deccan Horse, while his father retired as vice-president of the Council of India, at that time the 'highest post an Indian could occupy in government service'.[9] Baig himself spent most of his adolescence in comfort in England. Only Kaul came from a relatively poor, non-martial family.

The bias of the selection process was but one of many shortcomings in the recruitment, training and promotion opportunities noted by the Indian Sandhurst Committee (ISC), appointed in 1925 and containing a majority of Indian politicians including Motilal Nehru, Mohammed Ali Jinnah (henceforth referred to by surname only) and Sir Jogendra Singh. Surely, the subcontinent's over 300 million people contained more potential officers than the 85 Indian GCs admitted to the RMC from 1919-25. More worrying was that 30 per cent of Indian cadets, compared to only 3 per cent of British GCs, failed to graduate. Many in the ISC felt the low Indian pass rate existed largely because non-PWRIMC candidates were disadvantaged by insufficient and/or improper educational preparation. The PWRIMC's high fees and exclusivist admissions almost regardless of aptitude were also thought unfairly restrictive. Another major complaint was the lack of Indians in higher command positions, seen to be a direct result of limiting KCIOs to the army's 'Indianised' eight units (see below).

The ISC report of 1926 proposed various remedies. The number of RMC places reserved for Indians should be doubled from ten to 20, thereafter increasing annually by four. KCIOs should also be allowed to join the army's artillery, engineer, signal, tank and air arms. The limited 'eight unit experiment' should be replaced by a comprehensive programme of 'Indianisation' including the opening of a military college equivalent to Sandhurst on the subcontinent (see below). Finally, Indians of all communities, martial and 'non-martial', should be given an equal chance of admission for all of the above.

Although the British dragged their feet on implementing all of the unanimous proposals of the ISC (whose members they themselves had appointed), reforms did come. The RMC's annual intake of Indian candidates was doubled, and an additional five places (rising to ten if the number of direct entry candidates was lower than the allowed limit) were reserved for VCOs. Indians also were given six vacancies at the Royal Military Academy (RMA), Woolwich, for training in artillery, engineering and signals, and six places at the Royal Air Force College (RAFC), Cranwell (see below). Subsequent pressure from the first

Indian Round Table Conference's Defence Subcommittee resulted in a threefold increase in RMC places reserved for Indians (bringing the total to 60), and a widening of Indianisation. The subcommittee's most important result was the 1931 creation of a committee of experts under General Sir Philip W. Chetwode to investigate the establishment of an Indian equivalent of the RMC.

This landmark change came on 10 December 1932 with the establishment of the Indian Military Academy (IMA) at Dehra Dun. With the closure of Sandhurst to Indian GCs, all Indian officers henceforth would experience their military education wholly on the subcontinent. While graduates were to be known as Indian commissioned officers (ICOs), like KCIOs they would begin their careers with a year in a British Army regiment serving in India before transferring to the Indian Army. However, unlike KCIOs who had been commissioned by the king into 'His Majesty's Land Forces', ICOs were commissioned by the viceroy into 'His Majesty's Indian Land Forces', giving them complete authority over jawans anywhere in the world but British troops in India only.[10]

The IMA's admissions procedure was perhaps more rigorous and certainly less arbitrary than that of the RMC. After submitting his application through the collector or deputy commissioner of the district in which his parents resided, a candidate would attend a competitive examination held twice a year in Delhi by the Federal Public Service Commission (FPSC). The examination consisted of four compulsory subjects, three optional subjects, and an 'interview and record test' conducted by a board made up of a FPSC member, two Indian Army officers nominated by the commander-in-chief (C-in-C) in India, and two non-official gentlemen (one nominated by the government of India and one by the C-in-C).

The IMA was set up as a copy of the RMC. Its commandant was a senior British brigadier, his teaching and drill staff were overwhelmingly British, and they provided a virtually identical military education to officer candidates who would continue to be called GCs. However, due to the lack of suitable preparatory institutions on the subcontinent, IMA cadets would undergo five terms of training over two and one-half years instead of Sandhurst's three terms in 18 months. Many felt that the extra two terms spent at Dehra Dun often resulted in a more uniformly educated and knowledgeable second-lieutenant.

Socially, admission was no longer restricted. Admittedly, the make-up of the IMA's first half-yearly batch of 40 GCs (which included future

Indian Army Chief Field Marshal, S.H.F.J. Manekshaw) reflected the
military authorities' traditional bias for cadets of the martial races
and/or aristocracy: 15 (37.5 per cent) cadets were admitted by open
competition, 15 selected from Indian Army VCOs and other ranks (after
they had undergone a two-year course at the Kitchener College,
Nowgong), and ten from the Indian State Forces (ISF) drawn from the
Princely States. Nonetheless, the IMA's much lower, all-inclusive fees
made the academy affordable to a wider segment of Indian society,
especially the sons of the burgeoning, educated middle-class. A limited
number of scholarships provided by provincial governments provided
further access. (No fees were charged to army-nominated cadets.) Thus,
the first batch of IMA cadets included youths of 'all castes and creeds—
Hindus, Muslims, Sikhs, Christians, Parsis and Anglo-Indians—and
from the high and humble families'.[11]

Developing Professionalism

To a large extent, the British-led government of pre-independent India
ensured its supremacy-of-rule over the Indian Army's British officers
through what Samuel Huntington characterises as 'objective control';[12]
minimizing their influence by maximizing their professional
characteristics of expertise, responsibility and corporateness. While
these officers' expertise in what Harold Lasswell calls the 'management
of violence'[13] as measured by 'objective standards of professional
competence'[14] may argued to have been no better and perhaps poorer
than that of some European counterparts, it was superior to any found
on the subcontinent. The professional responsibility of British Indian
Army officers to deploy their expertise only at the discretion of their
client, society's legitimate rulers, under penalty of expulsion from their
profession was also respected, as evidenced by their unquestioned
obedience to the crown. Finally, corporateness, or that 'sense of organic
unity and consciousness of themselves as a group apart'[15] from the rest
of society, flourished among officers so obviously different to the
general population. Firmly under objective control, the British Indian
Army officer was the 'tool'[16] of his civilian masters.

To a greater extent, however, the Raj secured ultimate power over
British Indian Army officers through what Huntington describes as
'subjective control'[17], minimizing their power by maximizing their
identification with the institutions, character and/or objectives of the
regime. Britain's historical mistrust of a standing army meant only those

wealthy enough to purchase a commission and support themselves in a style unobtainable on a officer's meagre official salary could command troops in the British Army. Besides inhibiting a coup from within, officers owing their position to the status quo also discouraged any civilian radical reform movement. Although the purchase system was abolished by Royal warrant in 1871, and British Army officers increasingly professionalised after the respective Crimean and Boer Wars, British Indian Army officers retained their traditional, privileged and conservative character. Indistinguishable from the civilian elite by ethnicity, education or socioeconomic status, British Indian Army officers were a 'mirror'[18] of India's government, and little doubted the desirability, necessity and correctness of the Raj.

Theories of objective and subjective control are less clear when applied to the Indian Army's growing numbers of commissioned Indian officers. In Table 1, the questionnaire respondents appear to suggest the paramountcy of objective control by ranking 'professionalism of the armed forces' as the most important factor in the armed forces' non-involvement in independent India's politics. Yet follow-up interviews reveal most respondents as understanding an officer's professionalism to be composed simply of military expertise.[19] Questions concerning the nature of the military professionalism as bequeathed by the British to independent India's military officers, of Huntington's perception of professional responsibility and corporateness, and of larger civil-military questions are dismissed as the province of the very highest ranks only. Most officers, says Air Marshal 5, simply are too busy 'concentrating on the technical and other working aspects of the job'.[20] Where the respondents do discuss professionalism in the context of civil-military relations, opinion is divided as to whether it includes an implicit, explicit, or no understanding at all of officers' subservience to the government.

Despite most respondents' reticence to view professionalism as anything more than an expertise in training, tactics and command, their ranking of it as the prime factor ensuring civil supremacy-of-rule demands that professionalism be examined in a context of historical subjective and objective methods of control. To begin with, was subjective control relevant; that is, given their obvious ethnic and cultural differences, could commissioned Indian officers share their British counterparts' identification with the subcontinent's ruling elite? In terms of objective control, could British officers and KCIOs who had studied at Sandhurst have the same understanding of professional expertise as ICOs educated at the IMA? With the rise of the independence movement, would KCIOs and ICOs see their professional responsibility to the legitimate ruler of the subcontinent as laying with the British Raj or Indian nationalist leaders? Finally, given the many sources of conflict KCIOs and ICOs faced within the military, to what degree did they count themselves part of the overall corporate identity of the Indian Army?

During the interwar years, the Indian Army's British and Indian commissioned officers began their careers with the same military education intended to make them into the ideal 'officer and gentleman'. If the 'officer' half of this equation may be taken to entail professional expertise, responsibility and corporateness, or those qualities which make officers the tool of a government, the 'gentleman' half may be interpreted as that behaviour appropriate for those chosen to be the armed mirror of the ruling elite.

Before becoming an officer and gentleman, a young Indian cadet had to overcome any number of prejudicial attitudes and practices at the RMC. Living in England from 1910-23 had made Ambassador Baig English in all but skin colour. Only at Sandhurst did he first encounter racism: 'We did not belong and were made to feel it'.[21] Of course, most Indian GCs had never before travelled outside the subcontinent nor had to deal with British boys as equals. For them, Lieut.-General Thorat's experience of suffering an 'inferiority complex *vis-à-vis* British cadets'[22] was common. That British and non-British GCs hardly ever mixed compounded this new sense of not belonging, and President Ayub Khan recalls how Indian cadets 'all sensed that we were regarded as an inferior species'.[23] To protect themselves and to bolster their self-esteem, adds General Chaudhuri, Indian GCs developed their own

> unwritten code of conduct, a break from which would have meant ostracism. The rules were fairly simple. An Indian GC was to tip his servant 5 shillings weekly, which was double the normal rate. At the cinema, the Indian GCs were to use the more expensive balcony seats and not the cheaper stalls. Visiting 'Ma Hart', the RMC's favourite pawn shop was taboo. Attendance at the end of term ball, a very colourful, affair, was forbidden unless one could bring an Indian girl to it. Finally, cutting in on or filching another Indian GC's girlfriend was the greatest crime of all. I suppose the first three rules were designed to show that Indians were not a

poor race. Rule 4 made sense and rule 5, looking at the shortage of girls who in those days would be seen with Indians, was a safety device.[24]

Unwritten rules also applied in the 'open' competition between cadets for executive ranks: Indian GCs could rise to the honorary rank of a corporal and no higher, nor could they command any non-Indian cadets. That this discrimination was illogical is apparent, especially since as KCIOs, Indians would be entitled to command British troops and junior officers.

Despite the painful adjustment from India's privileged class to Sandhurst's underclass, many Indian cadets flourished under the RMC's strict regimen of training in academic, physical and leadership skills. They shared a privileged, conservative and, in the case of PWRIMC graduates, a public school background with the vast majority of British cadets which enabled most to assimilate, and the RMC to impart, those qualities necessary to a 'gentlemanly' military professionalism. Lieut.-General Kaul's recollection of his education includes descriptions of professional expertise, responsibility and corporateness:

> I had imbibed much at Sandhurst. I learnt a code of conduct, a sense of discipline and the significance of honour. I was taught a set of principles true to spiritual values by which can be judged what is right. I acquired the rudiments of military knowledge, the basic techniques of my profession and to appreciate the importance of turnout and skill at professional work and games and also to face agreeable and unpleasant situations alike. I was taught how to play the game, to know what the qualities of leadership were, the sense of many values and the honour of serving one's country selflessly and with devotion.[25]

Equipped with such an education, Indian GCs were intended to play an integral part of the ruling elite of the subcontinent.

While created in the hope of widening the intake, the IMA continued disproportionately to admit GCs from the north and northwest preserves of the martial races and train them according to the RMC ideal of an officer and gentleman. The IMA's course of instruction was intended to:

> (a) to develop in the Cadet the characteristics of leadership, discipline and physical fitness, and to instill in him a high sense of duty and of honour, and a realisation of the responsibilities of a servant of *the State,*
>
> (b) to ensure that a Cadet on joining his unit is in a position to discharge the essential duties of a platoon commander. [My italics.][26]

Although virtually identical in its emphasis on gentlemanly professionalism and professional expertise and corporateness, the fact that IMA cadets were all Indians and were taught wholly on Indian soil allowed the academy to lay greater stress on officers' professional sense of responsibility to their client, *Indian* society's legitimate rulers. The following extract from C-in-C General Sir Philip Chetwode's inaugural speech at Dehra Dun was later inscribed on the walls of the IMA for all GCs to see:

> The safety, honour and welfare of *your country* come first, always and every time.
>
> The honour, welfare and comfort of the men you command come next.
>
> Your own ease, comfort and safety come last, always and every time. [My italics.][27]

Despite the IMA's more explicit emphasis on officers' professional responsibility to their client, one awkward question remained: in pre-independent India which, exactly, was the client meant by 'the State' and 'your country', above? Was it the same as saying the British government of India or did it entail a higher loyalty to the 'nation' of India, and/or to her peoples?

Commissioned Indian officers' understanding of professional corporateness was also a matter for debate, especially after the 1923 imposition of the eight unit experiment which limited KCIOs to two cavalry regiments and six infantry battalions of the Indian Army. Moreover, these eight units would no longer accept newly commissioned British officers, and all KCIOs already serving elsewhere encouraged to transfer. Officially justified as an attempt to prove Indian officers could perform as efficiently as their British counterparts on a regimental scale, the Indianisation of the army unofficially ensured that, at least within the designated units, no British officer would have to serve under an Indian superior. And such was the paucity of higher positions now open to KCIOs that it would require over 25 years fully to Indianise the eight units![28]

The increasing number of KCIOs entering the Indian Army soon forced the eight units to replace their VCOs with KCIOs of second-lieutenant rank. Although British Army subalterns began their careers by leading platoons, KCIOs deeply resented the 'platoonism'[29] of having to command the Indian Army's smallest body of men as demeaning their commissions, especially since non-Indianised units retained their VCOs. Platoonism also greatly increased competition for promotion within the battalion, kept static the number of Indian officers in the army as a whole, and angered jawans by reducing their prospects. The extension of Indianisation attained by the Round Table Conference Defence Subcommittee still forced KCIOs and, later, ICOs to begin their careers at platoon level.

In addition to the formal career restrictions of Indianisation, commissioned Indian officers, especially the pioneering KCIOs, attempting to develop a sense of professional corporateness had to face the challenge of informal prejudice. As the army was admitting Indians to positions of significant responsibility much later than other government services, many British officers had difficulty adjusting to the idea of Indians as their professional equals. KCIOs expecting to assume a social position commensurate with their responsibilities often came up against unspoken barriers as they became the first Indians to break the colour-bar at military clubs and social functions (and this often only if a sympathetic commanding officer took it upon himself to intervene on their behalf). For the sons of India's elite, accustomed to deference and lives of ease, such treatment could not have been easy to tolerate, much less serve under.

Some coped by visiting their frustrations with professional and social discrimination upon fellow Indian officers. IMS Lieut.-General D.R. Thapar recalls a mess dinner discussion on the new ICOs at which a young KCIO asked the guests to 'imagine our feelings when we have to call these [Dehra] Doon [sic] Pansies our brother officers....after all these pseudo-officers are young men who could not afford to go to Sandhurst'.[30] KCIOs and ICOs also differed in their respective contact with British officers. While KCIOs had at first been scattered throughout the Indian Army, ICOs were posted to units long Indianised and had much less contact with British officers. Sceptics thought their lack of professional intercourse with British comrades would result in ICOs being of inferior quality. IMA supporters hoped instead that the onset of ICOs would signal the end of the tragicomic 'Brindian' officer who, though Indian by birth and background, heedlessly aped British ways.[31]

The gloomy picture of Indian-British commissioned officer relations lessened during the later interwar years and the Second World War. Indeed, as represented by the questionnaire respondents and/or interviewees, a majority of ICOs commissioned up to and including 1945 describe a mutually positive professional relationship with their British counterparts. Of course, there were some difficulties; for instance, the obvious prejudice involved in transferring Indian officers upon promotion so that they would not be in a position to command British officers. More common, however, is the memory of mutual respect and regard. 'Once you proved [to British superiors] you were good, you were good', recalls Major-General 20.

That KCIOs and the majority of pre-1945 commissioned ICOs disagree as to the state of Indian-British officer relations may be ascribed to their respective dates of joining-up. While pre-war commissioned British officers tended to display the inbuilt prejudices of the *koi-hai* (who's there?) types who felt the subcontinent their natural preserve, those entering the Indian Army just before the Second World War usually had a more liberal upbringing and joined without previously having formed censorious attitudes towards the capabilities of Indian personnel. These significant differences mean the older Sandhurst-educated group of KCIOs' description of a relationship full of pitfalls is more accurate of interwar Indian-British commissioned officer relations than that of the majority of pre-1945 commissioned ICOs who describe such relations as generally positive.

Despite the multitude of obstacles, commissioned Indian officers acquired a high degree of professional expertise and corporateness during the interwar years. Surprisingly, it was Indianisation which provided the motivation and conditions for KCIOs and ICOs to develop more quickly high professional standards. Initially, this was because the scepticism of British authorities (and, initially, jawans) pushed the first commissioned Indian officers to work twice as hard to learn the basics of military expertise. Indianisation also encouraged a kind of professional corporateness by forcing the small number of commissioned Indian officers to compete not only with themselves, but as a group apart from the mainstream of British Indian Army officers. General Chaudhuri explains:

> Had a handful of Indians been scattered round the whole army, their impact would have been minimal and, swamped by the British officers, they would have found it difficult to establish an identity of their own. Concentrated in the Indianising units their impact was much stronger and easier to evaluate as a successful, long overdue step.[32]

Thus, Indianisation ultimately helped to spur KCIOs and ICOs to pursue only the highest professional standards of expertise and to develop a distinct corporate identity within the Indian Army.[33]

For commissioned Indian officers in pre-independent India, the question of professional responsibility began with the Indian soldier. To a large extent, the jawan, like the sepoy before him (and the NCOs and VCOs who rose from the ranks), enlisted for the security and rewards offered first by the Honourable East India Company and then by the crown. The martial races enjoyed their designation as men of special fighting ability, the army's steady pay, and being pensioned off with newly irrigated land in Punjab. Their communities were pleased with receiving their sons' remittances, having army pensions spent locally, and the knowledge that future generations were virtually guaranteed military careers. While the long-term benefits may have been less obvious to the military's non-martial races, their personal rewards were equally attractive. Finally, no stigma was attached to serving under a leader not of one's own background; the 'mercenary' tag which later dogged Indian men (and officers) had not yet surfaced.

Yet on the battlefield, company and crown soldiers fought not just for pay and pension but to defend their *izzat*, a complex mix of personal, familial, caste, religious and even generational honour melded with that of the unit in which they served. In the Indian Army, a close identification with regimental honour was encouraged with the development of a unique internal structure of 'class' and 'class company' regiments; units made up entirely of the same caste or ethnic group *versus* those containing a different class in each of its three companies, respectively. As well as ensuring a measure of *divide et impera* within each unit, class and class company regiments allowed a British commander to do his recruiting simply by sending his NCOs to their villages with orders to get 'more of the same'. He then would then have troops united by speech, religion, caste, and blood to their immediate superiors who were, in turn, conscious of proving to their commander that his faith in their judgment of recruits was fully justified. The boundaries between individual, clan and unit identities were then blurred by incorporating men's traditional social and religious observances into regimental functions, and the bond between officers, men and their unit further reinforced by emphasizing the solemnity of the oath upon enlistment, the precision of guard-mounting, and the sacredness of the colours as the symbol of honour.

For the pre-independent Indian Army, a close identification of the jawan with his unit was extremely important as there was no obviously patriotic reason to join and fight, even after British control over the subcontinent became near total. The Indian soldier may have felt a kind of loyalty to a distant white ruler, but he understood his place in society more as a client or an associate of an alien ruler.[34] Therefore, it was crucial that throughout their career, jawans could feel that their regiment was their home, and their British commander their *mai bap meherbani* (benign mother and father). No problem would be too small to ignore, none too big to overcome—together. When the troops were well led, fairly treated and respected, the intensely personal nature of the Indian Army's unique system of class and class company regiments and dependence on martial races created a virtually unbreakable bond of loyalty between a man and his unit in which was tied the very definition of his existence.

Despite the huge gulf in their respective political and socioeconomic classes, commissioned Indian officers developed just as powerful a loyalty to their respective regiments' *izzat* as did the jawans. Like the troops, KCIOs were of specific communities and usually served out their careers in one regiment, with every opportunity to develop an intensely proud, proprietal attitudes towards it. Although many ICOs differed from KCIOs in their respective families' political and socioeconomic status, most continued to come from British-designated martial races' areas. Those with previous familial or community martial histories desired to add to them, while those without such traditions were anxious to start new ones. Whatever their backgrounds, ICOs, like KCIOs, shared a stake in their regiment's *izzat* and felt just as strong a desire to succeed in their prestigious profession. In the end, an army based on recruiting selected martial races into strictly segregated class and class company regiments created a keen sense of personal and professional responsibility among jawans, NCOs, VCOs and commissioned Indian officers alike towards their client, not society but the regiment and, through the regiment, the army.

The close personal identification of Indian Army men and officers with their regiment and, through it, the army, might pose a danger to independent India's future civil supremacy-of-rule. Huntington argues that military professionalism's corporate characteristic lends officers a shared consciousness of themselves as a group apart from society. With its unique *izzat*, specialized recruiting and distinctive internal structure, the Indian Army could be characterized as an impenetrable inner society. While very effective in battle, its personalized corporate loyalty might adversely affect commissioned officers' understanding of their proper role in civil-military relations. Come independence, how would Indian officers react to government decisions affecting their corporate well-being? Would their personal, regimental loyalty be transformed into a corporate allegiance to the central government, or further, to loyalty to some higher notion of India?

Indian Naval and Air Forces

An examination of the potential actors in a military coup which ignores or dismisses naval and air forces on the basis that only the army has the equipment and manpower necessary to take power and/or fill multiple government positions is incomplete. Experience shows that non-army officers, especially those in the air force, can lead a military intervention to replace the legitimate government.[35] On the other hand, such has become the destructive power, range and efficiency of modern air forces that this branch of the armed forces may itself severely damage or even prevent an attempted takeover of government by the army. The perceptions of naval and air force officers also indicate how military officers in general feel about government actions directed at the armed forces. Finally, as a significant number of the officers answering the questionnaires and/or interviewed are either naval or air force officers, a brief examination of their professional origins follows.

Like the Indian Army, the Royal Indian Marine (RIM), as the British-led Indian naval force was known until well into the twentieth century, owes much of its traditions, tactics and professional character to the British. It, too, sprang from Honourable East India Company origins, served faithfully in the conquest of the subcontinent and abroad, and fulfilled imperial duties in the First World War. The RIM also recruited selected Indian communities to serve in the ranks—Hindu Ratnagiri seamen and stokers (descendants of the sea-going Angria clan of the Mahrattas) and Goanese galley, wardroom and paymaster staff giving way to a Punjabi Muslim majority by Independence—while reserving commissioned officer positions for British personnel only. Only after Sandhurst's example did the RIM consider opening its commissioned officer corps to Indians. The first step came on 1 December 1927 when the RIM Dufferin was re-dedicated as a mercantile marine officer-training vessel for Indian cadets (who included R.D. Katari, later independent India's first Indian naval chief).[36]

Opportunities for Indians to win commissions in what, from 1934 became the Royal Indian Navy (RIN), remained inconsistent, limited and expensive. While British candidates could opt for an examination held in London and valid for all three Indian armed forces, Dufferin graduates sat a special test conducted by the FPSC, and other Indian candidates appeared for an examination in Delhi held conjointly with the IMA entrance test. The (historically) limited size of the officer corps in the sea-going branch of the British-led Indian naval forces also meant the annual intake of all new officers, British and Indian, was tiny, and permanent vacancies arose only from natural wastage and the like. Whether selected in India or England, all RIN officers were trained in UK naval establishments for which they had to deposit in full a personal share of their fee.

Although few in number, the RIN's commissioned Indian officers represented a wider geographic and socioeconomic background than the Indian Army's KCIOs and ICOs. To a large extent, this was because the RIN's technically demanding posts demanded educated youths who, by the late 1920s, were to be found among the Westernized middle-class in any of subcontinent's larger cities. Moreover, while the RIN continued to favour Punjabi Muslims as seamen, its lack of NCO positions and the subcontinent's relatively meagre sea-going tradition combined to curtail the growth of a naval martial races' lobby.

With no pre-British predecessor on the subcontinent, the air force of modern India perforce had traditions, tactics and professional character based on British origins. The subcontinent's first military flying school was established in 1913 at Sitapur. A Royal Flying Corps (RFC) detachment arrived two years later and slowly grew into a body of some strength until 1919 when, like its UK counterpart which became the separate Royal Air Force (RAF), it too split from the army to become the Royal Air Force in India (RAFI). Although the RAFI remained closed to the few Indians who had learnt their aviation skills at civil flying clubs set up in Delhi, Bombay, Calcutta, and Lucknow in the late 1920s, several Indian pilots had managed to become RFC commissioned officers during the First World War, distinguishing themselves in European theatre combat and winning gallantry medals.

The gallantry of the RFC's Indian pilots added weight to the argument that Indians should be allowed to train as air force commissioned officers. The ISC recommended giving selected Indians king's commissions to form an air arm of the Indian Army and, pending the establishment of proper flying training facilities on the subcontinent, sending them to Cranwell. As with RIN candidates, Indians hoping to attend the RAFC sat their entrance examination alongside prospective IMA cadets. After paying their fees, successful Indians then endured the same course as their British classmates. The first batch of six Indian cadets went to Cranwell in September 1930 and five passed out as pilots (including Subroto Mukherji, independent India's first Indian air force chief) two years later into what on 8 October 1932 became the Indian Air Force (IAF).

Unlike the Indian Army and RIN, the IAF granted commissions only to Indians. Because of nationalist fears expressed in the India's legislative assembly that the creation of a third, separate defence service could be used as an additional means of continuing British domination of the subcontinent, the Indian Air Force bill had insisted that only 'genuine' Indians as opposed to 'statutory' Indians be permitted to join the IAF. However, as there were very few commissioned Indian officers, a number of senior British officers and technicians sufficient to run a separate service were seconded to the IAF from the RAF. The Indian Air Force bill also stated that the IAF be open to all suitable Indian candidates. This requirement, combined with military aviation's technical demands and the lack of any significant domestic tradition of flying, produced an IAF officer corps more educated and nationally representative than the Indian Army.

Conclusion

The Indian Army's great strength remained the relationship of trust, loyalty and pride which jawans and their officers felt for one another and their regiment. With the exception of the Great Mutiny of 1857, this shared *izzat* grew and flourished through the conquest of the subcontinent, shift to martial races' recruitment, unification of the

Honourable East India Company's three respective presidency armies into one Indian Army, participation in the First World War, and introduction of commissioned Indian officers. The exploits of the British-led Indian armed forces would provide independent India's military with a long history of glorious fighting tradition on three continents.

The credit for much of this tradition must go to the small group of pre-independence commissioned Indian officers. Despite a multitude of formal and informal challenges—including the trials of Sandhurst, the racist eight unit experiment, the prejudice of British officers and polite society, and even the discrimination visited by KCIOs upon ICOs—the RMC and IMA turned out officers who were quick to master military professionalism's qualities of expertise and corporateness. Their prowess was crucial as immediately upon independence these relatively inexperienced officers were rapidly promoted to senior command positions with responsibility for repulsing considerable threats to national security.

Independence would also reveal wherein lay commissioned Indian officers' professional responsibility. Chosen for their loyalty to the Raj and then trained to feel full members of the ruling elite, would KCIOs and ICOs be able to transfer their sense of professional responsibility to the new rulers of independent India? General Chaudhuri does not doubt that jawans would be able to transfer their loyalty:

> Having been recruited and maintained in India, and having been recruited almost wholly from the rural areas where their land and its produce were their essential livelihood, Indian soldiers had their roots deep in the country. Once India became real and tangible, once it became their own, it was quite clear that they would fight as fiercely for their country as they had once fought for their good name, their community and for gain.[37]

Yet for commissioned Indian officers, the departure of the British ruling elite meant their 'membership' lapsing and subjective methods of controlling the military lessening. At the same time, depending solely on objective methods of control meant allowing the Indian Army's 'mercenaries' (in that officers and jawans volunteered to serve for security, rewards and status) wider corporate autonomy. Might such a course threaten independent India's civilian supremacy-of-rule? Much would depend on Indian officers' understanding of the relationship, discussed in the next chapter, between themselves and those nationalist leaders who were poised to take over the reins of government.

---

[1] Jawan, strictly translated as 'youth' or 'lad', replaced sepoy, from the Persian *sipah* or 'army', during the late nineteenth century as the common term for Indian soldiers in the British-led Indian armed forces.

[2] Indian Army NCO positions included *lance-naik*, equivalent to a British Army corporal, *havildar* or sergeant, and *havildar-major* and *quartermaster-havildars* of various levels. Indian Army VCO positions included *jemadar* or second-lieutenant, *subedar* or lieutenant, and *subedar-major* or major.

[3] From 1914-18, Indian Army personnel increased from 150,000 to almost 600,000 in number. In all, over 700,000 Indian troops served on the Western front, in Mesopotamia, Egypt, Macedonia, East Africa, Aden, Singapore, Hong Kong and China. They suffered 36,000 killed and 70,000 wounded while winning 16 Victoria Crosses and 99 Military Crosses.

[4] Lieut.-General S.P.P. Thorat, *From Reveille To Retreat*, (New Delhi: Allied Publishers Private Limited, 1986), p. 2.

[5] General J.N. Chaudhuri, *General J.N. Chaudhuri: An Autobiography*, as narrated to B.K. Narayan (New Delhi: Vikas Publishing House, 1978), pp. 24-25.

[6] Thorat, *From Reveille To Retreat*, pp. 3-4. See also A.L. Venkateswaran, *Defence Organisation in India: A Study of Major Developments in Organisation and Administration since Independence* (Government of India Ministry of Information and Broadcasting, 1967), p. 159.

[7] S. Cohen, *The Indian Army: Its Contribution to the Development of a Nation* (Berkeley: University of California Press, 1984), p. 119.

[8] The martial races' pattern of preferential recruitment into the rank-and-file of the Indian Army was based on the British authorities designating certain Indian communities as such due to any number of arguments, from the historical to the fanciful. Many of these communities did have a tradition of serving in the forces of local rulers long before the advent of the Raj. Hindusim also boasts a specific *kshatriya*, or warrior, caste. Other justifications were more species; for instance, the belief that soldiers hailing from the cold, 'hard' north of the subcontinent were tougher than those raised in the hot, 'enervating' south. The geography of military actions, limited from the mid-eighteenth century to the Second World War mainly to the subcontinent's northwest border, was used to argue that only troops drawn from this region were capable of facing the fierce, local enemies. Parade presentation also counted as British commanders seeking an idealized image of soldiers as tall, fair and sturdy, favoured men who are in the subcontinent found chiefly in the north and northwest. Finally, officers sought out the rural male, the yeoman and peasant farmer, plentiful in the north and northwest, whom they felt were much more easily impressed, trained and

unquestioning of orders than those relatively well-off, educated and high caste soldiers drawn from east India who had made up a large proportion of mutineers in the Great Mutiny of 1857.

[9] M.R.A. Baig, *In Different Saddles* (Bombay: Asia Publishing House, 1967), p. 10.

[10] ICOs were not accorded completely equal powers of command until the Second World War and the impending arrival of Japanese forces on India's borders in 1942.

[11] V.I. Longer, *Red Coats to Olive Green: A History of the Indian Army 1600-1974* (Bombay: Allied Publishers, 1974), p. 210.

[12] S. Huntington, *The Soldier and the State: The Theory and Politics of Civil-Military Relations* (Cambridge: Harvard University Press, 1957), pp. 83-85.

[13] H.D. Lasswell, 'The Garrison-State Hypothesis Today' as cited in S. Huntington, *Changing Patterns of Military Politics* (New York: The Free Press of Glencoe, Inc., 1962), p. 51. See also Lasswell, 'The Garrison State', *American Journal of Sociology,* 46:4, January 1941, pp. 455-458.

[14] Huntington, *The Soldier and the State*, p. 8.

[15] Huntington, *The Soldier and the State*, p. 10.

[16] Huntington, *The Soldier and the State*, p. 83.

[17] Huntington, *The Soldier and the State*, pp. 80-83.

[18] Huntington, *The Soldier and the State*, p. 83.

[19] Lieut.-General Dr. M.L. Chibber breaks this expertise down into: '(1) the organizing, equipping, and training of this [military] force; (2) the planning of its activities; and (3) the direction of its operation in and out of combat'. See Lieut.-General Dr. M.L Chibber, *Military Leadership to Prevent Military Coup* (New Delhi: Lancer International, 1986), p. 75.

[20] This and all following quotes from numbered officers are taken from their respective responses as written on the questionnaire and/or noted in oral interviews (see Appendix A).

[21] Baig, *In Different Saddles*, pp. 32-34.

[22] Thorat, *From Reveille To Retreat*, p. 5.

[23] M.A. Khan, *Friends Not Masters: A Political Autobiography* (London: Oxford University Press, 1967), p. 10. Sandhurst had hosted a number of foreign nationals from the Middle East, Siam and the Far East for many years before the arrival of Indians.

[24] General J.N. Chaudhuri, *General J.N. Chaudhuri: An Autobiography,* As narrated to B.K. Narayan. (New Delhi: Vikas Publishing House, 1978), p. 36.

[25] Lt. General B.M. Kaul, *The Untold Story* (Bombay: Allied Publishers, 1967), pp. 30-31.

[26] Venkateswaran, *Defence Organisation in India*, p. 190.

[27] As cited in P. Mason, *A Matter of Honour: An Account of the Indian Army, Its Officers and Men,* pbk. ed. (London: Macmillan Publishers Limited, 1986), p. 465.

[28] Cohen, *The Indian Army*, p. 107.

[29] B. Farwell, *Armies of the Raj: From the Mutiny to Independence, 1858-1947* (New York: W.W. Norton & Company, 1990), p. 299.

[30] Lieut.-General D.R. Thapar, *The Morale Builders: Forty years with the Military Medical Services of India* (Bombay: Asia Publishing House, 1965), p. 126.

[31] Thapar remembers one such officer who, though born and raised in Rawalpindi, pretended to forget Hindustani with such insistence that his British commander put him up for the relevant language test where he 'sang quite a different tune'. Another Brindian officer kept his drawing room clock set to Greenwich time 'just to know what people at home are doing at this time', although he himself had never having travelled further west than Egypt. Although Brindian entered common usage as a derogatory term, the British authorities approved, believing that commissioned Indian officers 'must resemble British officers—and what is more British officers from public schools—in every respect except the accident of birth'. Anything else would imply a lowering of standards. See Mason, *A Matter of Honour*, p. 458; and Thapar, *The Morale Builders,* pp. 93, 123.

[32] Chaudhuri, *General J.N. Chaudhuri*, p. 54.

[33] Not all commissioned Indian officers enjoyed successful military careers as evidenced by General Chaudhuri's account of the initial KCIOs to join his regiment (the 7th Light Cavalry). The first, a Burmese, 'must have disliked both India and soldiering for in a couple of years he left for home and a job with the Burma Police'. The second displayed 'a total inability to pass his promotion examination from Captain to Major' and eventually 'faded out via the Army Service Corps'. The third, the future Ambassador Baig, resigned for a mix of political and personal reasons. The fourth, too fond of alcohol, 'had to go' and ultimately ended up as an officer in an army of one of the Princely States. The fifth was killed in the 1935 Quetta earthquake. The sixth, Niranjan Singh Gill, 'fell out with the Colonel and was transferred to an infantry battalion'. After capture in the Second World War, he joined the Indian National Army (see chapter three). After independence, Gill held a 'number of minor ambassadorial appointments very successfully'. Although Chaudhuri does not describe the three KCIOs who joined the regiment before him, he points out that, 'If the Indian officers were rather a mixed bunch, that mixture was well matched by the British officers on the books of the 7th Light Cavalry at that time'. See Chaudhuri, *General J.N. Chaudhuri*, pp. 62-63.

[34] T.A. Heathcote, *The Indian Army: The Garrison of British Imperial India 1822-1922* (Vancouver: David and Charles, 1974), p. 105.

[35] See, for example, Flight Lieutenant Jerry Rawlings' 1981 coup in Ghana.

[36] Although British cadets of two similar naval training vessels located in the UK had long been eligible to sit the entrance examination for direct entry into the RIM, Dufferin graduates could join private shipping companies or various

government port authorities in India only. Not until 1931 were the first Dufferin cadets allowed to sit for the RIM entrance test (when four were admitted, including Admiral B.S. Soman, the second Indian naval chief). Indeed, the first two Indians to become RIM officers bypassed training on the Dufferin altogether.

[37] Chaudhuri, *General J.N. Chaudhuri*, p. 82.

2. THE INDIAN NATIONALIST MOVEMENT

The likelihood of a military coup depends as much on commissioned officers' perception of the civilian leadership as on their understanding of professional responsibility. If a regime is perceived as incompetent and/or illegitimate, civil supremacy-of-rule is endangered. So long as the viceroy and his administration represented the universally acknowledged governing authority on the subcontinent, questions concerning professional responsibility remained straightforward and commissioned Indian officers were free to concentrate on loyalty to their unit. However, steadily more forceful and responsible nationalist leaders were questioning the British right-to-rule. Could military *izzat* continue to shield Indian officers from the changing political landscape, or would the freedom struggle cause their professional responsibility to shift from the king-emperor to the nation?

Participation and Involvement

The independence movement interfered little with the military careers of KCIOs. Like young officers in any army, KCIOs were kept busy with their professional duties and responsibilities. Whether they were taught under diffident *koi-hai* types or helpful and tolerant British officers, the small number of KCIOs were very aware that as the first members of the army's Indianisation experiment, they were under close scrutiny by both British authorities and Indian politicians to see if Indians could handle command responsibilities as well as their British counterparts. So learn they must, and to the highest standards.

Conforming to the Indian Army's professional practices also meant assiduously ignoring politics, especially of the nationalist variety. As most army cantonments were located far from urban centres where nationalist politics were most prevalent, KCIOs became isolated from mainstream Indian thought after joining the military. More importantly, in the regimental mess, that particularly British military institution where 'decorum and regimental customs were taught and observed'.[1] Political discussions of any sort were judged wholly inappropriate. What little political awareness was allowed consisted of contrasting the internal racial and religious harmony of the army with the often ferocious communal violence afflicting Indian society at large. KCIOs worked just as hard as British officers to shield their men from any external attempts at highlighting religious and political differences which could destroy their regimental *izzat*.

The absence of nationalist sentiments amongst the majority of KCIOs was also connected with their conservative, privileged upbringing. With very few exceptions,[2] the families of KCIOs viewed nationalist politics as upsetting the status quo from which they profited and their privileged, commissioned officer sons accepted these sentiments. That the better Indian families continued to send their sons to Sandhurst despite the high failure rate of Indian GCs was but one indication of their unwavering enthusiasm for British institutions.

The general lack of nationalist sentiments among KCIOs is reflected in their reasons for joining the Indian Army. Take the seven illustrious RMC GCs discussed above. General Thimayya, Lieut.-General Thorat and Ambassador Baig enlisted in the military with boyish enthusiasm after little prompting from families and/or clans with a tradition of government service. President Khan was eager to follow in the footsteps of his *risaldar-major* father. Despite his strong nationalist sentiments, even Lieut.-General Kaul chose the military because he 'sought a life of adventure'.[3] While General Chaudhuri enlisted mainly as a means of getting away from his extended family circle of lawyers and doctors, he told his army interview board he wanted to join-up because 'the military profession was an honourable and necessary one while the importance of Indians joining the army of their country could not really be ignored'.[4] Lieut.-General Verma (who to a much lesser degree than Kaul displayed some nationalist sympathies) does not give any particular reason for his choice of career. Of the six out of seven KCIOs above who give a specific reason for choosing an army career, five do so because of a family/clan tradition of government/military service and/or to seek adventure. Only one, Chaudhuri, explains his decision in what may be deemed patriotic terms.

Not surprisingly, Indians with overt nationalist sentiments were hard to find once commissioned into the army. Lieut.-General Kaul (perhaps enhancing a tattered reputation; see chapter seven) remembers

> that whilst I and a few other Indians, in extreme minority, used to argue for our nationalist cause or in support of our nationalist leaders, many of our compatriots who rose later to occupy the highest military posts...poured unwarranted and critical comment on our national leaders...[5].

Although Kaul's compatriots may have included a number of Brindian officers who believed in the superiority of all things British, others must have been playing safe since Indian officers deemed particularly unsuitable to serving the Raj were sometimes forced to resign. A few KCIOs also resigned their commissions voluntarily, though this was usually the result of a disillusionment with the harshness of military life, the debilitating effect of entrenched racism, and/or because one could not make the grade rather than any appreciation of the nationalist cause.

A combination of all of the above factors led to Ambassador Baig resigning his captain's commission. From a very westernized and privileged background, Baig was deeply resentful of the racism he encountered in the Indian Army. Moreover, he clashed on two occasions with the same superior British officer, the second of which cost him a sufficiently high grading to be appointed adjutant. The politics of the freedom movement also entered his life when, while stationed at Allahabad, he visited leading nationalists. Soon afterwards, and despite the protestations of his fellow KCIOs that leaving would only add to arguments that Indians were unfit for king's commissions, Baig resigned.

Yet the vast majority of KCIOs concentrated on conforming to the professional standards and established practices of military life. Most were keen to achieve excellence in a career previously reserved for British officers which meant learning the methods which continued to bond all commissioned officers to each other, their men, and the regiment. Even Lieut.-General Kaul admits that his British company commander, Major Rees, 'was my idol and I tried to emulate his example throughout my professional life'.[6]

If KCIOs had little compunction about dismissing nationalist politics in favour of advancing their career, what of ICOs? Unlike the former, trained in England largely in the 1920's, the latter imbibed their professional education at the Dehra Dun-based IMA from the early 1930's onwards. Moreover, ICOs entered the Indian Army at a time when the freedom struggle had been active for some time; when the question of the British leaving India was rapidly changing from a context of 'if' to 'when'. Would their personal politics be more in sympathy with the goals of Indian nationalism than with the KCIOs' status-quo conservatism? If so, would this affect the continued loyalty and discipline of the British-led Indian armed forces?

The rising popularity of Indian nationalism is reflected in the experiences of ICOs as represented by those officers answering the questionnaires an/or interviewed. Fully a fifth of those commissioned before 1945 knew of participation in independence movement activities, mostly by their friends and/or family. Nonetheless, a few took part themselves, usually in the form of youthful, student-day exploits, joining 'demonstrations, shouting slogans and being thrilled when chased by the police!' A few were more daring (or foolhardy) in their nationalist exploits. While a University of Lucknow student, Lieut.-General 95 formed 'a small secret party of six in 1942...[which] carried out violent activities on a fair scale—[we] burnt some police stations, destroyed by explosives communications' channels, cyclostyled and secretly distributed revolutionary material'. They only narrowly escaped execution after arrest under the Defence of India regulations which allowed only death by hanging as punishment.[7] Despite such dramatic stories, the vast majority of ICOs did not have first- or even second-hand experience of the independence movement and joined the armed forces without censure from their family or friends.

Indeed, pre-war commissioned ICOs chose a career in the armed forces for much the same reasons as had KCIOs. To a large extent, this was because ICOs continued to be drawn from families where the father was employed in government service or the military. 'My great grandfather was wounded during [the Great] Mutiny in 1857 [and] we knew no other profession', writes Major-General 86. The adventure and glamour of a military career also continued to lure young men into a profession which still enjoyed an excellent status. Yet, for all their background similarities, ICOs were being drawn from a slightly lower strata of society than their predecessors and thus an increasing number cite career prospects as the prime motive in joining the armed forces (especially when, to entice educated young men to fight in the Second World War, recruitment to non-military all-India government services was suspended from 1942 until the end of the war).

There were also a small but growing number of ICOs who, like General Chaudhuri above, chose a military career for 'patriotic' reasons. However, because of their respective times of commissioning, just what KCIOs and ICOs understood to be 'patriotism' was very different. For the former, concerned with finding their place in a British-ruled subcontinent, there could be little sense of 'Indianness' exclusive of king and empire. Yet for many of the latter, the rise of nationalism during the interwar years meant that to be truly 'Indian' entailed imagining a subcontinent free from British rule. Such sentiments were potentially explosive in an army still commanded by a British C-in-C and a country ruled by a British viceroy. By the end of the war, there was less argument over what patriotism meant. Entering the armed forces just before the end of the Raj, Brigadier 90 'felt a sense of participation and belonging to the army of free India'.

Yet that was in the future; in the armed forces of British-ruled India, a growing nationalist awareness did not prevent ICOs from choosing a career in the armed forces for much the same reasons as had KCIOs, nor did it colour their actions once in uniform. There were a few exceptions: reflecting the conservatism of families used to government service, some ICOs looked down upon the credentials and abilities of nationalist leaders; at the other extreme, officers who openly voiced their support for the nationalist movement continued to be forced out of the armed forces. The rest, adhering strictly to professional military discipline, either ignored nationalist politics altogether or offered only passive support. Like KCIOs, ICOs concentrated on developing professionalism, ignoring any open support for nationalist politics which might interfere with their career prospects, and living to the full the pampered lifestyle of the hard-drinking, polo-playing, *shikari* (hunting)-mad 'Poona colonel'.

That a majority of ICOs were sympathetic but passive supporters of the nationalist movement and its leaders would be crucial to civil supremacy-of-rule in independent India. See Table 1 in which officers rank 'wisdom and stature of national leaders' as the joint eighth contributing factor in India never having experienced a military coup. The development of a core group of political leaders, including Mahatma Gandhi, Jawaharlal Nehru (both henceforth referred to by surname only), Vallabhbhai Patel, and Maulana Azad, belonging to one party, the Indian National Congress (henceforth referred to as Congress), which could unite and command both urban intellectuals and the uneducated masses in the campaign for independence was its greatest achievement. Moreover, mass participation in the freedom struggle over many years would give Indians an understanding of *swaraj* as rule by those popular political leaders who had led the movement. The stability crucial to ensuring civilian rule free from military interference was almost guaranteed as nationalist leaders, via Congress, would govern during India's formative years as a sovereign nation with the overwhelming consent of the people.

Nationalist Politicians' Understanding of the Military

Nationalist politicians' concern for the armed forces of the subcontinent began early. At Congress' inaugural 1885 session members expressed their concern at the excessive cost of maintaining the Indian Army, and a year later Raja Rampal Singh complained that prevailing military practices were 'systematically crushing out of us all martial spirit...converting a race of soldiers and heroes into a timid flock of quill-driving sheep'.[8] In 1886, Congress resolved that

> the military service in its higher grades should be practically opened to the natives of this country, and that the Government of India should establish military colleges in this country where the natives of India, as defined by statute, may be educated and trained for a military career as officers of the Indian Army.[9]

Six years later, G.K. Gokhale lamented that 'India is about the only country in the civilised world where the people are debarred from the privileges of citizen-soldiership and from all voluntary participation in the responsibilities of national defence'.[10] Even extremists like B.G. Tilak supported the participation of Indian military personnel during the First World War: 'If you want Home Rule be prepared to defend your Home....You cannot reasonably say that the ruling will be done by you and the fighting for you...'.[11] Tilak understood that self-government without the will or expertise for self-defence meant nothing.

Nonetheless, even those nationalist politicians most interested in military matters felt that increasing Indians' administrative, legislative and socioeconomic opportunities took precedence over defence issues. The efforts of those 'instrumental gradualists',[12] loyal members of the opposition interested in military matters, did achieve important gains in expanding Indian participation in the armed forces. Yet their more conservative members' 'jobbery',[13] or narrow preoccupation with opening up particular positions to Indians, eventually became seen as an unnecessary drag on the greater goal of independence.

As instrumental gradualists became consumed by the gathering pace of the nationalist movement, defence matters were increasingly left to the British authorities and 'traditional militarists',[14] Indian representatives of communities which had been previously, or were presently being recruited into the armed forces. In seeking enhanced enlistment opportunities for their members only, they hindered efforts at promoting a truly representative Indian Army. The combined pressure of traditional militarists and conservative British commanders ensured that the Indian Army's commissioned Indian officer corps continued to remain disproportionately drawn from traditional, British-designated martial races' recruiting areas.

Despite their waning interest in defence matters, instrumental gradualists consciously decided to allow commissioned Indian officers to learn their profession free from external political interference (and from being labelled as 'mercenaries'). Their reasoning is perhaps best expressed in the following conversation between Motilal Nehru and the young (then Lieutenant) General Thimayya where the latter has just asked if he should continue in with his army career:

> 'We're going to win independence. Perhaps not this year or the next, but sooner or later the British will be driven out. When this happens, India will stand alone. We will have no one to protect us but ourselves. It is then that our survival will depend on men like you'.
> 'You mean that we should stay with the army to learn as much as we can?'...
> 'Exactly...'.[15]

Lieut.-General Thorat describes a very similar conversation with the senior nationalist leader Lala Rajpat Rai.[16] Despite his frequent social contact with leading nationalist politicians and thinkers, Ambassador Baig also reports no direct attempt to influence his military career for political ends. By never trying to wean commissioned Indian officers (and soldiers) away from unquestioning obedience to their British commanders and towards nationalist politics, Congress' instrumental gradualists not only allowed KCIOs and ICOs to learn a degree of professionalism essential come independence, but ensured that India's future civilian governments did not have to contend with a politicized officer corps.

This happy outcome was in great part due to the beliefs and actions of nationalism's three great leaders; Gandhi, Nehru and Subhas Chandra Bose. Contrary to popular belief, Gandhi did not forswear violence.[17] Indeed, he raised and served in a volunteer ambulance corps in the Boer War as a rebuke to the 'average Englishman [who] believed that the Indian was a coward...'.[18] Gandhi also formed a Indian volunteer corps for ambulance duties in the First World War, and helped with army recruiting efforts upon his return. Despite his hope that the subcontinent's loyal service during the First World War would hasten the day of self-government, peace brought not freedom but an extension of wartime's harsh Rowlatt Act and the infamous Jallianwala Bagh massacre. Still Gandhi did not then, or ever afterwards, resort to violence in fighting for *swaraj*. That he did not may be traced to Gandhi's first-hand knowledge of the horrors of war in South Africa, his frustration with military discipline, [19] and scathing opinion of the Indian Army's lowly soldiery:

> Many weavers of the Punjab have left the handloom for the sword of the hireling [during the First World War]. I consider the former to be infinitely preferable to the latter. I refuse to call the profession of the sepoy honourable when he has no choice as to the time when and the persons or people against whom he is called upon to use his sword. The sepoy's services have more often been utilised for enslaving us than for protecting us, whereas the weaver to-day can truly become the liberator of his country and hence a true soldier.[20]

That Gandhi's military experience helped him reject armed struggle in favour of *satyagraha* as the chief means of mobilizing the masses against the Raj boded well for civil supremacy-of-rule in independent India since it precluded the use of commissioned Indian military officers' expertise in the management of violence. When independence came, there was little chance of the Indian public accepting any officer as a worthy rival to the highly respected civilian politicians who had led the fight for *swaraj*. Table 1 shows that officers agree; the 'independence struggle's non-'violent nature' is ranked in joint fourteenth place as a factor contributing to India never having experienced a military coup. As arms were unnecessary in successfully combating the British Raj, no public associations were made between might and right.

Like Gandhi, Nehru also had seen the positive side of military action and tasted military discipline. Along with the rest of the subcontinent, he had reveled in Japan's 1905 defeat of the Russian fleet, the first time in modern history an 'uncivilized' Asian people had beaten a major European power. Later, at Harrow, Nehru made 'sergeant' in the Officer Training Corps (OTC). That he must have enjoyed his duties is borne out by his helping to set up a committee in Ahmedabad to back the new Indian Defence Force (IDF), a sort of Indian version of the UK's Home Guard. Just at this time, however, Annie Besant was arrested for her Home Rule League activities and an angry Nehru persuaded his fellow committee members to cancel their activities. But for this coincidence Nehru would have become a soldier (albeit a reserve)! Despite the above, mostly favourable military experiences, a *shikari* expedition the young Nehru undertook after his return from England is more pertinent to an understanding of his later views on the military. He describes wounding an antelope: 'This harmless little animal fell down at my feet, wounded to death, and looked up at me with great big eyes full of tears. Those eyes have often haunted me since'.[21] Nehru's inability to forget the ugliness of killing only fortified what was to become a lifelong disapproval of military methods.

Nehru's pre-independence views and post-independence actions regarding the military reflect the classic liberal belief in the basic rationality and innate charitable behaviour of all men. He admired democratic societies in which politicians had to respond to the wishes of the people. In contrast, he wrote:

> The soldier is bred in a different atmosphere where authority reigns and criticism is not tolerated. So he resents the advice of others and when he errs, he errs thoroughly and persists in error. For him the chin is more important than the mind or the brain.[22]

Moreover, this reliance on brute strength rather than reason caused a military man to lose his basic civility: 'The soldier, stiffening to attention, drops his humanity and, acting as an automaton, shoots and kills inoffensive and harmless persons who have done him no ill'.[23] Nehru's rejection of the armed forces' Hobbesian view of society in favour of stressing the individual goodness to be found in all men and, hopefully, harnessed for the good of all, meant he never fully understood military thinking or its justification for unpleasant actions.[24]

Turned off by the military mind, Nehru readily appreciated Gandhi's belief that the armed forces were unnecessary in the fight to oust the British from India. For, though he viewed non-violence as a political tool rather than a moral obligation, Nehru disdained violence as inimical to Indian interests. Like the Congress' mainstream instrumental gradualists and Gandhi, Nehru rejected the military and militarism as viable instruments or targets for nationalist propaganda.

Indeed, Nehru never gave military matters much serious thought. He was far more interested in wresting fundamental political, social and economic control over the subcontinent from the British than in wasting time with the jobbery of opening up army recruitment or speeding up military Indianisation. However, Nehru did understand that the armed forces would have to be changed to suit the needs of an independent nation: although 'our present [1931] army is efficient, we must bear in mind that we shall have to re-organise it completely and create out of it and out of fresh material a truly national army, with a national purpose and a national outlook'.[25]

For Nehru, India's freedom would ultimately depend on the will of its people, not the strength of its armed forces. Raised and educated on British ideals of law, justice and democracy, and displaying the typical liberal's aversion to the military mind, he perhaps naively, never questioned that with supreme political authority would come complete control over the military. Only then would armed forces' concerns demand the attention of the political leadership.

The one prominent nationalist leader to appreciate the utility of violence was Subhas Chandra Bose. Deeply influenced by Swami Vivekananda's 'muscular Hinduism',[26] he believed Indians should not be afraid of defending their rights by force if necessary. In 1916 Bengal, where youths were physically combating petty racism on public transport, Bose observed that the 'effect was instantaneous. Everywhere the Indian began to be treated with consideration. The word went round that the Englishman understands and respects physical force and nothing else'.[27] For him, violence as a instrument for winning respect was effective—and stimulating.[28] Bose's belief in Indians standing up for their rights as equals extended to learning military skills. Upset that Bengalis were denied opportunities to receive the training necessary to defend the country, Bose applied to join the Indian Army's newly formed 49th Bengali Regiment (instituted as a concession to Bengali sentiment that they be allowed to participate in the First World War) to prove they were not the non-martial race the British believed.[29] Though rejected for his poor eyesight, Bose went on to gain military experience as a member of the University of Calcutta branch of the IDF.[30] That he reveled in the experience reinforced what was to become a life-long love for military methods and uniforms.

Bose's background, beliefs, military training and considerable charisma combined to propel him as a real alternative to the nationalist leadership duo of Gandhi and Nehru whose non-violent tactics too often appeared to delay winning independence. Recalling the terrorist tactics of early Bengali revolutionaries, he boasted: 'We in Bengal represent the real revolutionary force. Jawahar[lal Nehru] only talks. We act'.[31] Later, when faced with many Indian nationalists' caution at the first Round Table Conference, Bose pressed for the setting up of parallel administrative and legislative institutions: 'I am an extremist and my principle is—all or none'.[32] His radicalism made him very popular, both within Congress and especially among the Bengali public. Yet his sometimes overbearing militaristic streak and unwillingness to toe the Gandhi/Nehru religious/liberal line led Gandhi to force him out of Congress in 1939 and into the political wilderness. Early in 1941, Bose left India to fight British rule with methods considerably more militant than those of the mainstream independence movement (see chapter three).

Commissioned Indian officers were aware that nationalist leaders had a mixed opinion of the military and its methods. A significant minority of pre-1945 commissioned questionnaire respondents and/or interviewees remember a 'positive' attitude towards the armed forces based on the recognition that officers were professionally competent, inwardly sympathetic to the independence movement, and necessary for the defence of a future independent India. Yet a strong majority of their comrades recall nationalist leaders as displaying an indifferent or even negative attitude towards the armed force. For many, this was because Indian politicians simply were ignorant of military matters; for others, the latter were openly hostile, looking down upon officers 'as slaves of the British'. The perception that nationalist politicians had a lowly opinion of the armed forces could prove dangerous to continued civil supremacy in an independent India. As described above, most officers in pre-independent India held the freedom struggle and its leaders in high, if undeclared, esteem. If, at the same time, a majority felt that their admiration was not reciprocated by the nationalist politicians, civil-military relations could become tense.

The Public's Understanding of the Military

Throughout the interwar years, relations between the general Indian public and the armed forces remained distant and static. As Brigadier 44 explains, to a large extent, this was because officers and jawans lived in secluded cantonments apart from society:

> The Indian soldier was kept in a cocoon, totally divorced from all side-effects of civil administration. When he went on leave, he spent all his time in the company of ex-soldiers of the same regiment, caste and community. If he had a civil problem, his status as a soldier gave him immediate and favourable dispensation. The civilian never understood what made the soldier tick; the soldier disassociated himself from all civilian aspects of life. The two sides dressed differently, spoke differently and had almost nothing in common except family ties which, for the army man, was all military.

Even though KCIOs and ICOs had some opportunities to mix with both the people and polite society, the relationship, as it existed, was usually a variant of each party's respective station in life. On the subcontinent as elsewhere, simple rural folk were impressed by the stories of heroic derring-do and foreign campaigns which most soldiers tell. Those areas which provided the 'martial races' soldiery were particularly impressed with military life. Remember, writes Lieut.-General 49, 'India has been ruled for a thousand years by big and small kingdoms...Mercenary armies were the rule and the common Indian took them all in his stride for centuries'. The burgeoning Indian middle-class, chiefly interested in enlarging their educational and career possibilities, took their cue from instrumental gradualist politicians and gave little thought to the armed forces except when pressing for more commissioned officer places. Even the intelligentsia for the most part disregarded the importance of the military as the enforcer of British rule, thinking, like Nehru, that with political independence would come control of the military. For now, they shunned the armed forces as a tool of imperialism. Perhaps only the aristocratic families which supplied the KCIOs both knew of, and appreciated, the efforts of the Indian Army and its men as guardians of the status quo.

The importance of the public following their nationalist leaders may be seen on Table 1 where the officers rank 'political awareness of masses' in joint eighth place among factors which have contributed to India never experiencing a military coup. Although it may be argued that the Indian electorate's political sophistication is less than that in contemporary Western democracies, elections on the subcontinent have proved repeatedly that people understand the power of their vote to change governments. Again, the particular methods of the Indian independence movement—*swadeshi* (supporting Indian-made goods), *hartals* (the cessation of all normal activity) and *satyagraha* (non-violent non-cooperation)—demanded the participation of many millions of people from all across the subcontinent's geographic, ethnic, linguistic and socioeconomic boundaries. If nothing else, the struggle for *swaraj* gave the diverse communities of the subcontinent a novel sense of political unity, of together belonging to an entity called 'India'.

Conclusion

The paramount political importance of the nationalist movement on the subcontinent during the interwar years had minimal affect on the loyalty and discipline of commissioned Indian officers. While the conservative backgrounds of KCIOs made many indifferent to the politics of *swaraj*, many ICOs had first- and/or close second-hand experience of participating in nationalist activities. Yet, although some KCIOs and ICOs questioned the morality of their chosen career as demands for independence grew, once commissioned their desire to prove their professional competence and the armed forces' internal discipline of an apolitical outlook checked most displays of nationalist sympathies, however deeply felt. For some, this outward indifference was not easily achieved. Brigadier 40 recalls how commissioned Indian officers

> seemed to have a split personality: a favourable attitude towards the [nationalist] movement trying to overcome... [their] 'loyalty' to the crown...[and this] dichotomy building up a diffidence in them. While in private they were with the movement...they seemed to have been aggressively against it in their public posture. They generally had a very reverential

attitude towards the leaders of the movement at the time—
the latter were not yet politicians! [My italics.]

Despite such internal struggles, commissioned Indian officers' notions
of professional responsibility never shifted from the king-emperor to
nationalist leaders during the interwar years.

The indifferent attitude of most nationalist leaders towards military
matters was also crucial in ensuring the continued loyalty of Indian
armed forces' personnel. Rather than question the role of the army as
the chief instrument of British rule, most Indian politicians sought only
to open military careers to all Indians, or to better the advancement
chances of preferred martial races' recruits. Even Nehru disdained
thoughtful reflection of the present and future role of the armed forces
in favour of assuming that with independence would come the armed
forces' subservience to civil supremacy-of-rule. Those few nationalist
politicians interested in defence issues made it clear that a young
officer's prime duty was to learn his profession to the best of his ability
as his knowledge would be essential come independence.

Nationalist politicians' generally indifferent attitude towards the
military was shared by the general public. The common man remained
ignorant of the armed forces, the educated middle-class were interested
only insofar as to employment possibilities, while the wealthy and/or
aristocratic Indian families sending their sons to the RMC and IMA
were unwilling to see their social position reduced by challenges to the
status quo. The protective shield of objective control which separated
the Indian military from the general societal upheaval caused by the
independence movement remained firmly in place up to the eve of the
Second World War.

That both nationalist politicians and the general public could afford a
lackadaisical attitude towards the armed forces was due to the unique
non-violent nature and methods of the independence movement. With
no battles to be fought, the military officer's professional expertise of
tactics and weaponry was superfluous. *Swaraj* would be attained by
appealing over the heads of armed forces' jawans and officers, as it
were, and directly to the people.

With the exception of the Indian national armies of the Second
World War (see chapter three), the exclusion of the military in the
struggle for independence boded well for the future of civil supremacy-
of-rule in India. As no arms were necessary to overthrow the Raj, there
was no popular mystification of the soldier as hero. Instead, both jawans

and commissioned Indian officers had to defend themselves against the charge of doing nothing to hasten *swaraj* in contrast to the personal participation of millions of common people active in the nationalist movement. When independence came no one, least of all the military man, would be in a position to challenge the right-to-rule of those nationalist leaders who became India's democratically elected representatives.

---

[1] Lieut.-General S.P.P. Thorat, *From Reveille to Retreat* (New Delhi: Allied Publishers Private Limited, 1986), p. 14.

[2] A few KCIOs were themselves involved in freedom movement activities while youths. Lieut.-General Kaul recalls pasting up a 'nationalistic poster at the entrance of a British official's residence', delivering 'a parcel to a mendicant in the Old Fort [of Delhi]...at the dead of night', and making frequent visits to the legislative assembly where he heard 'stirring speeches' by leading nationalist politicians. Kaul was also in the gallery when Bhagat Singh and B.K. Dutt exploded two bombs in the legislative assembly and, along with many others present, was detained briefly on suspicion of having helped the conspirators. Lieut.-General Verma recounts how his father, 'a strong nationalist', reluctantly consented to his son leaving school in response to Gandhi's call for a student boycott of British educational institutions. Verma returned after losing an academic year and went on to join the RMC from the famous Government College, Lahore. See Lt. General Kaul, *The Untold Story* (Bombay: Allied Publishers, 1967), pp. 9-11; and Lieut.-General S.D. Verma, *To Serve with Honour: My Memoirs* (Dehradun: Natraj Publishers, 1988), pp. 2-3.

[3] Kaul, *The Untold Story*, pp. 16-17.

[4] Lieut.-General J.N. Chaudhuri, *General J.N. Chaudhuri: An Autobiography,* as narrated to B.K. Nehru (New Delhi: Vikas Publishing House, 1978), pp. 2-3, 25.

[5] Kaul, *The Untold Story*, p. 41.

[6] Kaul, *The Untold Story,* pp. 48-49.

[7] Lieut.-General 95's story is confirmed in T.N. Kaul, *Reminiscences Discreet and Indiscreet* (New Delhi: Lancers Publishers, 1982), pp. 93-94.

[8] As cited in V.I. Longer, *Red Coats to Olive Green: A History of the Indian Army 1600-1947* (Bombay: Allied Publishers, 1974), p. 124.

[9] Longer, *Red Coats to Olive Green*, p. 124.

[10] Longer, *Red Coats to Olive Green*, p. 136.

[11] From a speech at Poona, n.d., in B.G. Tilak, *His Writings and Speeches* (Madras: Ganesh, 1918), p. 365, as cited in S. Cohen, *The Indian Army: Its Contribution to the Development of a Nation* (Berkeley: University of California Press, 1971), p. 92.

[12] Cohen, *The Indian Army*, pp. 65-68, 78-85.

[13] J. Nehru, *Jawaharlal Nehru: An Autobiography* (New Delhi: Oxford University Press, 1980. First published at London: John Lane, The Bodley Head Ltd., 1936), pp. 293-294.

[14] Cohen, *The Indian Army*, pp. 58-65.

[15] H. Evans, *Thimayya of India* (Dehra Dun: Natraj Publishers, 1988. First published New York: Harcourt, Bruce & Co., 1960), p. 124.

[16] Newly graduated from Sandhurst, (then lieutenant) Lieut.-General Thorat found himself travelling back via ship to India on the same ship as the noted Indian nationalist leader Lala Lajpat Rai. He asked the latter:

> 'Sir, do you think that we have done wrong in joining the Indian Army, on the strength of which the British are ruling us?....
>
> 'No, I don't think so at all. How long will the British continue to rule us? One day India shall become a free country, and then we will need trained men like you. So work hard and qualify yourself for that moment'

See Thorat, *From Reveille to Retreat,* p. 8.

[17] In his article, 'The Doctrine of the Sword', Gandhi wrote: 'I do believe that when there is only a choice between cowardice and violence, I would advise violence'. See *Young India,* 11 August 1920, p. 3.

[18] M.K. Gandhi, *An Autobiography: The Story of my Experiments with Truth,* translated from the Gujarati by Mahadev Desai (London: Phoenix Press, 1949), p. 179.

[19] Gandhi served in a volunteer ambulance corps during the Boer War and helped nurse wounded Zulu prisoners during the Zulu 'Rebellion'. He had an unhappy time while serving briefly in an ambulance corps during the First World War. See Gandhi, *Autobiography*, pp. 179-180, 263, 293-296; and *Doctrine*, p. 3.

[20] M.K. Gandhi, 'Notes', in *Young India,* 27 October 1921, p. 338.

[21] As cited in M.J. Akbar, *Nehru: The Making of India* (London: Viking, 1988), p. 81.

[22] Nehru, *Jawaharlal Nehru*, p. 448.

[23] From J. Nehru, *Toward Freedom*, pbk. ed. (1941; rpt. Boston: Beacon Paperback, 1958), pp. 3-4; as cited in Cohen, *The Indian Army*, p. 105.

[24] See Nehru, *Jawaharlal Nehru*, p. 446.

[25] J. Nehru, 'The Defence of India', in *Young India*, 1 October 1931, pp. 284-285.

[26] M. Bose, *The Lost Hero: A Biography of Subhas Bose,* pbk. ed. (First published London: Quartet Books, 1982), p. 8.

[27] S.C. Bose, *An Indian Pilgrim* (reprint ed.; Bombay: Asia Publishing House, 1965), pp. 65-66 as cited in Cohen, *The Indian Army*, p. 100. See also Bose, *The Lost Hero*, p. 15.

[28] Bose himself was involved in physical violence while a student at Presidency College, Calcutta, when, according to various accounts, he either master-minded, led or simply witnessed the beating of an English history professor critical of Indian nationalism and accused of manhandling a student. Held responsible and expelled, Bose recalled the incident with pride. See Bose, *The Lost Hero*, p. 15; and G.H. Corr, *The War of the Springing Tigers* (London: Osprey, 1975), p. 79.

[29] Unfortunately, writes Chaudhuri, the 49th Bengali Regiment 'went to Mesopotamia, World War I's most ill managed campaign where they mutinied'. See Bose, *The Lost Hero*, p. 16; Chaudhuri, *General J.N. Chaudhuri*, p. 13; and Cohen, *The Indian Army*, pp. 99-100.

[30] During his student days at Cambridge, UK, Bose was unsuccessful in his attempt to have Indian undergraduates admitted to the university's OTC. See Bose, *An Indian Pilgrim*, p. 91 as cited in Cohen, *The Indian Army*, pp. 100-101; and Corr, *The War of the Springing Tigers*, p. 80.

[31] M. Edwardes, *Nehru: A Political Biography* (London: Allen Lane The Penguin Press, 1971), p. 73.

[32] M. Edwardes, *Nehru*, p. 78.

3. THE INDIAN NATIONAL ARMIES

With the exception of the formation of the Indian national armies (see below) and a few minor mutinies,[1] the Second World War saw commissioned Indian officers and men serve with distinction on Allied fronts throughout the world.[2] The tremendous wartime expansion of all three defence services necessitated new patterns of recruitment and posting which appeared to signal the end of the Indian Army's over-dependence on traditional martial races.[3] The war also afforded commissioned Indian officers new opportunities as the Indianisation experiment was ended, KCIOs and ICOs granted equal powers, and equal pay instituted for British and Indian officers entering during wartime. In the rush to fill commissioned officer positions, the Indian Army recruited approximately 9,000 Indian emergency commissioned officers (ECOs), many of whom were retained in the services.[4] The differences in the numbers and responsibilities of commissioned Indian officers before and after the war were staggering. For instance, whereas the seniormost KCIO had been a major, now over 220 Indian officers were lieut.-colonels and above, including four temporary or acting brigadiers. Whereas from 1920 to 1934, 214 Indians had become KCIOs and, from 1936 to 1939, 279 ICOs, by the war's end 9540 Indians held commissioned officer positions in the Indian Army (this huge numerical increase saw the ratio British to Indian officers excluding those in the IMS fall from 10.1/1 before the war to 4.1/1 by its end). On 22 October 1945, C-in-C (then General) Field Marshal Claude Auchinlek announced that permanent commissions in the Indian Army henceforth would be granted to Indians only.

Yet, a small but significant minority held in Axis prisoner-of-war (POW) camps joined tens of thousands of jawans imprisoned with them to form various Indian 'national' armies with the express purpose of invading the subcontinent and overthrowing the Raj. Although these forces proved to be no match for the Allies in combat, their mere existence and raison d'état worried a British Empire contemplating defeat on both the European and Far Eastern fronts while facing a nationalist 'Quit India' movement on the subcontinent.[5] How did Indian officers—and men—react to national armies' demands that they switch allegiances and join their brethren in fighting for *swaraj*?

Formation and Deployment

KCIOs, ICOs, Indian ECOs and jawans alike had to face the unique test of conflicting loyalties posed by the various Indian national armies. The Free India Legion (FIL), raised by Subhas Chandra Bose during his stay in Nazi Germany from Indian military personnel captured in North Africa, and the Centro Militare India, mustered by Mohammed Iqbal Schedai under the patronage of Benito Mussolini from Indians held in Italian POW camps, were relatively small forces and of negligible military consequence.[6] More formidable Indian national armies were to be raised in the Second World War's Eastern theatre.

The Indo-Japanese Indian National Army (INA) was led by General Mohan Singh, an Indian Army captain of the 1/14th Punjab Regiment who the Japanese had placed in charge of the 55,000 Indians POWs separated from their British officers after the fall of Singapore in 1942. Detecting their disillusionment with the British performance in the region, Singh began thinking of forming a revolutionary army and fostered a new spirit of 'Indianness' among the men through inclusive measures such as the abolition of caste divisions and a common kitchen. Singh eventually convinced the Japanese that this new, universal Indian identity could be used as the basis of a fighting force and up to 40,000 Indian POWs volunteered to serve, although a lack of resources and suitable officer numbers and experience limited the INA to approximately 16,000 armed personnel.

Whilst Singh hoped the heroic exploits of a battle-hardened, revolutionary liberation force close to India's frontiers would inspire the wholesale defection of Indian Army troops to the INA, his men were never allowed to demonstrate this theory. Despite some success in recruiting Indian Army jawans from among the remnants of the Slim River engagement and the POW camps in Kuala Lumpur, the INA was used mainly for propaganda purposes and the mundane tasks of guarding concentration camps, constructing runways and acting as camp followers to Japanese troops. Singh's protests over Japan's unwillingness to respect and equip the INA as a fighting force, the transportation of its personnel to far-flung labour camps, and the ill-treatment of Indian civilians in Japanese-controlled territories eventually led to his arrest and exile at the end of 1942. The INA now contracted to approximately 10,000 men as thousands of its soldiers reverted to POW status, a few hundred deserted, and all who remained were disarmed.

A brief stopgap force organized by the respected Japan-based Indian revolutionary Rash Behari Bose under the leadership of Singh's right-hand men, (Indian Army Lieut.-Colonel) Major-General J.K. Bhonsle and (Captain) Major-General Shah Nawaz (a.k.a. Shah Nawaz Khan) was re-energized by the April 1943 announcement that the nationalist hero Subhas Chandra Bose would be coming from Germany to lead the fight for *swaraj*. After his arrival in Singapore, Bose's reputation and charisma led around 10,000 Indian POWs to rejoin their comrades in a revitalized INA now renamed the Azad Hind Fauj, or Free India Army (FIA). From throughout Southeast Asia, 20,000 Indian civilians also enlisted.

Bose's dream of making the FIA into a full-fledged fighting force of 3,000,000 men the equal of the Indian Army was checked by the Japanese failing to accord it adequate arms and other resources. Whereas Bose wanted the FIA to act as the vanguard in the Japanese Army's forthcoming Imphal campaign, his hosts agreed only to accept small groups of men seconded to various formations for propaganda and espionage functions, and not to split the FIA's most potent force, the 3,000-strong 1st Guerrilla Regiment, into units of less than battalion size. Although a FIA unit briefly took Indian soil during the Japanese Army's Arakan operation, the Imphal campaign proved disastrous.[7] Crucially, Bose's belief that a British-led Indian Army personnel would not only desist from firing upon their countrymen in the FIA but throw their lot in with the national force was proved false.[8] The Allied counter-offensive was now in full swing and the Japanese were pressed to help themselves, much less the FIA. While some FIA units continued to fight, the battle now was for the defence of Burma and not the liberation of India; eventually, most quit the field, were captured or surrendered.[9] Those that remained lost their leader when Bose, while trying to reach the Soviet Union from where he planned to carry on the struggle against the imperialist Raj, died of burns suffered during the Taipei stopover on 17 August 1945.

The greatest achievement of the Indian national armies was getting Indian Army men and officers to switch their allegiance from the king-emperor to Indian military men. How was this done? Jawans joined the various Indian national armies for an assortment of reasons. FIL recruiters found that while some Indian troops expressed anti-British sentiments after their British officers had been taken away, the vast majority were unaware of their potential propaganda value to the nationalist struggle. Not until Bose ordered that the men be cut off from those NCOs championing the military discipline of loyalty did many consider his argument that to join the FIL was to fight as patriots rather than remain as captive British mercenaries. Nonetheless, the FIL's most effective recruiting method was promises of 'more money, more food, Red Cross parcels and access to women'.[10] The Centro Militare India may be assumed to have followed the same pattern in recruiting volunteer rank-and-file POWs.

Unlike their counterparts held by the European Axis powers, many of the jawans captured by the Japanese were recent wartime recruits, unused to combat and bewildered by their sudden change of circumstances. 'Alone with the Japanese conqueror',[11] and witness to the torture of commissioned Indian officers who refused to switch sides, many jawans enlisted in the INA/FIA from fear. Most Indian rank-and-file POWs, however, simply enlisted in the INA/FIA if and when their officers did. As described above, though jawans took an oath of loyalty to the king-emperor upon joining the Indian Army, their real trust extended only to their immediate outfit and its officers. After their British officers had been separated from them, the rank-and-file relied on the example of their Indian officers when deciding whether or not to enlist in the INA/FIA. As a result, several units such as 1/14th Punjab Regiment and the Garhwali Regiment went over virtually *en bloc;*[12] the men replacing their oath to the king-emperor with one sworn to the INA of General Singh.

Commissioned Indian officer POWs needed more convincing to switch allegiances. Several underwent torture but did not succumb to Japanese pressure to join the INA. Many were unconvinced of Mohan Singh's suitability as an army commander. Others, having seen the harsh treatment meted out to Allied soldiers and civilians in Malaya before their own capture, were suspicious of Japanese intentions towards both the INA and India. Yet a variety of factors eventually combined to cause a number of Indian commissioned officers to join the INA and, later, the FIA. Singh won over his skeptics by replacing Indian officers' long-standing grievances with the Indian Army's racial discrimination, slow pace of Indianisation, and differentiation of pay and allowances in a complex hierarchy of officers[13] with non-communal practices, one class of officer, one scale of pay, and a liberal promotion policy. A 'very large number'[14] of officers switched allegiances to protect their men—and themselves—from torture. The scope and suddenness of Japanese victories and the paucity of British-led forces left to defend the subcontinent led many officers to enlist in the INA/FIA to help protect Indian civilians from the invasion they believed was imminent. Any remaining reluctance to break their oath ended after officers learned of nationalist calls for the British to Quit India; thus Captain P.K. Sahgal 'joined the I.N.A. from purely patriotic motives. I wanted freedom for my motherland and was ready to shed blood for it'.[15]

After the removal of British officers, there remained only about 250 Indian officers—KCIOs, ICOs, Indian ECOs, VCOs and those seconded from the ISF—among the 55,000 Indian POWs at Singapore. Approximately 150 of these officers eventually enlisted with the INA and/or FIA (along with a large number of IMS officers, many of whom joined so as to care for the men). The vast majority consisted of VCOs who, because of the great shortage of experienced officers in the INA and FIA, were promoted to fill positions normally held by commissioned officers (both the INA and FIA then abolished this intermediate class of officers). These armies' remaining staff and higher command positions were filled by a 'handful' of KCIO majors and lieutenant colonels and 'score' of ICO and Indian ECO lieutenants and captains. ISF officers also accounted for a number of commissioned officers. Fifteen captured commissioned Indian officers who did not switch allegiance remained POWs for the duration.[16]

Courts-Martial

After the surrender of the Axis powers, the government of India had to decide what to do with the Indian military personnel who had joined the various Indian national armies. Although all were guilty of 'mutiny, desertion and waging war against the king-emperor' for which the Indian penal code prescribed the death penalty, the authorities could hardly execute tens of thousands of men.[17] Yet the steadfastness of the almost equal number of Indian military personnel who preferred enduring the hardship of POW life had to be shown to be respected.[18] In the end, the various Indian national armies' personnel were divided into three categories depending on their degree of guilt: 'Whites' were those who had simply joined-up; 'Greys' had displayed some additional acts of disloyalty; while 'Blacks' had taken on leadership roles and/or committed atrocities on their comrades. While the 3,880 Whites were reinstated in the Indian Army without loss of seniority, and the 13,211 Greys discharged with the loss of pay and allowances due during their period of captivity but with the retention of their pension, the 6,177 Blacks were scheduled for courts-martial.

Although nationalist politicians and the Indian press initially accepted the above punishments as fair on enemy collaborators, the Indian public soon perceived Indian national armies' personnel to be patriots. Despite opposing the Indian national armies during wartime, all the major nationalist parties soon followed suit and Congress provided the 'Red Fort Three',[19] the first three Blacks to face a court-martial, with a high-powered defence team (which included Nehru himself). The defence argued that the accused had acted out of a patriotic love for Indian freedom and, as such, demanded leniency.

As C-in-C, Field Marshal Auchinlek had to balance calls for showing leniency against what effect this might have on the men and officers of the armed forces. Crucially, he recognized that the future cohesiveness and effectiveness of the Indian armed forces depended on those Indians who by the end of the Second World War formed the majority of the Indian Army's commissioned officer corps. For Auchinlek, *'Every Indian commissioned officer is a Nationalist and rightly so,* provided he hopes to attain independence for India by constitutional means....their feelings are much the same as those of the public at large'. [My italics.][20] And the public saw the men of the Indian national armies as patriots.

Public sympathy, nationalist defence arguments, and the perceived pro-*swaraj* sentiments of commissioned Indian officers effectively guaranteed a compromise punishment of the Red Fort Three. All were found guilty of waging war against the king-emperor (and INA/FIA Major-General Nawaz of the additional charge of abetment to murder), cashiered, ordered to forfeit all pay and allowances, and sentenced to transportation for life. While confirming the guilty verdicts and other punishments, C-in-C Auchinlek freed the three by remitting the transportation order. He appears to have had little choice; later describing how the majority of commissioned Indian officers 'are sure that *any attempt to enforce the sentence* [of transportation] *would have led to chaos in the country at large and probably to mutiny and dissension in the Army culminating in its dissolution*, probably on communal lines'. [My italics.][21] In the end, the military authorities authorised the court-martial only of those Indian national armies' personnel suspected of atrocities and ordered any resultant death sentences to be commuted to rigorous imprisonment. Only 15 such men—two commissioned officers, four VCOs and nine other ranks— were tried and sentenced before C-in-C Auchinlek ended the operation altogether.[22]

The question of whether KCIOs favoured or disapproved of leniency for those who joined the FIL, Centro Militare India, INA and FIA is difficult to ascertain. The recorded experiences of the KCIOs used above show these officers most circumspect in revealing their opinions on this matter; in the respective (auto)biographies of President Khan, Field Marshal Cariappa, General Chaudhuri, and Ambassador Baig there are no more than passing references to these forces despite, in the respective cases of the first two, personal involvement in the battle theatres in which the national armies were active.[23] The remaining KCIOs—General Thimayya and Lieut.-Generals Kaul, Thorat and Verma—approach the issue from very different angles.

General Thimayya's main concern is the pull of opposite loyalties created by the mere existence of the Indian national armies. Upon hearing rumours of Indian POWs joining the Japanese in order to help oust the British from India, he recalls that Indian officers felt pride at their patriotism. If so, however, 'then we who served with the British must be traitors'.[24] For Thimayya, this dilemma was resolved as he learned more of Japan's future plans for the subcontinent. Professional and personal loyalties also came to the fore: 'to sign with the British, to learn from them, and then to go over to the enemy was reprehensible; I doubt if I could have done it'.[25] He also makes the argument that to stay and fight with the British would teach Indian officer valuable skills for the defence of independent India.

As two of the battalion commanders in the famous 'All-Indian Brigade' operating in the Arakan, General Thimayya and Lieut.-General Thorat had the possibility of fighting fellow Indians in Bose's national army. Thimayya recalls how FIA propaganda efforts—tapping telephone lines, cutting in on radio communications—came to naught since those targeted were Allied officers who, knowing more than the enemy about the war situation, could shrug off such actions. When, however, intelligence reports warned him that the Japanese were set to deploy FIA combat forces against his battalion, Thimayya became worried that his men might become demoralized. In the event, the situation did not arise, and Thimayya was spared having to lead his men against fellow Indians. Thorat mentions only his plan to say that he was a FIA man escaping from Indian Army captivity if caught by the enemy while out on a two-man reconnaissance patrol.

Lieut.-General Thorat does, however, offer an apology for those joining the Indian national armies. Saddened that his former regiment, the 1/14th Punjab, went over to the INA *en masse,* Thorat points out that

> the officers and men whose loyalty had failed or quailed [sic] under the Japanese heel...and what they did or did not do, had no connection with their fine record of duty in the Malayan campaign until it was lost. Prior to their capture 1/14th Punjab had lost three officers, five VCOs and one hundred and thirty-eight men killed in action. Thereafter a further one hundred and twenty men died in captivity.[26]

For Thorat, the men of the 1/14th Punjab Regiment may be partly excused their switch of allegiance after having been reduced to a state of utter bewilderment by the time of their surrender.

Lieut.-General Verma, who also saw action in the Eastern theatre, has little sympathy for those enlisting in the various Indian national armies and none for the politicians defending the Red Fort Three. Although he allows that many who broke their oath might have done so as a result of being told of the imminent defeat of the British worldwide, while some others may have been motivated by patriotism, 'by and large the majority gave in to avoid harsh treatment and to have an easier, more comfortable life'.[27] Verma backs this up by pointing out the discrepancy between the brave, fighting words and the timid, actual deeds of the national armies. He also castigates the military authorities for staging the first courts-martial in the politically charged venue of the Red Fort, therefore ensuring that the defendants were 'let off and put on a pedestal'.[28] For Verma, neither the Indian national armies nor their politician defenders emerge with any credit.

In contrast, Lieut.-General Kaul believes those joining the Indian national armies were, with some exceptions, true nationalists and stoutly defends the Red Fort Three's switch of allegiance. He also discounts those like C-in-C Auchinlek and 'some senior Indian officers'[29] who thought that freeing designated Indian national armies' Blacks would damage Indian Army discipline. As with his strongly pro-independence sentiments and activities described earlier, Kaul's views on the Indian national armies appear indistinguishable from those of nationalist politicians.

The differences in the four above officers' respective approaches to the Indian national armies are reflected in the actions of the 'about...half a dozen'[30] KCIOs surrendering in Singapore. Two of these six, Captains K.P. Dhargalkar and H. Badhwar, refused to switch allegiances. The four who did were hardly fervent converts. Captain Gurdip Singh Dhillon, for example, enlisted in the INA with the express—and later realized—purpose of getting closer to the front lines from where he could re-defect to the Indian Army. Major N.S. Bhagat refused to join the INA as he 'did not trust the Japanese at all'.[31] Though he later enlisted in the FIA to escape the deprivations of captive life in Borneo and make himself 'more useful in resisting the Japanese',[32] his insistence on opposing the Japanese whenever possible pushed Bose to dismiss him in 1944 for 'insubordination and disloyalty'.[33] Lieut.-Colonel Singh Gill, the highest-ranking Indian officer POW, enlisted in the INA after 'just drifting along':[34]

> I was puzzled and confused, unprepared to meet the circumstances that suddenly faced me. On the one hand there was the attraction of doing something for one's country. And my attachment to the British was not strong enough to prevent me trying. On the other hand all my life had been spent in a pro-British atmosphere, the effects of which still remain with me. I could not suddenly get away from it and start hating the British as Premier Tojo said we must do....Again, there was the question of safeguarding the lives and interests of the Indian soldiers and civilians...[35].

Later, Gill testified 'that this I.N.A. was not genuine and I could not believe that this will [sic] result in [the] freedom of the country'.[36] Lieut.-Colonel Bhonsle's motives for joining the INA are unclear.

KCIOs, then, constituted a far from monolithic bloc on the issue of the Indian national armies. General Thimayya concentrates on these forces' effect on Indian officers' loyalties. Lieut.-General Thorat looks to post-war reconciliation efforts. Lieut.-General Verma unhesitatingly condemns both those switching their allegiances and the politicians defending them after the war. Lieut.-Generals Kaul commends the motivation of national armies and the efforts to lessen their personnel's punishments. Yet the almost unanimous reluctance of those six KCIOs surrendering at Singapore to switch allegiances points to Thimayya's understanding of the paramountcy of personal and professional loyalties, scepticism of Japanese aims, and patience for the future good of independent India's armed forces as the most widely held view of KCIOs. Certainly, the highly individualistic responses to the national armies of all the officers described above, especially those with the opportunity to join them, suggest the British had little reason to question the loyalty of KCIOs.

The Raj had better grounds to challenge the loyalty of ICOs and Indian ECOs as these types accounted for the vast majority of commissioned Indian officers who joined the INA/FIA. Perhaps loyalty was a function of Indian officers' contact with the British? KCIOs, educated in English public schools (in the UK or India), trained at Sandhurst and embracing a Western lifestyle, were thought to share British officers' extreme disapproval of the Indian national armies. In contrast, ICOs and Indian ECOs, whose only close contact with the British may have been during their IMA training, were more likely to view those who joined the Indian national armies as patriots. Proof of this argument lay in the fact that 1/14th Punjab, one of the Indian Army's original eight Indianised units which by the time of the British surrender at Singapore was almost fully staffed by commissioned Indian officers, provided the bulk of the INA/FIA's leadership.[37] Yet thousands of ICOs, Indian ECOs, VCOs and ISF officers remained loyal to the Raj throughout the Second World War. Did they keep their allegiance only because they lacked an opportunity to join the Indian national armies?

Pre-1945 commissioned officers as represented by the questionnaire respondents and/or interviewees have mixed views of those who joined the Indian national armies, ranging from revulsion at their switching allegiances to admiration for their 'patriotic' motives. For many, the shift from war to peace is the key to their understanding, as Lieut.-General 49 explains:

> during the war we did not have sympathy with them—they were shooting at us. Also, we suspected that many had joined the INA[/FIA] to find a life easier than that of a POW. As time passed we found they were poorly motivated at the soldier's level and tended to desert from the INA[/FIA] to the Indian side at the first opportunity. They

> never fought well as a cohesive team...[After the war] we
> individually contributed towards their legal defence. In 1948
> many rejoined the army and performed well. There was no
> stigma but also no credit for INA[/FIA] service.

Despite this softening of attitudes, the majority opinion of pre-1945
commissioned officers is that their comrades who joined the Indian
national armies were unprofessional and their post-war justifications
insincere. 'You don't become a patriot at the end of a gun', argues
Major-General 97. Thus, while Indianised units like the 1/14th Punjab
could be expected to contain higher concentrations of disgruntled Indian
officers prepared to reconsider their ultimate personal and professional
responsibilities when circumstances allowed, most ICOs and Indian
ECOs agree with the anti-national forces sentiments held by KCIOs.
Given the anti-Indian national armies sentiments of all types of
commissioned Indian officers described above, C-in-C Auchinlek need
not have been so concerned with commissioned Indian officers equating
their own pro-nationalist sentiments with the necessity of leniently
treating the Indian national armies' designated Blacks.

Aftermath

The question of what to do with former Indian national armies'
personnel continued to vex the authorities. The new Interim government
met demands that the 15 imprisoned for committing atrocities be freed
by referring each case to federal court. After India became independent,
the government released all national armies' personnel still in prison
and offered them reinstatement into the Indian Army at the respective
levels at which they had left.[38] Yet both army HQ and the defence
ministry continued to oppose public pressure to reinstate Indian national
armies' personnel of all 'colour' designations.

This opposition to reinstating Indian national armies' personnel had a
sound basis. Military coups may be triggered as a result of corporate
grievances such as a perceived threat to the army's 'monopoly...[or]
functional claim to existence as the nation-state's principal, legitimate
organization of armed force'.[39] Might Indian Army officers see the
resurrection of FIL, Centro Militare India, INA and FIA units as just
such a threat? There is also the concern that 'a mission that
differentiates between service to "the government" and service to "the
nation" encourages the armed forces to move directly into politics'.[40]

Subhas Chandra Bose, Mohammed Iqbal Schedai and Mohan Singh recruited men into their forces with the 'patriotic' argument that the Indian Army was serving the interests of the Raj and not Indians themselves. Might re-admitted Indian national armies' personnel again differentiate between loyalty to a government and loyalty to the nation? Military coups may also be the result of clientelist motives. With their unique shared experience, the more committed Greys and Blacks of the Indian national armies may have been more ready to find occasion to organize themselves into a cohesive clique(s) than other Indian Army personnel.

Despite his personal sympathies, Nehru, now Prime Minister (PM), was aware that re-admitting Indian national armies' personnel into the regular army might create problems for civil supremacy-of-rule. The future Defence Secretary P.V.R. Rao recalls a 1948 meeting at which Nehru 'patiently listened'[41] while he and senior military officers advised that those men and officers who joined the Indian national armies should not be reinstated into the Indian Army. Rao paraphrases the PM's response as

> I do not agree with your arguments but I agree that the Indian National Army should not be reinstated. Do you know why? I do not want politics to enter the Services, which will be the result if these men are reinstated. The day politics enters the army, it will be a sad day![42]

Nehru could not have articulated better the military's own fears and the Indian national armies soon faded from public consciousness as their Grey and Black rank-and-file returned to village life (and other members found a future in public service).

Conclusion

While most Indian nationalists demanded the termination of the Raj before coming to Britain's aid in the Second World War, Indian military personnel fought for the king-emperor all over the globe. IMS Lieut.-General Thapar describes how this stark difference was possible:

> My [British] brigadier asked me what my mental reaction and that of the average Indian officer would be if suddenly we found Congressmen bossing over us. As I hesitated a bit,

he said he wanted to know the real feelings and did not want a sophisticated answer. I told him that our loyalty was to the government in power and not to any particular people or party. We had been trained from the very beginning to keep out of politics and have only one loyalty.[43]

What if there was an alternative claim to governing legitimacy?

The creation of the FIL, Centro Militare India, INA and FIA tested the loyalty of the British-led Indian armed forces' Indian men and officers. By defecting to the Indian national armies, argued Mohan Singh and then Subhas Chandra Bose, Indian military personnel would hasten an Axis invasion of the subcontinent and thus *swaraj*. Although some tens of thousands of Indian POWs, including the great majority of Japanese-held commissioned Indian officers, did eventually switch their allegiance, almost as many chose to endure the harsh regime of Axis prison camps.

More importantly, those jawans and commissioned Indian officers on active duty with the British-led Indian armed forces remained loyal to the Raj, believing their allegiance to the government in power and efforts during the war would have to be rewarded by independence. General Thimayya describes how, after the peace had been won,

> We Indian officers felt the excitement of great expectations....We knew that we had made a good showing in the war. We no longer lacked confidence. We knew, also, that the British Raj was irrevocably finished. We were impatient for the day when the Indian Army would serve its own country under its own leaders.[44]

The feeling that *swaraj* would not be long in coming buried post-war qualms about those who had joined the various Indian national armies. So long as this 'clique' of ostensibly politicized men were not allowed back into the armed forces—and they were not—even commissioned Indian officers could agree with the public and nationalist politicians that such men had been true, if misguided, Indian patriots.

---

[11] In September 1939, a group of 35 jawans and NCOs deserted from the 31st Punjab Regiment just before its departure for Egypt, and three months later there was a mutiny of Sikhs in the 25th Motorised Transport Company already

in Egypt. In July 1940, the most serious indiscipline of the war happened when 106 men of a Sikh unit attached to the Central India Horse refused to embark at Bombay for overseas service. Other acts of indiscipline included: two VCOs and 24 jawans of the 1/11th Sikh Regiment surrendering and/or deserting after being inadequately prepared for immediate action in Burma; seven Indian gunners mutinying and then surrendering to the enemy on Christmas island in 1942; and three Indian bombardiers trying to instigate an armed uprising on RAF bases in the Cocos-Keeling islands. All of the above incidents were isolated and the eventual punishment severe.

[2] Up to August 1945, the Indian Army suffered 179,935 casualties including 24,338 killed, 64,354 wounded, 11,754 missing and 79,489 POWs. Twenty-eight of the army's 31 Victoria Crosses were won by Indians, including 20 of the 27 awarded for the Burma campaign. The RIN and IAF also participated fully in the war effort, as did the ISF which by January 1944 had grown from 47,000 to 98,00 personnel.

[3] From 1939 to 1945, the Indian Army expanded from under 200,000 to over 2,000,000 men and officers, while the RIN and the IAF grew from 1,590 and 200 to 27,650 and 28,540 personnel, respectively. For the first time, previously separated communities of jawans were mixed together (with the exception of *harijans*—today known as *dalits*—who, although recruited for the first time in large numbers, were usually kept apart from higher caste soldiers). The military authorities found that proportionate representation of all classes from all provinces was not only necessary in terms of numbers, but desirable in promoting a national spirit of contribution. The Indian Army's stuttering adoption of modern military technology also convinced the authorities of the need for better educated jawans who were more readily found outside traditional recruiting areas. All of the above changes made for an Indian Army more like the RIN and the IAF in that recruits were chosen in a more meritocratic and non-discriminatory way.

[4] Emergency commissions ceased in 1946. That those Indian ECOs found fit to retain their commissions were high-quality officers was shown when one, General K.V. Krishna Rao, served as chief of the Indian Army from 1981-83.

[5] On 8 August 1942, Congress passed what became known as the 'Quit India' resolution which demanded the immediate end of the British rule in India.

[6] The 4,000-strong FIL was used chiefly for propaganda purposes (apparently inspiring 47 desertions from the Indian Army in North Africa during July-August 1942) and not as a combat army as Field Marshal Rommel refused to accept it into his *Afrika Korps.* Two months after Subhas Chandra Bose, fed up with his hosts' cavalier attitude towards both the FIL and Indian nationalism, left for Japan, the force moved to Holland where its personnel refused to go on active service (despite their newly sworn allegiance to Adolf Hitler). Its three battalions were then absorbed into the German Army as infantry Regiment No. 950 and posted to Bordeaux for non-combat duties. Later, during the Allied

offensive, the remnants of the FIL were incorporated into the Waffen SS where they remained until Germany's surrender and their subsequent repatriation to India. Trained as saboteurs, the two companies of the Centro Militare India under the command of Italian Major Avrea mutinied on 9 November 1942 when they—falsely—thought they would be sent back to Libya to help counter Allied landings. As a result, the force was dissolved.

[7] Of the 6,000 FIA men involved, 400 were killed, 1,500 died of disease and starvation, 715 deserted or went missing in action, and 800 surrendered. Of the 2,600 who returned, 2,000 had to be hospitalized.

[8] Although an intelligence/reconnaissance unit under FIA Major L.S. Misra subverted a picket of the ISF Gwailor Lancers on 4 February 1944, no regular Indian Army troops switched allegiance during the Imphal offensive.

[9] According to the British, in the Second World War the INA and FIA combined suffered 715 killed, 1500 dead from disease or starvation, 2,000 escapees to Siam, 3,000 surrendered or deserted, and 9,000 captured. See J. Connell, *Auchinlek: A Biography of Field Marshal Sir Claude Auchinlek* (London: Cassell, 1959), p. 797.

[10] M. Bose, *The Lost Hero: A Biography of Subhas Chandra Bose, pbk. ed.* (First published London: Quartet Books, 1982), pp. 186-187.

[11] Lieut.-General Sir F. Tuker, *While Memory Serves* (London: Cassell and Company, Ltd., 1950), p. 57.

[12] This was not always the case; for example, while all three ICOs—Captain Prem Kumar Sahgal, Captain Burhan ud-Din and Captain(?)/Major(?) K.P. Thimayya—of the 2/10th Baluch Regiment switched sides, the men did not.

[13] In the Second World War, there were KCOs, KCIOs, ICOs, British and Indian ECOs, VCOs, ISF officers, warrant officers (WOs)—introduced as replacements for VCOs, they were withdrawn by the end of the war—and NCOs.

[14] K.K. Ghosh, *The Indian National Army: Second Front of the Indian Independence Movement* (Meerut: Meenakshi Prakashan, 1969), p. 69.

[15] Moti Ram, ed. *Two Historic trials in Red Fort: An Authentic Account of the Trial of Captain Shah Nawaz Khan, Captain P.K. Sahgal and Lt. G.S. Dhillon and the Trial by a European Military Commission of Emperor Bahadur Shah* (N.p.: Moti Ram, n.d.), p. 115.

[16] See S. Cohen, *The Indian Army: Its Contribution to the Development of a Nation* (Berkeley: University of California Press, 1971), p. 155; M.W. Fay, *The Forgotten Army: India's Armed Struggle for Independence, 1942-1945* (Ann Arbor: University of Michigan, 1993), pp. 81, 140, 208-209; and Ghosh, *The Indian National Army*, p.59.

[17] The huge numbers of Indian national armies' personnel who surrendered and/or were captured before the end of the Second World War dissuaded the Indian Army from giving them the maximum punishment. Nonetheless, 30 such men, captured in battle or trying to enter India by parachute or submarine

during the war were sent for court-martial and nine, found guilty of espionage or sabotage activities, were executed.

[18] According to Viceroy Lord Wavell, the 25 per cent casualty rate for Indian POWs was almost four times that of Indian national armies' personnel. While the figures may be contested the point of the argument is obvious. Note that fully 11,000 of the 15,000 Indian POWs in the Western theatre did not join the FIL.

[19] These were (Indian Army Captain) INA/FIA division commander Major-General Shah Nawaz and two of his battalion commanders, (Captain) Lieut.-Colonel Prem Kumar Sahgal and (Lieutenant) Lieut.-Colonel Gurbaksh Singh Dhillon. Nawaz had been an Indian Army 1/14th Punjab Regiment ICO captain (and former winner of the Sir Pratap Memorial Prize for best IMA cadet), Sahgal a 2/10th Baluch Regiment ICO captain and Dhillon a 1/14th Punjab Regiment ICO lieutenant. Besides the charge of waging war against the king-emperor, Khan was accused of abetment in the murder of three comrades, Dhillon of four counts of murder and Sahgal of abetting the four murders. All of these charges, however, stemmed from the officers' carrying out, or passing on, the orders of their superiors according INA/FIA procedures. Selecting a Muslim, Hindu and Sikh defendant, respectively, to show religious impartiality only served to unify Indians of all faiths behind the defendants. Picking New Delhi's Red Fort, the historical seat of Mughul rule and the prize of the mutineers of 1857, as the courts-martial site was seen as a deliberate provocation to nationalist sensibilities. Finally, opening the trial to the public ended any hopes of a non-contentious resolution. NB: The authorities' first choice to face a post-war court-martial was (Indian Army 2/10th Baluch Regiment ICO Captain) INA/FIA Lieut.-Colonel Burhan ud-Din. Charged with arbitrarily ordering two men who had attempted to desert to be flogged by a whole battalion (which resulted in the death of one), his trial was postponed on a late technicality. Ud-Din was eventually sentenced to seven years rigorous imprisonment.

[20] Connell, *Auchinlek*, pp. 813, 946.

[21] Connell, *Auchinlek*, pp. 813, 946.

[22] Though he spent six months in British custody (after two years and eleven months under Japanese arrest), and came up before a court of inquiry, INA General Mohan Singh himself never faced a court-martial and was freed on 4 May 1946.

[23] While President Khan saw action in the Burma campaign, he did not come up against any Indian national forces. He notes only that some officers of his old battalion, the 1/14th Punjab, 'joined the Indian National Army, a Japanese-inspired force'. General Chaudhuri, also in Burma and usually expansive on matters concerning the professionalism of the Indian Army, offers no comment on the Indian national armies. Although Ambassador Baig resigned from the army in 1930, he describes meeting Mrs. Ammu Swaminadhan whose daughter

Laxmi (a.k.a. Lakshmi) 'won great renown as the Commander of the [FIA's all-female] Ranee of Jhansi Brigade', and briefly describes the career of Bose's ADC, Abid Safrani. Field Marshal Cariappa's biographer mentions but does not elaborate on Cariappa's service as one of the Red Fort courts-martial 'Presidents'. See M.R.A. Baig, *In Different Saddles* (Bombay: Asia Publishing House, 1967), pp. 78-79, 102; General J.N. Chaudhuri, *General J.N. Chaudhuri: An Autobiography,* as narrated to B.K. Narayan (New Delhi: Vikas Publishing House, 1978); I.M. Muthanna, *General Cariappa: The First Indian Commander-in-Chief* (Mysore: Usha Press, 1964), p. 33; and Lt. General B.M. Kaul, *The Untold Story* (Bombay: Allied Publishers, 1967), pp. 13-14.

[24] H. Evans, *Thimayya of India* (First published New York: Harcourt, Bruce & Co, 1960; Dehra Dun: Natraj Publishers, 1988), pp. 180-181. Thimayya's inner conflict was exacerbated by the knowledge that the older of his two brothers in the Indian Army, Captain(?)/Major(?) K.P. Thimayya, called up from the reserve OTC to 2/10th Baluch Regiment, had joined the INA.

[25] Evans, *Thimayya of India*, p. 181.

[26] Lieut.-General S.P.P. Thorat, *From Reveille to Retreat* (New Delhi: Allied Publishers Private Limited, 1986), p. 84. Thorat also mentions that both Mohan Singh and Shah Nawaz of the 1/14th Punjab Regiment joined the INA. Thorat, *From Reveille to Retreat*, p. 39.

[27] Lieut.-General S.D. Verma, *To Serve with Honour: My Memoirs* (Dehradun: Natraj Publishers, 1988), p. 45.

[28] Verma, *To Serve with Honour*, p. 46.

[29] Kaul, *The Untold Story*, p. 74.

[30] Ghosh, *The Indian National Army*, p. 63.

[31] From [FIA] Col. Bhagat's statement to the defence counsel of the first INA court martial, INA defence papers, as cited in Ghosh, *The Indian National Army*, p. 63.

[32] From [FIA] Col. Bhagat's statement to the defence counsel of the first INA court martial, INA defence papers, as cited in Ghosh, *The Indian National Army*, p. 63.

[33] From [FIA] Col. Bhagat's statement to the defence counsel of the first INA court martial, INA defence papers, as cited in Ghosh, *The Indian National Army*, p. 63.

[34] As used in G.H. Corr, *The War of the Springing Tigers* (London: Osprey, 1975), p. 103. Although there were some IMS Indian officer POWs of higher rank, Lieut.-Colonel Gill was the highest-ranking combat officer.

[35] As cited in Corr, *The War of the Springing Tigers*, p. 103.

[36] As cited in Ghosh, *The Indian National Army*, p. 64.

[37] INA/FIA officers drawn from 1/14th Punjab include (Indian Army KCIO Captain) Gurdip Singh Dhillon, (ICO Captain) General Mohan Singh, (ICO Captain) Major-General Shah Nawaz (ICO Adjutant GSO 3 Intelligence) Major-General Zaman Kiani (a.k.a. Mohammed Ziani Kiani), (Indian ECO

Captain) Major Abdul Rashid, and (ICO Lieutenant) Lieut.-Colonel Gurbaksh Singh Dhillon.

[38] As this meant forfeiting up to three ranks relative to those Indian military personnel who had remained true to their oath, only one man took up this offer.

[39] W.R. Thompson, *The Grievances of Military Coup-Makers* (Beverly Hills: Sage Publications, 1973), p. 15.

[40] C.E. Welch Jr. and A.K. Smith, *Military Role and Rule: Perspectives on Civil-Military Relations* (North Scituate: Duxbury Press, 1974), pp. 12-13.

[41] P.V.R. Rao, *India's Defence Policy and Organisation since Independence* (New Delhi: United Service Institution of India, 1977), p. 4.

[42] Rao, *India's Defence Policy*, pp. 4-5.

[43] R. Thapar, *A History of India: Volume One,* pbk. ed. (First published Harmondsworth: Penguin Books, 1966), p. 179.

[44] Evans, *Thimayya of India*, p. 230.

4. THE TRANSFER OF POWER

After the test of the Indian national armies came the challenges brought by the transfer of power and independence including immediate post-war strikes and mutinies, the division of the armed forces between India and Pakistan, the departure of British military personnel, and immediate actions in Punjab, Junagadh, Hyderabad, and Jammu & Kashmir (J&K). *Swaraj* also saw an Indian political and administrative elite assume governing power. This chapter will examine commissioned Indian officers' confidence in their own personal and professional abilities to meet these challenges, and in the capabilities of the new governing elite. Would independence necessitate any changes to the country's established civil-military relationship boundaries?

Mutinies, Partition and Immediate Actions

On 18 February 1946, Indian ratings of the RIN training ship, HMIS Talwar began a mutiny which in days encompassed nearly 3,000 sailors on naval ships in Bombay harbour. While its flashpoint was Talwar Commander F.W. King's mendacious denial of having used abusive language towards ratings, the sailors had long-standing grievances over their food, pay and conditions. The mutiny took on a nationalist character and three days of unprecedented violence swept Bombay as sailors and protesters shouting 'Jai Hind' and 'Quit India' fought running battles with British Army troops. Seamen on vessels and in shore installations in Karachi, Madras, Vizagapatam, Calcutta, Cochin, and the Andaman islands also committed acts of indiscipline, and other units of the Indian armed forces vented their own grievances.[1]

Yet the British nightmare of a general Indian Army uprising never appeared likely. Some thought the simple jawan had less time for indiscipline than their more educated and politically aware counterparts in the RIN and RIAF (the IAF won the 'Royal' prefix in March 1945). Others felt commissioned Indian officers' professional sense of responsibility to the government helped keep jawan discipline. Most importantly, Indian officers opposed post-war strikes and mutinies not because they underestimated their men's grievances, but because discipline was, and in an independent subcontinent would be inviolable if the armed forces' fighting effectiveness was to be maintained.[2]

Most nationalist politicians themselves were unwilling to risk developing the Bombay mutiny into a general revolt against the Raj. The actions of the ratings and their civilian sympathizers, and the reaction of the British authorities occasioned extreme violence anathema to the Congress of Nehru and Gandhi. Widening the mutiny would also enhance the power and prestige of those communists increasingly influential in leading the strikers, a unpalatable development for both Congress and the now-powerful Muslim League (ML), neither of which wanted to endanger the future military discipline of independent India and Pakistan, respectively. When Nehru, ML leader Jinnah and other nationalist leaders advised the ratings to lay down their arms in return for promises that their grievances would be addressed and no retribution taken, the mutiny came to an end.

Despite the reluctance of most nationalist politicians to use the mutinies and strikes overtly to hasten the transfer of power, British politicians took the hint. On 18 February 1947, British PM Clement Attlee told the House of Commons that 'His Majesty's Government wished to make it clear that it is their definite intention to take the necessary steps to effect the transference of power into responsible Indian hands by a date not later than June 1948'.[3] Attlee's commitment and the work of Viceroy Lord Louis Mountbatten, Nehru, Gandhi, Jinnah and many others led to the 'partition' of the subcontinent into the independent nations of Pakistan and India on 14 and 15 August 1947, respectively.

Partition meant dividing the personnel, materials, stores, and fixed installations of the British-led Indian military in a general 2/1 ratio between India and Pakistan to form 'new' armies, navies and air forces. The Indian Army and Pakistan Army were allocated regiments roughly on a communal basis. In mixed regiments, each man in every unit or training institution was allowed to choose which new nation to serve. Muslims hailing from Pakistani territory could not, however, join the Indian Army nor could non-Muslims with roots in India opt for the Pakistan Army. The RIN and RIAF were similarly divided, and the ISF integrated into the new forces of India and Pakistan.[4] On 14 August 1947, C-in-C Auchinlek signed the last order of the British-led Indian

Army, and in December 1947 the second regular batch of post-war IMA cadets graduated into the army of independent India.[5]

On top of the expected organisational and logistical difficulties came worries that the severe Hindu *versus* Muslim disturbances sweeping civilian society were beginning to affect the military, especially after it became apparent that two independent nations were to be formed and each serviceman given the choice of which to serve. Pressures on Hindu and Muslim servicemen to choose 'correctly' became intense. For all the tensions, however, the break-up of the British-led forces was hard on officers who had served together on the subcontinent and all over the world, and a majority of pre-1947 commissioned officers recall that partition negatively affected their personal lives in the shape of moving and/or losing their home, giving up friends, etc. In the end, the break-up of the British-led Indian armed forces was completed with no major indiscipline, especially as the ever-quickening timetable for independence forced the quick resolution of most problems.

Of more concern was the armed forces' lack of experienced commissioned Indian officers, exposed by the departure of British military personnel upon independence.[6] For instance, the first Indian to hold an army HQ staff appointment, essential for learning the techniques of planning and strategy and the formulation of policy, did not do so until after the commencement of the Second World War. Despite wartime commissions, the Indian Army was left with just five substantive and 88 acting/temporary lieut.-colonels. Moreover, those Indian ECOs who were retained in the military had undergone a short training period geared to producing battlefield commanders, not peacetime 'managers'.[7] While the pre-partition RIN had 211 British commissioned officers, their Indian counterparts numbered just 25, the highest-ranking of whom were two captains. In addition, the RIN was to lose most of its mainly Muslim Indian WOs and senior ratings to Pakistan.[8] Although the RIAF was from the outset completely Indianised, wartime expansion had necessitated that 100 RAF officers (and 500 RAF airmen) be loaned to join its 33 commissioned Indian officers. All three services also had to deal with acute shortages of qualified technical officers. This shortage of experienced senior commanders was met by the loan of British officers formerly in the pre-*swaraj* Indian armed forces (with the exception of the RIAF which accepted RAF officers),[9] the rapid promotion of relatively inexperienced, junior Indian officers, and the re-admittance of Indian officers previously deemed unsuitable for retention at war's end. Inevitably, standards were lowered.

Despite this conclusion, the vast majority of pre-1947 commissioned officers as represented by the questionnaire respondents and/or interviewees refuse to acknowledge that partition had any negative effect on the professionalism of the independent India's 'new' armed forces (see **Table 2**). There are some exceptions; just over a fifth of officers cite factors such as the lack of senior officers, the plethora of less-experienced ECOs and the resultant quick promotion schedule as inimical to the effectiveness of the armed forces at independence. Yet this minority is dwarfed by the three-quarters majority who feel that the army, navy and air force of independent India were fully prepared for *swaraj*. The key to their confidence is the belief that, however inadequate were the military's organisational and command resources at independence, professional expertise and corporateness would remain high enough to provide a solid foundation on which to base the defence of the nation. Indian officers rose to the challenge, satisfactorily filling the top command and staff positions in all three services: on 15 January 1949, (then General) Field Marshal Cariappa was appointed the first Indian Indian Army C-in-C; on 1 April 1954 Air Marshal Subroto Mukherji became the first Indian head of the air force;[10] and on 22 April 1958 Admiral K.D. Katari became the first Indian naval chief.

TABLE 2: Prepared for Independence?*

	Armed Forces		Political Leadership		Civil Service	
	Per cent (Number)					
Yes	72.24	(34)	61.27	(29)	78.73	(37)
No	23.40	(11)	34.04	(16)	12.77	(6)
No Answer	4.26	(2)	4.26	(2)	8.51	(4)
Total	100.00	(47)	100.00	(47)	100.00	(47)

* Asked of Pre-1947 commissioned officers only.

Professional expertise and corporateness in isolation, however, may readily endanger civilian supremacy-of-rule if officers deem their own personal and/or organisational needs supreme. Yet the pre-1947 commissioned officers clearly recall that that independent India's officers retained their professional characteristic of responsibility; that is, using their expertise only at the discretion of their client, society. Although, writes Brigadier 31, 'most of us did not have long experience, our seniors were top class, devoted patriots'. Every officer, adds

Brigadier (Justice) 47, was 'very well trained, well led and disciplined—and fully dedicated to their new role of guarding the freedom of the country'. Other officers stress the military's inherited tradition of being 'apolitical'. What remained to be seen was whether independent India's commissioned officer corps understood professional responsibility to mean loyalty to the legitimate government of the day, thereby decreasing the likelihood of military intervention, or to a higher sense of 'nation', thus increasing the chances of an armed forces' coup.

The testing of the professional expertise, corporateness and responsibility of commissioned Indian officers began even as independence was being won. In the midst of partitioning its personnel and resources, the British-led Indian Army set up a Boundary Force to try to stem the communal atrocities which killed up to half a million of the refugees moving between the two new nations of India and Pakistan.[11] Immediately after independence India's armed forces were deployed to help integrate the Princely States of Junagadh, Hyderabad and J&K.[12] In the first, the ruling Muslim nawab's decision to opt for Pakistan—despite Junagadh being wholly inside Indian territory and having a population 80 per cent Hindu and Jain—failed when Indian military forces threatened invasion and forced him to flee. In the second, the ruling Muslim nizam's declaration of independence—despite Hyderabad's size, geographic position and predominantly Hindu population—and failure to control the Razakars (a 200,000-strong militant armed wing of the Ittehad-ul-Musilmeen party of feudal Muslim landowners) led to the Indian Army forcing his surrender in 'Operation Polo'. In the third, procrastination by J&K's Hindu maharaja over which country his strategically located and overwhelmingly Muslim populated state would join led to a bloody 15-month war between Pakistani proxies and Indian military forces, the repercussions of which continue to this day.

The Junagadh, Hyderabad and J&K actions demonstrated the ability of Indian officers to meet professional commitments at all levels. In Junagadh, they massed forces on the state's borders while awaiting higher political machinations. In Hyderabad, they commanded an operation which overwhelmed the state's army and the Razakars in just 100 hours, and (then Major-General) General Chaudhuri went on to serve a 13-month term as military governor. In J&K, they successfully repelled a proxy-Pakistani invasion in extreme conditions and at very short notice. It was a source of pride that this operation was carried out under Indian officers operating at the highest command positions.[13] The RIAF and RIN also provided a measure of support in J&K, and Major Som Nath Sharma became the first (posthumous) recipient of independent India's supreme gallantry award, the Param Vir Chakra.

The performance of all personnel in the armed forces' immediate actions, especially in J&K, also established the reliability and loyalty of those Muslim men and officers who had opted to serve independent India,[14] and thereby helped ensure civil supremacy-of-rule. Although, in terms of their share of the national population, some communities are over-represented among officers of one or more of the defence services (see the case of Sikh officers in the Indian Army as described in chapter nine), virtually all of India's communities are represented in the officer corps. [15] The ability to admit and promote to the highest positions a wide mix of officers free from doubts that their personal background might overrule their professional behaviour has kept the Indian armed generally free from the influence of ready-made, homogenous cliques or clientelist groups which are more amenable to unite around a common regional, ethnic, religious, economic or other grievance and therefore more likely to further their own agenda at the expense of the military, the government, and/or the state. That Indian officers recognize the importance of recruitment open to all may be seen in Table 1 in which 'nationally representative military personnel' is ranked as the fourth most important factor contributing to India never having experienced a coup. Put bluntly, the 'heterogeneity' of the over 40,000 Indian Army officers currently serving has helped prevent the formation of intra-military cliques on a sufficient scale to organize a forcible take-over of government.

Civilian Counterparts

History shows that newly emerging states suffering from ineffective and therefore vulnerable civilian rule are particularly prone to military takeovers. In India, however, a core group of nationalist leaders brought to government a deeply held, personal belief in the moral superiority of democratic rule which they enshrined in a national constitution, and long experience of political responsibility at the provincial and central levels in which the techniques essential to self-rule were absorbed. In addition, mass participation in *satyagraha* had given many people an understanding of *swaraj* as government by the popular political leaders and the one party, Congress, which had led the nationalist movement.

Yet, however popular and experienced the nationalist politicians may have been fighting the Raj, India would not long enjoy stable democratic rule if its military officers did not also perceive the political leadership as fully prepared for the challenges of *swaraj*.

As describe above, relations between commissioned Indian officers and politicians was somewhat mixed before independence and this is reflected in Table 2. Over a third of pre-1947 commissioned officers believe the political leadership was not prepared for *swaraj*. In reference to the frequent arrest of Gandhi, Nehru and other nationalist leaders, Brigadier 60 argues that 'going to jail does not train you in administration'. Others cite the act of partition as the most glaring example of Indian politicians' unpreparedness to rule. Nonetheless, this group is greatly outnumbered by the three-fifths of their comrades who feel that politicians were ready to meet the challenges of independence. Respect for the political leadership's personal qualities is the touchstone for this group of officers. 'At that time', says Brigadier 63, 'India had a galaxy of great men'. Lieut.-Colonel 80 adds that 'there was one Indian in whom every serviceman had the utmost faith...Nehru [and] all that [he] did and stood for was accepted'.

This majority belief in the personal experience, eminence and integrity of independent India's initial political leadership went a great way to ensuring civil supremacy-of-rule. See Table 1 in which the officers rank 'initial political stability, quality and/or democratic rule', and 'wisdom and stature of national leaders' as the third and joint eighth most important factors, respectively, in India never having experienced a military coup. Commissioned Indian officers' recognition of the political leadership's quality at independence meant their professional sense of responsibility was not limited to loyalty to the state as separate from the government, but embraced the country's civilian political leadership as well.

The third arm of government was the bureaucracy. Unlike the British-led Indian armed forces, the Indian Civil Service (ICS) had always been open to Indians. However, not until the development of widespread Indian educational facilities along British public school-lines and the passage of the Government of India Act of 1919 which allowed ICS examinations to be held in India and Burma as well as in London did Indian candidates begin to win a significant proportion of ICS places. Indian representation in the ICS further increased with the suspension (never to be rescinded) of British recruitment in 1939. (From 1942 to the end of the Second World War, Indian recruitment into the ICS was also stopped in an effort to get educated young men to join the military.) Like commissioned Indian officers, however, Indian ICS officers had to deal with the complexities and prejudice of representing the British ruling elite while their countrymen struggled for *swaraj*.

Whatever their personal working relationships and/or opinions of the freedom struggle, Indian ICS officers provided their new nation with an invaluable cadre of top administrative experience in the new Indian Administrative Service (IAS). Indeed, just before independence, 43 Indian ICS officers were secretaries, joint secretaries or their equivalent in the Indian government of secretariat, compared to 14 British and European personnel (with 13 others on leave) holding such offices.[16] Indian representation in the provincial civil services was even more numerous and experienced. Still, as in the case of the political leadership above, Indian democracy would not long endure if military officers themselves remained unconvinced of the civil service's readiness for independence.

As seen in Table 2, this was not an issue as almost four-fifths of pre-1947 commissioned officers believed the country's administrators were ready for independence. There are a few exceptions, and the complaint of several officers that Indian bureaucrats were trained to run a top-down, colonial administration rather than one suited to a democracy of the people is an important one. Yet most have nothing but praise for a civil service composed, recalls Air Marshal 3, of 'well trained and experienced men of integrity and administrative capability'.

The vast majority's confidence in the respective preparedness of the civil service is reflected in Table 1 where officers rank 'administrative efficiency' as the joint eighth most crucial factor contributing to India never having had a military coup. The confidence of Indian military officers in the respective abilities of the civil service and political leadership at independence goes some way in negating the common characterisation of newly independent nations as struggling to modernize because of ineffective governmental leadership. However, it remains to be seen whether civilian politicians and bureaucrats would fulfill the armed forces' high expectations. Failing to do so might certainly endanger the democratic civil-military relationship.

The Structure of Civil-Military Relations

The transfer of power raised questions as to the role of the armed forces in an independent India. Gandhi saw no use for conventional armed forces and argued that a police force could keep internal order while the 'good-will of the whole world'[17] would be sufficient to defend India. Failing that, the military's organisational skills and manpower should be harnessed for domestic duties and soldiers should 'plough the land, dig wells, clean latrines and do every other constructive work that they can, and thus turn the people's hatred of them into love'.[18] Along with relief/rescue functions, aid in times of national disaster, maintenance of essential services, and assistance in quelling internal disturbances, such developmental activities fall under the remit of any armed forces' secondary role of 'aid-to-the-civil authority' duties.[19] Yet nationalist leaders were well aware that these detracted from the military's organisational efficiency and effectiveness in its primary role as the nation's defender and hence must be kept to a minimum. Thus, for all his talk of transforming independent India's military into 'a truly national army, with a national purpose and a national outlook',[20] and belief that 'all barriers between the armed forces and the civilian population must disappear',[21] Nehru left the services virtually unchanged, allowing officers to get on with perfecting their professional expertise in the management of violence.

Indeed, despite some rumours as to the political intentions of commissioned Indian officers in the run-up to independence,[22] the Indian military retained virtually all its British organisation and traditions come *swaraj*.[23] Keeping old regimental practices, including the mess and other trappings of the British officer and gentleman, reinforced commissioned Indian officers' historical understanding of themselves as apolitical servants of the ruling civilian government during the awkward transfer of power. As the first Indian Indian Army C-in-C, (then General) Field Marshal Cariappa constantly sought to reinforce his British predecessors' avoidance of 'politics in the mess' while at the same time promoting a new nationalism, saying:

> Politics in the Army is a poison. Keep off it. But as citizens
> of India you must know, only know, about it.

[The] Army is there to serve the Government of the day, and we should make sure that it does not get mixed up with party politics.

A soldier is above all politics and should not believe in caste or creed. As to myself, I am an Indian, and to the last breath would remain an Indian. For me there are only two STHANS, Hindusthan and Foujistan (the Army).

At all times, in everything you do and say, be an INDIAN first and Indian always. DO NOT disintegrate the country into little 'penny-packets' of your own class, your community or your religion.[24]

Thus, the traditional British ideal of military professionalism would continue to be the guiding ethos for independent India's officer corps.

Like the British officer and gentleman, the established civil-military hierarchy of the Raj, with certain modifications, continued as the model for independent India. After assuming formal control of the Honourable East India Company's holdings on the subcontinent, the crown had set up a governing structure—from monarch (later emperor) to prime minister, cabinet and secretary of state for India to governor-general (later viceroy) of India advised by an executive council which excluded the Indian Army C-in-C but included a high-ranking officer— embodying the principle of civil supremacy over the military. Having a military member inferior in rank but superior in influence to the C-in-C caused numerous confrontations. The most serious of these, the C-in-C Kitchener *versus* Viceroy Curzon controversy in the early twentieth century, resulted in the former being made principal defence advisor to the Raj as well as the armed forces' supreme administrator and operational commander. While Kitchener felt able to decide on all matters under his authority, the demands of the First World War led later C-in-Cs to accept advice from various military and civilian quarters. Nonetheless, all policy, administrative, operational and financial decisions concerning Indian defence matters were ultimately taken by the C-in-C (see **Illustration 1**).[25]

Fortunately for civil supremacy-of-rule in independent India, Nehru understood the dangers of one man acting as both the government's chief defence advisor and armed forces C-in-C, especially in a young democracy where politicians, administrators and military officers are

MILITARISM IN INDIA

ILLUSTRATION 1: The defence hierarchy in India, 1938

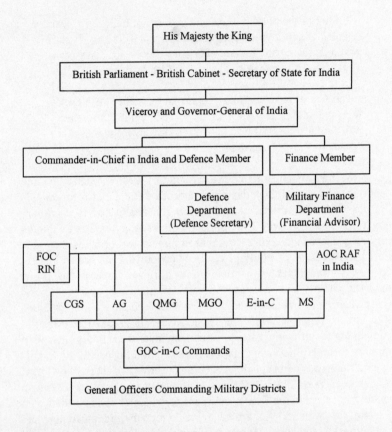

AG	= Adjutant General	MGO	= Master-General of Ordnance
AOC	= Air Officer Commanding	MS	= Military Secretary
CGS	= Chief of the General Staff	QMG	= Quarter-Master General
E-in-C	= Engineer in Chief	RAF	= Royal Air Force
FOC	= Flag Officer Commanding	RIN	= Royal Indian
GoC-in-C	= General Officer Commanding in Command		

Adapted from: A.L. Venkateswaran, *Defence Organisation in India: A Study of Major Developments in Organisation and Administration since Independence* (Government of India Ministry of Information and Broadcasting, 1967).

ILLUSTRATION 2: The defence hierarchy in India, 1949

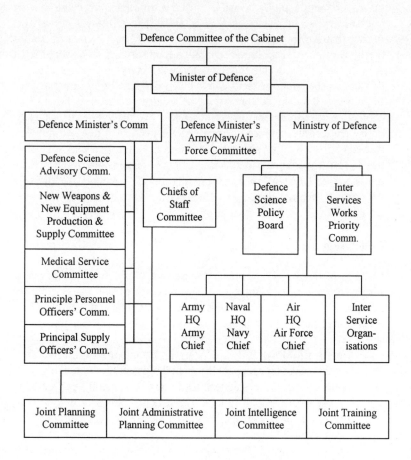

Comm. = Committee

Adapted from: A.L. Venkateswaran, *Defence Organisation in India: A Study of Major Developments in Organisation and Administration since Independence* (Government of India Ministry of Information and Broadcasting, 1967).

daily learning the limits of their respective organisations' powers. He modified the civil-military defence hierarchy by appointing an elected civilian politician as defence minister with responsibility for obtaining the government's policy decisions, then transmitting and seeing to their implementation by the three service HQs. The military's power was further reduced by replacing the office of C-in-C with a chief of staff at the head of each of the three separate armed services who would meet with the defence minister and the defence secretary only in this capacity and not as the supreme field commander(s).[26] The army, navy and air force were thus under three tiers of civilian control: political—the cabinet and parliament as represented by the defence minister; bureaucratic—the defence secretary at the head of a defence ministry staffed entirely by civil servants; and financial—the financial advisor at the head of the ministry of finance (defence) responsible to the finance minister (see **Illustration 2**). Nehru also began a process of adjusting the warrant of precedence to reflect the armed forces' loss of power compared to government civilians.

Conclusion

Upon their victorious return from the Second World War, Indian armed forces' officers faced military mutinies and strikes, and the partition of personnel and materials into the respective military forces of newly independent India and Pakistan. And yet, marvels Major-General 20,

> We got rid of the British officers from the units within two months of independence [by rapidly promoting relatively junior officers to the highest positions of command], carried out the most difficult task of evacuating millions of people from India and Pakistan, restored normalcy, brought the erring Princely States within India, quelled communal riots, and still fought a full-fledged war in Kashmir...No other army in the world could have achieved so much in so little time.

The navy and air force shared in the army's proud record of achievement, the basis of which was the constant belief of Indian officers that their professional expertise and corporateness were equal to any challenge. In great part this confidence was due to the armed forces enjoying a virtually unchanged tradition of professional training and organisation through the transfer of power. IMA GCs continued to be taught British standards of military efficiency while regiments kept their centuries-old battle honours and intermediate officer class, and the army its martial races (though increasingly tempered by efforts to recruit nationally representative personnel) and *izzat*.

Armed forces' officers were also confident that their new political and administrative leaders were fit to meet the challenges of independence. (Indeed, as shown in Table 2, pre-1947 commissioned officers gauge the latter as more equipped for *swaraj* than the military.) The high marks gained by all three government institutions bode well for the future of civil supremacy-of-rule in independent India. Remember that in Table 1, officers rank 'professionalism of the armed forces' as the number one factor in preventing a military coup in India.' While a belief that their professional expertise and corporateness equipped military officers to cope with the many challenges of independence, their faith in the ability of the country's new political and bureaucratic elite to govern effectively after *swaraj* allowed them to transfer their professional responsibility from the British Raj to independent India's new civilian rulers and to accept their downgrading in the reorganized civil-military hierarchy.

The loyalty of the Indian armed forces to their new civilian masters was re-affirmed when India became a sovereign democratic republic on 26 January 1950. Previously, only VCOs, NCOs and soldiers, as well as and their equivalent ranks in the naval and air forces, had been required to take an oath of allegiance to the king-emperor. Henceforth, all personnel of the Indian Army and the renamed Indian Navy (IN) and Indian Air Force (IAF) would share in a new pledge:

> I do swear in the name of God/do solemnly affirm that I will bear true faith and allegiance to the Constitution of India as by law established and that I will, as in duty bound, honestly and faithfully serve in the Navy/Regular Army/Air Force of the Union of India and go wherever ordered by sea, land or air and that I will observe and obey all commands of the President of the Union of India and the commands of any officer set over me even to the peril of my life.[27]

Only time would tell if the armed forces' personnel of independent India would take this new oath to heart.

[1] Indian airmen of RIAF Kohat refused to obey a supposed order to take aerial action against Bombay's naval mutineers, and less serious strikes occurred at Secunderabad and at Delhi's Factory Road camp and Palam air base. The Indian Army also experienced minor acts of indiscipline. In Calcutta, two units of Pioneers refused orders and assaulted their officers. In Jabalapur, the men of the signal training centre staged a city-centre protest; in Santa Cruz, Bombay, an infantry battalion vociferously complained of bad food and the over-zealous customs examination to which it had been subjected to on its return from active service. In addition, large numbers of personnel of the ex-Middle East and Central Mediterranean Forces loudly grumbled about returning from overseas duty to markedly inferior living conditions in India.

[2] That the RIN's Indian chief petty and petty officers (equivalent to Indian Army VCOs) shared their superiors' feelings may be seen from their refusal to join in the ratings' mutiny. Discipline was also evident in the use of Indian Army units in often bloody actions against mutinous naval personnel in Bombay, Karachi and Calcutta with no breakdown of discipline.

[3] As cited in L. Collins and D. Lapierre, *Freedom at Midnight* (London: Collins, 1975), p. 67.

[4] In a separate agreement, the 20 Gurkha regiments were allotted in a 12/8 ration to India and Britain, respectively.

[5] The first post-war regular class of cadets had graduated from the IMA in December 1946.

[6] British troops began leaving on 17 August 1947 and, except for those officers volunteering to stay on in the new Indian and Pakistani forces, the last British serviceman departed the subcontinent on 28 February 1948. Post-Second World War demobilisation reduced the Indian Army to approximately 400,000 men of whom about 260,000 went to India and 140,000 to Pakistan.

[7] Immediately after the war, there were only 242 commissioned Indian officers, just 17 of whom had been trained pre-Second World War, qualified to fill the undivided Indian Army's approximately 500 graded staff appointments.

[8] See Admiral R.D. Katari, *A Sailor Remembers* (New Delhi: Vikas Publishing House Pvt. Ltd., 1987), p. 62; and A.L. Venkateswaran, *Defence Organisation in India: A Study of Major Developments in Organisation and Administration since Independence*, (Government of India Ministry of Information and Broadcasting, 1967), p. 168.

[9] Initially, 1,200 British officers stayed on in the Indian Army, including the new C-in-C, Sir Rob Lockhart. Although almost all the approximately 300 British officers remaining in the army in January 1948 left soon after, a few held technical appointments until 1956. In the RIN, about 60 commissioned and 70 Warrant Officers stayed on, including Rear Admiral J.T.S. Hall in the new post of RIN C-in-C. Indianisation was only complete when the British chief of naval aviation left in 1962. In the air force, Indian officers assumed all senior staff and operational appointments with only a few technical posts given

to RAF officers. The RIAF's need for highly specialized knowledge did, however, result in an increase of RAF personnel in some years after 1947. Not until C-in-C Air Marshal Ivelaw Chapman's departure in 1954 was the force completely Indian.

[10] From 15 January 1966, heads of the air force were upgraded to the rank of air chief marshal. See Venkateswaran, *Defence Organisation in India*, p. 140.

[11] Set up in July 1947 to keep peace in the Punjab border area, the Boundary Force consisted of approximately 50,000 men under the command of British Major-General T.W. Rees. The Boundary Force did much good work before concomitant pressure from Indian and Pakistani quarters to hand over its duties to their respective own military forces resulted in just this step on 1 September 1947.

[12] Travancore, the only other Princely State (out of 565) not to have acceded to India or Pakistan by 15 August 1947, accepted Indian rule on 17 August 1947.

[13] In October 1947, the Indian Army C-in-C was General Auchinlek and the army commander with responsibility for J&K General Dudley Russell. By the 1 January 1949 cease-fire, these posts were filled by (then General) Field Marshal General Cariappa and (then Lieut.-General) General S.N. Srinagesh (already the second Indian to command the area army), respectively.

[14] Perhaps the most conspicuous example was provided by Brigadier Mohammed Usman, CO of 50th Parachute Brigade, who led his unit to glory in J&K and was feted as a national hero after his death in battle.

[15] The religious mix of the Indian armed forces is reflected in those officers answering the questionnaires and/or interviewed who, in addition to Hindu officers, include the Christians Brigadier 44 and Lieut.-Colonel 80, the Roman Catholics Vice Admiral 6 and Brigadier 83, the Buddhist Major-General 85, the Zoroastrian Brigadier 76, the Jewish Lieut.-General 101, the Muslim Air Marshal 5, and 16 Sikh officers.

[16] These numbers do not include European and Indian officers serving in the Indian Political Service.

[17] M. Gandhi, Editorial, *Harijan*, 10 February 1940.

[18] From *Harijan*, 21 April 1946 as used in S. Cohen, *The Indian Army: Its Contribution to the Development of a Nation* (Berkeley: University of California Press, 1971), p. 103.

[19] K.F. Rustomji, *Aid to Civil Authority*, USI Seminar (Number Twelve), (New Delhi: United Service Institution of India, 1986).

[20] J. Nehru, 'The Defence of India', *Young India,* 1 October 1931, p. 284.

[21] S. Gopal, *Selected Works of Jawaharlal Nehru: A Biography: Volume 1, 1889-1947* (Cambridge: Harvard University Press, 1976), p. 412.

[22] As a member of the post-war armed forces' Nationalisation Committee, General Thimayya recalls British colleagues warning nationalist leaders that Indian officers 'were getting too ambitious', that the Indian Army was a powerful organisation capable of taking control of the country', and that 'in

Burma army officers had assassinated the new premier'. As a result, Thimayya and other Indian officers had to spend some time convincing nationalist leaders that they were without political ambitions. British officers were not alone in suggesting unusual potential scenarios. Lord Ismay, Viceroy Mountbatten's closest advisor, recalls how

> [then Brigadier, later Field Marshal] Cariappa came to see me yesterday [9 May 1947] and volunteered the amazing suggestion that [the] Indian Army with either Nehru or Jinnah as commander-in-chief should take over power when we left in June 1948. I at once said that the proposal was dangerous, that throughout history the rule of an army had always proved tyrannical and incompetent, and that the army must always be servants and not masters. I added that the Indian Army, by remaining united and refusing to choose sides, could wield a tremendous influence for good in disturbed days that lie ahead but that they must always be subservient to civil power. I concluded by begging him to put the idea right out of his mind and never to mention it again even in the strictest secrecy...It is hard to know whether Cariappa in putting forward this idea was *ingenuous and ignorant* or *ingenuous and dangerous.* [My italics.]

'Ingenuous and ignorant' is the more likely characterisation; Cariappa's suggestion was just the most extreme manifestation of the frustration he and many of other officers felt at the impending partition of both the subcontinent and the armed forces. See H. Evans, *Thimayya of India* (First published New York: Harcourt, Bruce & Co, 1960; Dehra Dun: Natraj Publishers, 1988), p. 246; M.J. Akbar, *Nehru: The Making of India* (London: Viking, 1988), p. 407; M. Ayub Khan, *Friends not Masters: A Political Autobiography* (London: Oxford University Press, 1967), pp. 19-20.

[23] The respective armies of India and Pakistan are the only such institutions to have retained an intermediate officer class to serve as a buffer between commissioned officers (former KCIOs, ICOs and Indian ECOs) and troops; that is, those VCOs re-designated after independence as junior commissioned officers (JCOs).

[24] I.M. Muthanna, *General Cariappa: The First Indian Commander-in-Chief* (Mysore City: Usha Press, 1964), pp. 47-50.

[25] There were some constraints on the power of the C-in-C. As the defence member on the executive council, the C-in-C listened to the defence department secretary, an officer of the ICS who also had access to the viceroy. As the armed forces' chief administrator and supreme operational commander, the C-in-C was advised by the Indian Army chief of staff and three other principal staff officers (PSOs). The C-in-C's power was further circumscribed by the finance advisor of military finance, a senior ICS officer directly responsible to

the executive council's finance member, a position which ensured that any military demand which necessitated the government's approval was first discussed with its civilian financial representatives before being put to the army department for approval.

[26] The official title for these three posts were chief of the army staff and commander-in-chief, Indian Army; chief of the naval staff and flag officer commanding, Royal Indian Navy; chief of the air staff and air marshal commanding, Royal Indian Air Force. On 1 April 1955, these offices were re-designated as chief of the army staff , chief of the naval staff, and chief of the air staff, respectively, although all three are commonly referred to as simply 'chief'.

[27] Venkateswaran, *Defence Organisation in India*, p. 225.

5. THE FIRST DECADE OF INDEPENDENCE

In newly independent countries, the first decade of independence is *the* crucial period in establishing the pattern of civil-military relations to be followed henceforth in the life of the state. For, however well or badly the system inherited from the colonial power served the colonial power, the new state is now on its own. Its native political leaders, senior administrators and commissioned armed forces officers must themselves decide to re-negotiate, retain or reject the civil-military relationship inherited at independence.

Civil-military relations in the partitioned states of India and Pakistan could not have been more different at the end of the first decade of independence. Less than ten years after they had served side-by-side in the Indian armed forces of the Raj, commissioned Indian officers saw Pakistan Army C-in-C General Ayub Khan lead their former comrades into government with the justification that the civilian leadership had completely mismanaged the country. To see if Indian officers were tempted to follow this example, this chapter will compare the general state of civil-military relations in India and Pakistan in their respective first decades of independence, paying particular attention to differences in the professional and societal experiences of officers in both countries and to Indian officers' perceptions of the (in)competence of their country's political and administrative elite.

Neglect in India

Being called upon to perform in actions in Punjab, Junagadh, Hyderabad, and J&K surrounding the transfer of power did not stop Indian military officers from perceiving that the armed forces were neglected during the first decade of independence. Even their relatively junior positions at the time did not shield a majority of officers answering the questionnaires and/or interviewed from perceiving that the political leadership held an poor opinion of the armed forces during this period. A number of factors are cited as contributory factors, including: the continuing 'hangover' of the effectiveness of non-violence in the struggle for *swaraj* which continued to give politicians a low opinion of force and those who managed it; civilian leaders' all too common ignorance of how to deploy the military as an effective instrument of the state; and a government emphasis on civilian economic development instead of maintaining defence preparedness. Indeed, Nehru saw national defence as more a function of long-term economic planning than immediate military might. The armed forces also lost out due to the PM's championing of a new, non-aligned movement (NAM) not beholden to the American or Soviet superpowers which effectively froze them out of lucrative defence pacts. Nehru's fervent belief that international disputes should be handled by the United Nations (UN) and diplomacy further contributed to governmental disinterest in the armed forces. Although most officers accepted that in the new, democratic India the needs of the armed forces must take a backseat to the economic development of the people, Air Marshal 5 accurately sums up the political leadership's attitude towards the armed forces in the first decade of independence as 'very much as that of a teetotaler who had inherited a brewery'.

Civil-military relations also suffered from Nehru's unwise choice of defence ministers during this period. The first, Sardar Baldev Singh, joined the cabinet more as a compromise Sikh member than for any knowledge of military matters and left the day-to-day running of the ministry to a civil servant, IAS Secretary H.M. Patel. Unfortunately, 'His Majesty' (a nickname given by colleagues in the defence ministry) Patel and the proud and stubborn Indian Army C-in-C (then General) Field Marshal Cariappa did not get along personally, setting the mood of bureaucrat-officer relations for years to come. Although matters improved when N. Gopalaswami Ayyangar, an able administrator respected by military officers for his work as chairman of the armed forces' Nationalisation Committee, became defence minister after the 1952 general elections, he died after just ten months in office. Relations again suffered when Nehru assumed the defence portfolio for the next two years but left (junior) Minister for Revenue and Expenditure Mahavir Tyagi, in his role as minister for defence organisation (MDO), to run the ministry. While the next defence minister, Dr. Kailash Nath Katju, was a Congress stalwart and the first in this position with a full political background, his ignorance of military matters continued to impair civil-military relations and he gained a reputation for not being able to decide upon anything—careful to do nothing wrong, he did little right. After two years he became chief minister of Madhya Pradesh and for the next three months Nehru again held the defence portfolio.

It was not just the defence minister who comes in for criticism; with very few exceptions, those officers answering the questionnaires and/or interviewed hold all of India's senior civil servants responsible for what they perceived as the general neglect of the military in the first decade of independence. These bureaucrats, complains Brigadier 76, had no conception of proper civil-military boundaries:

> In a democracy, it is accepted that the military remain subordinate to the supremacy of the civil government. However, whereas in Western democracies the term 'government' meant the parliament and its elected members, in India, unfortunately, it also encompassed the civil servants, which was never the intention when we became a republic. Thus there was a constant battle between the bureaucrat and the soldier.

Other officers describe how this battle was soured further by civil servants who took advantage of the political leadership's ignorance of military matters to promote unfounded fears of an Indian military coup—especially after the army seized power in Pakistan in 1958 (see below)—in order to reduce the budgetary resources of the armed forces and the status of officers *vis-à-vis* other government employees. India's top civil servants, concludes Brigadier 76, had a 'bad, positively bad' attitude towards the military.

Officers were not alone in perceiving Indian civil-military relations in the first decade of independence to be suffering because of a generally negative attitude towards the armed forces on the part of both the political leadership and senior civil servants. As early as 1954, even ex-Defence Secretary Patel admitted the that 'ignorance of civilian officials of defence matters is so complete as to be a self evident and incontrovertible fact'.[1] This was a time, adds Ex-Defence Secretary P.V.R. Rao, when the armed forces 'eked out their existence...like a neglected wife. She was there, her presence was comforting, on occasions, even useful...but essentially Governmental policy did not prescribe any definite objective for the Services'.[2] Irregardless of which branch of civilian government was more responsible, the poor state of Indian civil-military relations during the first decade of independence might endanger civil supremacy-of-rule in India, especially if officers were confronted by the example of a successful armed forces' coup next door.

A 'Coup' in Pakistan

On 7 October 1958, Pakistan President Iskander Mirza abrogated the constitution, proclaimed martial law, dismissed the central and provincial governments and assemblies, and appointed army C-in-C General Ayub Khan (henceforth referred to by forename only) as chief martial law administrator (CMLA). Twenty days later, Ayub pressured Mirza into surrendering all governing power to the armed forces in what he described as a 'Revolution'[3] but more commonly known (and henceforth referred to) as a coup. The government had already weathered one attempted military coup when, in spring 1951, it uncovered the 'Rawalpindi conspiracy', a plot led by Major-General Akbar Khan to assassinate PM Liaquat Ali Khan, Pakistan Army C-in-C General Sir Douglas Gracey and other top officials. Seven years later, Ayub's main justification for his own actions was to halt what he perceived to be years of political mismanagement of the country, especially evident in the deteriorating the law-and-order situation of the last few months as political parties geared up for forthcoming elections. The Pakistan Army, he wrote, was 'the only disciplined organization that could give the country the necessary covering fire, in order to enable it to steady itself and extricate itself from the evils which had surrounded it'.[4] Paradoxically, Ayub also justified leading the army into government in order to protect its officers from becoming affected by the turmoil of domestic politics.

Ayub's actions found a mixed response from those officers answering the questionnaires and/or interviewed. Virtually equal numbers report their thoughts at the time were that the Pakistan coup was not a surprise and necessary, a surprise and unnecessary, and of no particular interest. The first group supports their views by pointing to the country's dearth of politicians of either national stature (Jinnah, long-time leader of the ML and 'father' of Pakistan, died 13 months after independence while Liaquat Ali Khan was assassinated in 1951) or basic competence. They note that Ayub's initial elevation to CMLA was at the request of the government and conclude that the military was virtually 'pushed' into assuming politics. The second set of officers recall their shock at hearing of Ayub's coup and some worried about its knock-on effect in the region. Others, underscoring the importance of India's 'nationally representative military personnel' as shown on Table 1, understood the coup as a dynamic of the dominance of one community of both country and army: at independence, Punjabi Muslims accounted for approximately 60 per cent of both Pakistan's total population and its army personnel. A few Indian officers, like Major-General 20, express regret for their former comrades-in-arms and the inevitable consequences of Ayub's action:

> We felt that the military coup in Pakistan will bring the end of the high military traditions of the Pakistan Army. We felt that once the army entered politics and started ruling Pakistan, the army will deteriorate and its officers and men will get involved in corruption, nepotism and unmilitary [sic] professions. All this came out true.

A final group of Indian officers took no particular notice of Ayub's coup, saying that it was none of their business to think about the politics of another country.

The above responses reveal most commissioned Indian military officers as able to dispassionately observe the political upheaval taking place next door by their comrades-in-arms of only 11 years before. 'The army was simply [the] most organized actor in Pakistan', opines Lieut.-Colonel 25. Yet, however necessary and/or unsurprising, the particular circumstances perceived to have led to Ayub's takeover of government—incompetent political and administrative leadership, the dominance of one ethnic group in society and army, a feudal socioeconomic structure—were dismissed as irrelevant to India. 'Anything', writes Brigadier 69, 'could happen in Pakistan'.

Contrasting Experiences

The idea that 'anything could happen' in a state which just ten years previously formed an integral part of British India comes from the vastly different experiences of Indian and Pakistani military officers and society during this period. After the perceptions of officers themselves, the crucial determinant of an armed forces' coup is the quality, stability and popularity of a country's political and administrative leadership during what are often problematic post-independence attempts to modernize and the state and society. In Pakistan, political infighting after the death of its two outstanding leaders, Jinnah and Liaquat Ali Khan, soon after partition and the lack of agreement over a constitution (not framed until 1956) led to chronic government instability and the inability to respond to the desires of the people (the country's first free and fair general election did not take place until 1970). With the civil service increasingly politicized and the economy suffering, many people openly demanded intervention by the one remaining organisation, the army, seen as capable of uniting the country. India, in contrast, enjoyed a surfeit of experienced politicians belonging to one party, Congress, which by 1958 had won two general elections under an established constitution. India also inherited experienced senior civil servants confident of their ability to administer an independent nation. Most importantly, there stood throughout this time Nehru and his towering authority over the machinery of the state and the hearts of the people.

Just as glaring are the distinctly different 'reference-group' experiences of Indian and Pakistani armed forces' officers in the post-partition decade. Robert Price argues that, so powerful is the desire of third world officers to retain all aspects of their prestigious Western-academy training, they develop a positive reference-group identification with the officer corps of the educating state, sometimes to the extent of becoming 'non-nationalistic'—sharing the latter's dislike for politicians, especially anti-colonial leaders—and 'non-puritanical'—demanding first world standards of compensation and social liberties. If such officers judge their country's new leadership and/or status in society as inferior to that previous to independence, adds Price, they may forcibly overthrow the government.[5] Reference-group identification may be further cemented by a newly independent country's leadership's decisions regarding international co-operation and agreements which link their armed forces with those of other states. The chances of officers staging a coup are thought to rise, especially if 'external military assistance facilitates role expansion and greater autonomy for the armed forces'.[6] Were Indian and Pakistani officers affected by a too-strong identification with the ethos and/or corporate rewards of foreign military organisations?

There was little danger of independent India's commissioned officers becoming non-nationalistic and/or non-puritanical. Although they continued to be taught according to the ideal of a British officer and gentleman, since 1932 all Indian officers had received their professional academy training at the IMA. And, while a number of officers participated in UN operations in Korea, Indo-China, Egypt, and Lebanon and/or enjoyed higher command and technical training courses in the UK, the vast majority had no opportunity to compare directly their resource allocation, corporate status and/or rewards with their foreign counterparts. With the exception of some Brindians, officers did not ape British military attitudes nor expect to receive Western rates-of-pay. (Even so, the Indian armed forces continued to receive a significant share of public expenditure: from 1950 to 1958, defence as a percentage of current expenditure only slowly declined from 29 to 24.3 per cent, respectively.)[7] The poor quality of defence ministers also helped ensure that the military's corporate sphere of decision-making was left (perhaps too) inviolate. Most importantly, most officers had long appreciated the competence of their political and administrative leaders and had had complete confidence in their preparedness for independence.

In contrast, joining the US-sponsored Baghdad Pact and Southeast Asia Treaty Organisation (SEATO) exposed Pakistani military officers to the full force of the American defence establishment. In addition to receiving a great quantity of equipment, the armed forces revised their tables of organisation to US suggestions, switched their subscriptions from UK military journals to American competitors, and even modified the strict traditions of the mess—crucial in forging the professional qualities of a British officer and gentleman and regimental *izzat*—to accommodate American ways. Most importantly, Pakistani officers underwent a considerable amount of prestigious professional training in the US. In the end, their reference-group identification with the American armed forces combined with their role in US-led international alliances to give Pakistan's military officers the (over)confidence to think themselves capable of governing as well, if not better, than their erstwhile civilian masters.[8]

Those officers answering the questionnaires and/or interviewed also point to the respective majority religions of Pakistan and India as important factors in shaping the contrasting civil-military relations of each state. 'Islam, its faith, culture and tradition lend themselves to a military dictatorship the world over', opines Major-General 74; and armed forces' regimes have ruled Pakistan from 1958-71 and 1977-88. As recently as September 1995, over 30 military conspirators were arrested on charges of allegedly plotting to 'eliminate the army's high command and top politicians...declare martial law, and impose *sharia,* or Islamic law, in the country'.[9] In contrast, note these officers, India, with a population which is over 80 per cent Hindu, has remained a democracy since independence. Comparing their neighbour's experience with their own convinces officers to rank Table 1's 'dominant Hindu culture' as the sixth most important factor contributing to India never having experienced an armed forces' coup.

Are Islam and democracy incompatible? If Muslims believe that 'the heart of reality is Allah, one God who is creator and arbiter of all things',[10] they must strive to order their personal and public life as laid out in the holy Koran and by *sharia* as developed and taught by the *ulema* (Islamic scholars). Politically, this means creating 'a theocratic state, where God rules in practice because his ministers and law order life'.[11] In practice, most Muslim rulers, including Ayub, are unwilling to hand over power to religious leaders on the basis of non-political arguments. Yet they do appear ready to use Islam's 'well-formulated and powerful belief structure'[12] in absolutism to sustain autocratic rather than pluralistic rule. For example, of the 13 military coups occurring world-wide from 1950-57, five occurred in three Islamic states (a ratio of 1.67/1) compared to eight in seven other countries (1.14/1). From 1958-85, 32 coups occurred in 13 nations (2.46/1) where Islam is the chief religion, compared to 89 in 45 other states (1.98/1).[13] A 1994 survey of 39 Islamic countries found that just seven could 'in one degree or another even hesitantly be called democracies'.[14]

Although, for all its imperfections, India is certainly a democracy, the exact nature of its majority's Hindu religion is less sure. Unlike other world religions, Hinduism lacks a revelatory text, organized priesthood and congregational worship. More 'something to be done' rather than something 'to be believed', Hinduism is about the 'fundamental laws of existence, to which men and women must conform through performance of their own *dharma* or religious duty',[15] rather than a fixed interpretation of the will and wish of God. As such, Hinduism is more readily understood as a philosophy or way of life.

A number of the questionnaire respondents/interviewees argue that it is this Hindu *culture*, rather than religion in the strict Judeo-Christian and/or Islamic sense, which has helped prevent in a variety of ways a military coup in India. Firstly, it has instilled in Indians a higher than usual level of tolerance of otherwise distasteful or unsavoury situations, including governmental mismanagement. Hinduism has also given India a semi-rigid and highly complex caste system of *varnas* (at its simplest, a hierarchy of priests, warriors, traders and cultivators) and *jatis* (localised kinship groups) which helps to keep people, including armed forces' officers, fixed in their respective societal roles. A number of officers back up this argument by saying that, until the advent of Mughul (Muslim) rule, Indian kingdoms enjoyed a separation of governing power similar to modern ideas of civil-military relations.

How much a national religion or dominant culture affects the commissioned military officers of Pakistan and India is debatable. For Lieut.-General 94, the differences are obvious:

> In a Muslim culture soldiers see themselves as 'guardians of the nation', enjoying a unique position in society as defenders of the country's ideals, [i.e., those of] Islam. A Hindu soldier does not occupy a special place in society. Though he and his institution are respected, he is not thought of as particularly special or different. He does not think he has a special status. He sees his role purely as relating to his military advisors.

Yet, although Islam was used to unify the Pakistan Army on a general, emotional level (for example, in the introduction of Islamic battle cries), it played little part in the professional development of officers up to and including the 1958 coup. Indeed, the country's political and military leaders were more concerned with constructing a viable defence establishment than with revamping officers' ideology which continued to remain that of the British officer and gentleman. While senior military commanders under Ayub's government and General Yayha Khan's subsequent martial law regime of 1969-71 increasingly referred to the 'spirit of jihad [holy war] and dedication to Islam',[16] there was still no concerted effort to incorporate religious measures into the armed forces' training, organisation or strategy. Only during General/President Zia ul-Haq's period of military rule from 1977-88 were more formal measures adopted, such as the introduction of Islamic teachings into the Pakistan Military Academy (PMA). While the 'Islamic' coup attempt of 1995 described above may be seen as the extreme outcome of such steps, many Pakistani officers remain skeptical of the incorporation of religious strictures into their professional careers.

In contrast, the Indian armed forces always have followed the secularism and religious tolerance enshrined in the country's constitution. No one faith guides or dictates the recruitment, training, organisation and/or strategy practiced in the armed forces. However, officers and troops of all faiths are provided with appropriate priests and/or facilities for observing the rites of their respective religions.

Whatever the views of commissioned Indian officers as to the existence of a dominant Hindu culture in India and/or its role in helping to prevent a coup, there is no escaping the question of applicability. That is, while officers can point to the proliferation of coups in Muslim countries to support the view that a national religion of Islam predisposes a state to military rule, they can offer only India as an example of a nation with a dominant Hindu culture. That it has never experienced a coup is neither here not there: if there was a military takeover in India, would respondents still view Hinduism as an anti-coup influence? If, instead of a strictly Hindu culture it is an 'Indianness' created from the totality of the subcontinent's historical experiences in which a multitude of often competing religions and cultures have contributed which has helped prevent military rule, the Indian example is even more inapplicable to other countries.

TABLE 3: Should the Indian armed forces follow Ayub Khan's example?

	Civilians		Military Officers	
	Per cent (Number)			
No	81.25	(78)	92.71	(89)
Yes	15.63	(15)	4.71	(4)
No Answer	3.13	(3)	3.13	(3)
Total	100.01	(96)	100.01	(96)

The sharply contrasting post-independence experiences of Pakistani and Indian military officers, respectively, is reflected in the very few officers answering the questionnaires and/or interviewed who recall any discussion of emulating Ayub's coup (see **Table 3**). Fifteen of this group remember only some idle civilian gossip of the matter, usually from businessmen keen for more order in Indian society. Four, however, admit that military officers themselves discussed the possibility of an Indian coup. Brigadier 70 remembers some 'vague conversations among people both military and civil'. Major-General 72 protests that this was only an 'academic discussion amongst the military'. Brigadier 73 disagrees: 'Ayub Khan's action was favoured by a large portion of the army officers. I should say it [this view] was held fairly strongly'. Lieut.-Colonel 81 goes further: 'We could have done better with a form of military dictatorship for some time. We would be a better country'. Perhaps it is no coincidence that officer 81 retired a lieut.-colonel?

Indeed, in Table 3, the vast majority of officers recall no civilians or military personnel as desirous of replicating Ayub's coup in India. Many praise Field Marshal Cariappa, the first Indian Indian Army Chief, who, reports Brigadier (Dr.) 55, 'drummed into all officers day in and day out that our job is to protect the country, obey the government and protect the population from strife. Every officer had to carry these commandments in his pocket—[in] a small book'. India's officers, adds Lieut.-General 49, had both 'respect for our political leadership at that time...[and] a clear knowledge of our own incapability of running things other than the military'. The second factor in the preceding answer is also acknowledged in Table 1 where 'example of ineffectiveness of military rule in Pakistan and Bangladesh' is ranked as the joint fourteenth most important factor in India never having experienced a military coup.

Conclusion

Fears that the poor state of Indian civil-military relations in the first decade of independence might lead officers to copy the 1958 Revolution of their Pakistan neighbours proved unfounded. For, while Nehru disdained the military as almost irrelevant to his government's policies for domestic and international conflict resolution, he continued to respect the armed forces' corporate sphere of decision-making and adequately reward its personnel. For Vice Admiral 103,

> Any anger towards politicians was always of an indirect nature in that officers felt they had more time for the bureaucrats than the military. The military was upset with Warrant of Precedence and the open humiliation, unconcealed arrogance of the IAS regarding the military. But this is insufficient motivation for a coup. *One wants to change the [defence] minister, not the system.* [My italics.]

Although 'there was some grousing about pay and allowances being lowered', recalls Major-General 105, 'a good soldier always grouses'.

Indeed, the antagonistic relations between military officers and senior bureaucrats in the first decade of independence may have helped ensure civil supremacy-of-rule in India. R.E. Dowse argues that a developing country's military officers and 'bureaucratized middle class' share 'primary socialization and educational patterns....[and] structural positions....*vis-à-vis* the politicians'. As 'alternative elites' with 'a firm interest in ordered modernization and economic growth', one or both of these two groups 'must' assume leadership responsibility if the political elite fails to manage effectively. Since the military do not have the numbers nor expertise to administer the complex state machinery and civilians cannot physically overthrow a regime, continues Dowse, the most effective instruments for replacing regimes are 'military-bureaucratic coalitions'.[17] While India's military officers and senior civil servants shared a socioeconomic background of privilege and their respective organisations a history of elitism, their hostile relationship in the first decade of independence precluded developing a coalition against their political masters. So, whereas Dowse argues that the military-bureaucratic coalition most effective for ousting a regime is fostered by its two elements sharing a similar position *vis-à-vis* the politicians, Lieut.-General 101 points out that in India, 'the situation is civil servants and politicians *versus* the military. Contrast this with Pakistan where it is the civil servants and military *versus* the politicians'.

After partition, India and Pakistan developed in different ways. Contrasting experiences of political (mis)management, reference-group identification, and the influence of their respective countries' dominant religion/culture differentiated and distanced Indian officers from their former comrades in the British-led Indian military who seized the reins of government in Pakistan. Moreover, that those officers answering the questionnaires and/or interviewed rank the 'example of ineffectiveness of military rule in Pakistan and Bangladesh' in Table 1 as only the joint fourteenth most important factor contributing to India never having had a military coup shows their unwillingness to relate neighbouring countries' respective experiences to their own. In 1958, concludes Air Marshal 5, 'only a few nutters', civilian or military, suggested that Indian armed forces' officers copy Ayub's coup in Pakistan.

---

[1] From an article in the USI Journal of April 1954 as cited in Lt. Gen. S.K. Sinha, *Of Matters Military* (New Delhi: Vision Books, 1980), pp. 43-44.

[2] P.V.R. Rao, *India's Defence Policy and Organisation since Independence* (New Delhi: United Service Institution of India), p. 5.

[3] M. Ayub Khan, *Friends not Masters: A Political Autobiography* (London: Oxford University Press, 1967), pp. 70-76.

[4] Khan, *Friends not Masters*, p. 58.

[5] R. Price, 'A Theoretical Approach to Military Rule in New States: Reference Group Theory and the Ghanaian Case', *World Politics*, 23:3, April 1971.

[6] C.E. Welch, Jr. and A.K. Smith, *Military Role and Rule: Perspectives on Civil-Military Relations* (North Scituate: Duxbury Press, 1974), pp. 18-19.

[7] L.J. Kavic, *India's Quest for Security: Defence Policies, 1947-1965* (Berkeley: University of California Press, 1967), Appendix I.

[8] See Stephen Cohen's discussion of the 'British' *versus* 'American' generation of Pakistani officers in his *The Pakistan Army* (Berkeley: University of California Press, 1984), pp. 55-70.

[9] A. Rashid, 'Fundamental Problem: Islamic officers' coup plot shocks country', *Far Eastern Economic Review*, 26 October 1995, p. 18. Note, too, that in May 1996 high level civil-military machinations and the unauthorised mobilisation of troops led to fears of an attempted coup in another of India's neighbours, Muslim-majority Bangladesh. See Z.A. Chowdhury, 'Army trouble exposes diarchy in Bangladesh, *The Times of India*, 22 May 1996; and R. Zaman, 'Dhaka alert amid coup rumours', *The Times of India*, 21 May 1996.

[10] J.M. Brown, *Modern India: The Origins of an Asian Democracy*, pbk. ed. (1988. First published Oxford: O.U.P., 1985), p. 27.

[11] Brown, *Modern India*, p. 28.

[12] Brown, *Modern India*, p. 27.

[13] The nations and the year(s) of coups are taken from R.H.T. O'Kane, *The Likelihood of Coups* (Aldershot: Avebury, 1987), pp. 141-144. In judging which countries have Islam as their chief religion, I include Muslim-majority countries such as Nigeria, Sudan and Indonesia, as well as obvious choices such as Syria, Oman and Afghanistan. See also 'Dicing with Democracy', *The Economist*, 3 February 1990.

[14] In the 1994 survey, the seven countries described as democracies are Bangladesh, Iran, Jordan, Lebanon, Malaysia, Pakistan, and Turkey. The 32 non-democratic states in the survey are Afghanistan, Algeria, Bahrain, Brunei, Azerbaijan, Egypt, Gambia, Guinea, Indonesia, Iraq, Kazakhstan, Kirgizstan, Kuwait, Libya, Maldives, Mali, Maurutania, Morocco, Niger, Oman, Quatar, Saudi Arabia, Senegal, Somalia, Sudan, Syria, Tajikistan, Tunisia, Turkmenistan, United Arab Emirates, Uzbekistan, and Yemen. See 'The trickiest one of all', *The Economist*, 6 August 1994.

[15] Brown, *Modern India*, p. 23. Paul Younger argues that *dharma* has come to be used to mean '"order" and to describe all the religious, legal, customary and political efforts to identify an area of stability of both roots [primordial loyalties expressed in social institutions such as family and caste] and vision [a primordial commitment to the idea of a universal vision of human existence]'.

See P. Younger, *From Ashoka to Rajiv: An Analysis of Indian Political Culture* (Bombay: Popular Prakashan, 1987), pp. viii, 1-10, 20-24, 39-42.

[16] From a speech by Pakistan Army Lieut.-General Tikka Khan as cited in Cohen, *The Pakistan Army*, p. 86.

[17] Not that officers and bureaucrats 'plot coups with one another, [and] carry them out', writes Dowse, for the 'need for secrecy would preclude such an arrangement'. See R.E. Dowse, 'The Military and Political Development' in C. Leys, ed., *Politics and Change in Developing Countries Studies in the Theory and Practice of Development* (Cambridge: Cambridge University Press, 1969), pp. 228-232.

6. THE MENON-KAUL NEXUS

The time of greatest civil-military conflict in India began in the late 1950s with the rise of V.K. Krishna Menon (henceforth cited by surname only) and Lieut.-General B.M. Kaul to the top rank of the defence establishment. As defence minister and chief of the general staff, both used their close personal relationship with PM Nehru to undermine established civil-military procedures, playing favourites and upsetting colleagues to the point of being charged with politicising the armed forces. A Menon-Kaul nexus appeared to split the officer corps into pro- and anti-Menon-Kaul factions. Was there a danger of either bloc intervening against the civilian government to ensure the furtherance of their respective interests?

Defence Minister V.K. Krishna Menon

After a decade of governmental neglect of the armed forces, India's armed forces warmly welcomed the almost simultaneous appointments of Menon as defence minister (DM) and General Thimayya as Indian Army chief in the spring of 1957. Menon, highly intelligent, eloquent and admired for his London-based efforts in pursuance of *swaraj*, service as India's first high commissioner to the UK, and defence of Indian interests as head of the country's UN mission, was also known to be an influential confidant of Nehru. In turn, writes Lieut.-General 10, Thimayya was 'undoubtedly one of the Indian Army's best field commanders...[commanding] great respect for his professionalism and dynamic qualities as a leader of men. His becoming the chief added lustre to the office rather than the other way around'. When, in 1958, Admiral R.D. Katari and Air Marshal Mukherji joined Thimayya as heads of the IN and IAF, respectively, Indians commanded all three services for the first time. Expectations were great and India's defence establishment seemed poised to begin a new and fruitful era.

The Indian armed forces accomplished some notable achievements under Menon. Abroad, military personnel were deployed in peacekeeping missions in Lebanon, Laos, the Congo, and Gaza. At home, 'Operation Vijay' saw the armed forces forcibly liberate Goa, Daman and Diu, Portugal's remaining colonies on the subcontinent. Menon also carried out a number of important military reforms and initiatives, most notably in the field of indigenous defence production.

While Menon's successes as DM may be traced to his forceful personality and fierce concentration on the problem at hand, his working habits failed to impress colleagues, both civilian and military. 'Brash, impatient; [he] wanted quick results...[and therefore] rubbed people the wrong way', recalls ex-Defence Secretary Mr. C5. Ex-ICS officer Dharma Vira adds that for Menon, 'one who did not agree with him was either a fool or a knave'.[1] Air Chief Marshal P.C. Lal remembers the new DM's 'vitriolic, acerbic, unnecessarily devastating tongue and temper'.[2] Admiral Katari remembers Menon's 'supreme arrogance...[and] ill-concealed impatience with those less endowed [with intelligence]...I felt that he was something of a bully who took pleasure in harassing those who were prepared to take it lying down'.[3] Although at the time relatively junior and thus unlikely to know of Menon's personal working habits, those officers answering the questionnaires and/or interviewed include two who worked with the DM at close-hand. As director of one of the army's research and development (R&D) sections, Brigadier 76 worked closely with Menon and found him to be 'a brilliant man, whose major contribution was setting up the indigenous manufacture of military hardware and defence R&D'. Despite such acknowledged achievements, Lieut.-General 16, an officer in the military wing of the cabinet secretariat, describes Menon as 'bad at conducting conference; impatient, bad tempered....He could not run a happy team or carry people with him'. Unfortunately for India's defence establishment, it is the latter characterisation of unhealthy 'Menonitis'[4] that was most relevant to bureaucrats and officers who worked with the DM.

Lieut.-General B.M. Kaul

Like Menon, Lieut.-General B.M. Kaul captured Nehru's imagination by standing out from his peers in several ways. For one, he had engaged in nationalist acts while a youth and, contrary to all tenets of military professionalism, had continued such actions after being commissioned into the army.[5] Kaul's charitable attitude towards the Indian national armies' personnel and his confidence in the army's ability to overcome the commissioned officer shortfall at independence further pleased the PM. That Kaul, like Nehru, was a Kashmiri Brahmin, a small and readily identifiable community much in evidence in independent India's foreign service and higher administration, also did him no harm. Kaul soon became Nehru's advisor/confidant during his rapid rise in the army, impressing during his various official stints,[6] as well as enjoying unofficial duties as the PM's troubleshooter in J&K and sometime factotum. Kaul also caught Nehru's eye when, as commander of 11th Infantry Brigade and then of 4th Infantry Division, he twice led his men in constructing much-needed military housing and, at the request of Menon, oversaw the building of the defence pavilion at New Delhi's 'India Exhibition', a project inaugurated by the PM. With Nehru's patronage, Kaul appeared headed for the top of the military hierarchy and was even tipped as a potential future prime minister.

Despite Nehru's support, any number of factors combined to convince his fellow officers, senior and junior, that Lieut.-General Kaul lacked the 'right stuff' for high command. Unlike the majority of his senior (ex-KCIO) peers, he was not from a princely, privileged or martial races' family, nor did he play polo, hunt, smoke or drink alcohol. Kaul's support for the nationalist movement led him to break his professional code of non-involvement in politics, behaviour abhorrent to his fellow KCIOs. After independence, Kaul's political 'partiality towards the communist prisoners'[7] in Korea while serving with the Neutral Nations Repatriation Commission (NNRC) caused further embarrassment for his colleagues. Officers also disliked Kaul's ready access to Nehru and the building projects which, writes Major-General 85, 'turned soldiers into masons' but caught the PM's eye. While the former initially might be dismissed as mere jealousy, Nehru's willingness to see Kaul outside of normal civil-military channels would have grave implications for the defence of India's northern borders. Similarly, while the latter work may have been imperative, Kaul's seniors saw using troops for construction as detracting from the military's effectiveness in its primary role of defence of the nation.[8]

Most damaging in his colleagues' eyes was Lieut.-General Kaul's lack of combat experience. After graduating from Sandhurst and serving a mandatory year with a British Army regiment in India, Kaul was accepted into a prestigious Indian Army infantry unit. Although 'anxious to remain in the Rajputana Rifles in which I was not doing too badly',[9] he then requested a transfer into the army's service corps because its higher salary would enable him to service debts incurred by his 'constantly ill'[10] mother. Lieut.-General Thorat picks up the story:

> On the outbreak of World War II he [Kaul] asked my advice as what he should do. Naturally I told him to seek posting to a unit which was likely to proceed overseas on active service. To my utter surprise he argued that his talents would be far better utilised in the Public Relations set-up which he had decided to join....he certainly saved himself from being exposed to the dangers and discomforts of war. *Kaul was one of the few officers of his time who never served with combat troops in the field.* [My italics.][11]

This lack of combat experience was remarkable given the Indian Army's huge wartime expansion. Either the infantry judged Kaul incapable of fighting duties or he shied away from live action or both.[12] Although he returned to a fighting unit in 1948 as 11th Infantry Brigade CO and went on to lead the 4th Infantry Division, Kaul was never able to live down his lack of combat experience.

Indeed, Lieut.-General Kaul generated a remarkable amount of contempt from his comrades in all three defence service. For Air Chief Marshal 12, he was 'a totally self-centred officer with no professionalism or real patriotism', for Vice Admiral 2 'a strutting egoist', and for Brigadier 69, a 'piss-poor officer...who never heard a shot fired in anger'. Lieut.-General 4, a battalion commander in Kaul's division, 'knew him to be a hoax and a bully...just bloody mad...insane'. 'There is hardly any officer in the army who did not have contempt for this man', concludes Brigadier 76. Are these criticisms fair? Could Kaul's rapid rise be due to his acknowledged administrative drive, or was it attributable to political favouritism?

Politicisation

Any number of senior officers agree that Menonitis went beyond the DM's rudeness to his colleagues to include a disregard for professional advice and a deliberate manipulation of the civil-military decision-making hierarchy. Lieut.-General Verma recalls that any officer daring to disagree with Menon 'was branded an obstructionist'. When the DM, adds Lieut.-General Thorat, 'discovered that Timmy [General

Thimayya] was not as pliant a Chief as he would have liked him to be....[so he] started to bypass him and began to deal directly with his subordinate officers'.[13] 'Before long', continues Verma,

> it became generally known that the DM expected loyalty to his person even at the expense of the service and the individual's superior service officers. He started by making subtle promises, hinting at better future prospects to certain officers in reward for doing his bidding. This modus operandi was extended equally to the navy and air force as well. He would send for a junior officer and question him with regard to the advice given to him (DM) by the individual's superiors. He would get the junior officer to agree with his own views and thereby create a feeling of disloyalty among junior officers to their superiors....He was thus able to locate officers who would play ball with him and give him the answer he wanted.[14]

Director of Military Operations (DMO) Major-General D.K. Palit and Air Chief Marshal Lal, respectively, agree that 'to dominate the military bureaucracy by trying to make dent in the solidarity of its senior ranks'[15] Menon 'encouraged officers whom he liked to be in direct contact with him, ignoring the Chiefs, and that is not only unethical but a foolproof method of undermining discipline'.[16]

Notwithstanding this threat to military discipline, a number of officers appeared willing to 'play ball' with Menon and none more so than Lieut.-General Kaul. On the one hand, writes Lieut.-General Verma, Kaul was used by the DM as 'a quisling amongst senior officers to accomplish his own designs'.[17] On the other hand, adds Brigadier 44, Kaul avidly 'pandered to [the] politicians' willingness to believe that all other senior military commanders were fools' so as to fulfill his own ambitions. As someone 'very rightly' put it, continues Brigadier 60, '"B.M. Kaul, when he was amongst the politicians, he was a general and when amongst generals, he was a politician"'. For many, the proof of Kaul's undue influence in the armed forces came with his controversial May 1959 promotion to lieut.-general rank and appointment to quarter-master general (QMG) over the heads of two more highly recommended officers. Senior officers worried that the new QMG would use his seat on the army's selection board to hasten the rise of his followers dubbed 'Kaul-boys',[18] junior officers of 'mediocre capability, from whom he

[Kaul] demanded and obtained a personal and almost feudal commitment...'.[19] 'Are you pro-K. or anti-K.?' [20] soon became a question no officer needed explained.

Three months after Lieut.-General Kaul was appointed QMG, General Thimayya could no longer tolerate the DM's personal rudeness or professional disregard. On the afternoon of 31 August 1959, he walked into Admiral Katari's office brandishing his letter of resignation to explain that 'the only honourable course left for him was to quit....there was nothing I could say or do to alter his decision'.[21] Katari immediately sent an encrypted message to the head of the IAF, Air Marshal Mukherji, who was abroad at the time, relating Thimayya's decision and his own resolution to 'most probably follow suit'.[22] The next morning, *The Statesman* led with the news, adding that the 'likely' resignation of all three service chiefs 'is the result of prolonged but evidently unsuccessful efforts to keep politics out of the Army, Navy and Air Force...[and] other areas of disagreement, partly arising from reasons of temperament and personal preferences'.[23] That evening, Katari was summoned to a private meeting at which Nehru appeared

> grieved that the three Chiefs of Staff should gang up against the Defence Minister. I...pointed out that if the three of us, individually, were working under such severe disabilities that we found it difficult to function honourably, it could hardly be termed ganging up....[Nehru] went on to say that he realised that Krishna Menon was not the easiest of men with whom to get on. But, he said, Menon possessed one of the finest intellects that he, Nehru, had had come across, and it should be utilised for the benefit of the country. At that I quite spontaneously blurted out, 'But why as Defence Minister, Sir?' I was relieved to find that he laughed at that....as I was taking my leave at the end of about an hour, *he revealed that Thimayya had agreed to withdraw his resignation....*The question of [my] resigning was no longer immediate. [My italics.][24]

Thimayya, the 'simple soldier'[25] and long-time admirer of Nehru, had apparently been unable to resist the PM's promise of personally looking into every one of his complaints against Menon.

Instead, the day after General Thimayya withdrew his letter of resignation, Nehru appeared in parliament to castigate the army chief and praise Menon. The PM stated that, although the general had come to him a week ago 'not feeling very happy about various matters connected with the defence ministry', these were 'rather trivial and of no consequence' and therefore Thimayya's resignation the day before yesterday had been 'peculiarly unwise'. With the exception of Kaul's promotion to QMG, Nehru denied that his government had interfered with army recommendations in the promotion of senior officers. In any case, the government was entitled to have the final word as, under the constitution and in practice, 'civil authority is and must remain supreme'. The PM concluded by praising Menon for the 'great energy and enthusiasm he has put in his work and which has resulted in so much progress'. Only after being pressed by opposition members did Nehru acknowledge that 'Thimayya and our senior officers…are people who have done good service, whose experience and gallantry we have appreciated and we appreciate….That is why I went out of my way to get him to withdraw his resignation'.[26]

The Indian armed forces suffered two shocks. The first came when Nehru 'humiliated'[27] General Thimayya in parliament, upsetting the bulk of officers who respected both men and therefore could not understand the former's public censure of the latter. The second occurred when Thimayya failed to re-submit his resignation after his public castigation. Some of those officers answering the questionnaires and/or interviewed offer a variety of reasons for the army chief's motives, or lack thereof, for not offering to resign a second time. These range from the fairly plausible—Thimayya believed Nehru's personal promise that he himself would look into the military's dissatisfaction with Menon—to the frankly speculative—Major-General 75 wonders if Thimayya failed to act because the government now threatened to go public with a damaging personal file on the chief which may have included compromising photos of the 'reputed womanizer'. Whatever the reason, Thimayya's failure to understand the depth his fellow officers' sympathies for his original reasons for offering to resign both damaged his reputation among his supporters and allowed his opponents to grow stronger. Lieut.-General Thorat and Admiral Katari, respectively, recall how Thimayya's 'word carried but little weight'[28] before he 'retired [on 8 May 1961] practically unhonoured [sic] and unsung'.[29]

Accusations that a Menon-Kaul nexus effectively controlled the civil-military decision-making hierarchy gained strength in early 1961 with three contrasting promotions. The first confounded army expectations by using the principle of seniority to designate the inexperienced, 'lacklustre'[30] Lieut.-General P.N. Thapar instead of the battle-hardened, charismatic Lieut.-General Thorat as successor to General Thimayya as chief. In contrast, seniority was discarded in a second promotion when Lieut.-General Verma, associated with Thimayya and Thorat as an anti-Menon-Kaul officer, was superseded twice in the appointment of two army commanders (he then promptly resigned). The third promotion involved Lieut.-General Kaul's move to chief of the general staff (CGS), making him the effective head of the army's combat operations, after Thimayya had apparently 'given in'[31] by allowing the incumbent, Lieut.-General L.P. Sen, to supersede Verma and take up the post of general officer commanding (GoC) Eastern Command. On 5 April 1961, the *Current* printed a letter signed by 'Demoralized Army Officers' which accused 'the evil genius' Menon of tampering with military promotions in order to create a group loyal to himself and warned that Kaul was being cleared a path to promotion as army chief.[32] Six days later in parliament, former Congress President Archarya Kripalani charged Menon with 'having created cliques in the Army [and]...having lowered the morale of our armed services...'.[33] The DM managed to face down these accusations and Nehru himself replied with a spirited defence of Kaul. Menon and the new CGS now were free to cleanse the military of officers perceived hostile to their rule.

Lieut.-General Kaul's reign as CGS began with witch-hunts against those officers who crossed his and/or Menon's path. The first target was General Thimayya, on leave pending retirement but formally Indian Army chief until 8 May 1961. Although nothing came of a Kaul-instigated Intelligence Bureau (IB) investigation into Thimayya's 'alleged treason' over 'a number of careless and indiscreet remarks...regarding the army's possible role in a political emergency'[34] (and he died soon afterwards while serving as commander of the UN peacekeeping force in Cyprus), Lieut.-Generals Thorat and Verma also had to endure retributive attention from Menon and army HQ at the end of their military careers. Nor were serving officers immune from Kaul's attentions. In the most prominent case, (then Major-General) Field Marshal S.H.F.J. Manekshaw, a rising star under Thimayya, also underwent formal scrutiny for his alleged 'anti-Indianness'. While a military board dismissed the charges (including one of hanging portraits of British viceroys, governor-generals and C-in-Cs in his office) as ridiculous and recommended disciplining the accusing officers, Kaul escaped formal censure and Manekshaw continued to suffer, being twice superseded before having his career resurrected (he was to become the first IMA-trained chief of the army).

The reach of the Menon-Kaul nexus is illustrated by the personal experiences of two of those (then relatively junior) officers answering the questionnaires and/or interviewed. Air Chief Marshal 18, in 1960 in charge of policy and plans at IAF HQ,

> came into active and close contact with Mr. Menon. Due to his interest in R&D, he became instrumental in my having to serve a three year period with R&D much to my unhappiness and resulted in some misunderstandings with my superiors....He summarily ordered me back to my job at...Poona, after [Indian] Air [Force] HQ had deputed me to work in Assam with the Eastern Command.

Lieut.-General 4's career was also blighted:

> After commanding my battalion for five years with distinction, [and having] been GSO 1 (Operations) Eastern Command, and deputy leader of India's first mission to Bhutan, I was deliberately posted to command a girl's battalion on the NCC [National Cadet College] as a snub. I have personal knowledge that this posting was contrary to the military secretary's plan for my career, and occurred due to the personal intervention by Kaul. I was rehabilitated only because of the Sino-Indian conflict.

As the above experiences show, not even and junior levels of the armed forces were free from the machinations of the Menon-Kaul nexus in its attempt to bypass the established decision-making hierarchy and promote sycophantic officers. How long could the apparent politicisation of the Indian armed forces continue before a backlash occurred?

Coup d'État?

Military coups are often seen to be the result of officers acting to defend and/or enlarge any number of what they perceive to be their institutional, or corporate, interests. William Thompson describes ten corporate grievances which may provoke officers to stage a coup. Four are particularly relevant to the reign of the Menon-Kaul nexus; that is, when officers perceive that the civilian leadership is attempting to disrupt the military's hierarchical stability, render it less cohesive or united, attack its 'apolitical' preference, and/or threaten their own 'pay, promotions, appointments, assignments, and/or retirements'. As Thompson explains,

> less political and more professional personnel are aggravated by policies favouring incompetent and unqualified but loyalist officers, while those most directly affected by the personnel policies may realize that they must remove the incumbents before their own political control capabilities are seriously weakened. Either group or both in coalition may resort to the coup in order to eliminate a very direct threat to their career possibilities.[35]

Note that officers need only to *perceive* that civilian leaders' decisions are threatening their corporate interests before such concerns may manifest themselves as military coup. Did the Menon-Kaul nexus' definite and concrete disregard for the armed forces' decision-making hierarchy, cohesion, promotion of officers personally loyal to it and persecution of those opposed endanger civil supremacy-of-rule in India?

Just before he was due to go on leave pending retirement, a rumour circulated in government circles that General Thimayya, fed up with the Menon-Kaul nexus, would combine forces with Lieut.-General L.P. Sen, upset at being 'pushed out'[36] of the office of CGS in order to free it for Kaul, to stage a coup on 30 January 1961. Nehru and Minister of Home Affairs G.B. Pant became concerned about 'an order given by Thimayya moving a Division from Ambala to Delhi'[37] and asked Lieut.-General Kaul to investigate. In the end, it was found that the order had been sent directly from army command to the division commander, bypassing the principle staff officers (PSOs). However, the order was countermanded and nothing untoward happened.

The government was already nervous. (Then C-in-C) President Ayub Khan's 1958 coup in Pakistan had shaken India's political and administrative elite and caused a small number of civilians openly to wonder why their own officers did not 'do something'. Although he retired as army C-in-C in 1953, Field Marshal Cariappa's vocal public support for right-wing policies during this decade already had become more than just a nuisance. The former chief had suggested 'it would do good to have military rule under civil control in places where things had gone bad', and 'democracy and socialism could wait till India's teeming millions were assured of a square meal a day'.[38] Cariappa also admired some aspects of Ayub's military regime but stopped just short of advocating an Indian copy. Instead, he 'preferred President's rule in India for at least two years with the assistance of the Army, civil administration being made subordinate to the Army'.[39] With Cariappa also critical of Menon, Kripalani derided Nehru as 'our Hamlet [who] is terribly afraid of an expert man of action like General Cariappa, showing up the skeletons in the cupboard of the Defence Minister...'.[40] Did Cariappa's opinions reflect the mood of General Thimayya and his admirers in the military?

General Thimayya and his followers did have a history of speaking out of turn. Major-General 104 recalls that when Thimayya was promoted from GoC (general officer commanding) Western Command to army chief in May 1953, he 'did say...that you chaps must be ready to take over'. When Thimayya later offered his resignation as chief, Lieut.-General Verma, 'certain that my telephone was tapped and my mail censored under orders of Menon and [Lieut.-General] Kaul....rang him up to say that we were all with him'.[41] Two months after the supposed date of Thimayya's rumoured coup, Lieut.-General Thorat, still a serving officer, made 'a somewhat remarkable statement' critical of the government and asked that the rank-and-file show 'their loyalty to the Army Chief, with no word about loyalty to the Government or to the Constitution of India'.[42] Verma also relates being 'accused of having tried to incite the officers and men against the government in my farewell speeches, when I was leaving XV [15th] Corps'[43] subsequent to handing in his resignation.

A number of those officers answering the questionnaires and/or interviewed agree General Thimayya was the one officer who may have had the stature and popularity to lead a military coup in independent India. Brigadier 61 recalls the tensions surrounding the chief's letter of resignation episode when

> Nehru chided him [Thimayya] like a school boy in parliament. The general taking it like a man...showed tremendous moral courage and professional military leadership. This was the only occasion when his popularity in the army and the forces' reaction was so strongly felt...[that it] might lead to a military takeover.

Thimayya, adds Air Chief Marshal 18, 'might have been able to pull off a coup because of his immense popularity and respect [among officers]'. He was, agrees Lieut.-General 108, and the 'one and only chief who could have pulled off a coup with the military and civilians behind him'.

Despite the government's fears, all of the above events and opinions have more than sufficient counter-arguments. Although he reports General Thimayya as having warned army personnel to 'be ready to take over', Major-General 104 adds that '[Lieut.-General] Kaul started the rumours about Thimayya and a coup'. Perhaps Thimayya was advising his troops to be prepared to follow the orders of their next chief? He was unlikely to have been referring to the men intervening against the government. Indeed, Lieut.-General 94 recalls Thimayya

> talking to a closed-door session of army officers about the example of the Pakistani military coup. He asked, 'If soldiers saved Pakistan from chaos, why shouldn't we?' He illustrated the answer with a story. 'If a soldier is wounded in battle we give him immediate first aid to keep him alive for as long as it takes to get him to hospital. If we do not give him first aid he will die. If the hospital doctors do not treat him properly, he will die. To each his own specialty. We soldiers are trained to give first aid but we are not doctors'.

Finally, however popular with the armed forces, Thimayya's reputation hardly matched that of India's outstanding PM. 'If Nehru and Menon were worried about the popularity of Thimayya regarding leading a coup it was very silly', says Major-General 105; 'there was no comparison between the standing and esteem of Nehru *versus* that of Thimayya'.

Neither were General Thimayya's comrades trying to force him to lead a military intervention against his convictions. In telephoning Thimayya with his support, Lieut.-General Verma was only expressing a widely held feeling that Thimayya was in the right over his dispute with the Menon-Kaul nexus. And, although Verma remembers Thimayya as 'quite bitter about being let down by Mr. Nehru after he had withdrawn his resignation at the latter's behest',[44] the chief did not think to re-submit his offer. As described above, this failure to judge the depth of his colleagues' resentment with the Menon-Kaul nexus caused

Thimayya's once formidable prestige in the armed forces to rapidly drain away. Thus Lieut.-General Thorat's call for 'loyalty to the Army Chief', coming as it did during a Kumaon Regiment officers-only reunion mess dinner with Thimayya as the special guest in virtually his last official function, may be read simply as a personal wish for officers not to forget their once beloved leader.

Lieut.-Generals Thorat and Verma also dismiss suspicions that they themselves harboured any post-military ambitions. Thorat acknowledges that '[General] Thapar was one term ahead of me at Sandhurst, so I had no cause to nurse a grievance against the government—certainly none against Pran [Thapar]'.[45] Verma refutes any accusation that he 'tried to incite the officers and men against the government' by suggesting 'that a cross-section of the people who listened to my speeches might be examined on oath as to what they had heard me say. Of course, it was never done'.[46]

In the end, rumours that General Thimayya and/or Lieut.-Generals Verma and Thorat were planning to stage a coup may be dismissed an unfounded. Although Thimayya and Admiral Katari—and, most likely, Air Marshal Mukherji—were prepared to resign in protest at the Menon-Kaul nexus' interference in the armed forces' chain of command, promotions and appointments, neither contemplated violating their ultimate professional responsibility to their client, the legitimate government of India, because of such grievances. 'Those who at that time...spread stories about a projected coup did so out of sheer mischief and self advancement',[47] concludes Katari.

If General Thimayya was an unlikely candidate to enter politics, Lieut.-General Kaul was not. In Welles Hangen's *After Nehru, Who?*, Kaul is described as having 'an Indian's respect for horoscopes, and his foretells that he will one day rule India....He has none of the Indian officer's traditional disdain for politics. He is political to the end of his swagger stick'.[48] Kaul's only autobiographical reference to political ambition comes in response to the 1961 *Current* editorial quoted above which mentions him as possibly replacing Nehru when he describes how various 'politicians and soldiers...out of jealousy, wanted to rule out this possibility and took steps to assassinate my image in public by all possible manner and means'.[49] Of course, there would be nothing unprofessional about Kaul going into politics after retiring from the army.

Yet there did exist the spectre of Lieut.-General Kaul attaining the leadership of India through military intervention. In conversation, writes Hangen,

> Kaul makes no secret of his sympathy with what the military has done [i.e., assumed power] in Pakistan and Burma. He thinks the Army is mistaken to leave power in civilian hands in Indonesia. At the height of the Hindu-Moslem-Sikh communal slaughter in 1947, Kaul suggested privately to [Indian politician] Jayaprakash Narayan that a 'strong' government was needed to prevent Indian drowning in blood. Narayan interpreted this as a suggestion for army rule and he rejected it. Kaul might find more sympathetic listeners if India were again plunged into chaos. He has made it clear in private talks recently [1962] that *the Army should not hesitate to seize power if the civil government were incapable of ruling or India were about to fall prey to Communists, foreign or domestic.* [My italics.][50]

Thorat warns that Kaul had 'unbridled ambition—in the pursuit of which he was ruthless'.[51]

Unsurprisingly, Lieut.-General Kaul never publicly acknowledged the possibility that he or any other officer might end civil supremacy-of-rule in India. In his only comment on the subject, he writes that when asked about the chances of a coup in India by a member of a Harvard University audience to which he had been invited to speak soon after his 1962 resignation from the army, he

> snapped back at my questioner whether a coup was likely to succeed in a big democracy like [the] USA. Also, whether he had seen a picture recently exhibited called 'Seven days in May'. I said if a coup could fail in [the] USA—as shown in this movie—it was unlikely to succeed in democratic India.[52]

Was the possibility of failure the only factor holding Kaul back?

If Lieut.-General Kaul did entertain the notion of ruling India as a man on horseback he would have had to have been certain of the backing of his fellow officers. Would the Kaul-boys suffice? With Kaul as CGS, recalls Admiral Katari, there were already signs that a parallel line of command was insidiously developing in the army with its own power group gradually taking shape. It was the fortuitous shake-up created by the Chinese invasion of 1962 [see below] that fortunately arrested what was becoming an alarming split down the middle in that service.[53]

Katari is unduly pessimistic. Despite General Thimayya's loss of prestige and retirement, Lieut.-General Thorat's retirement and Lieut.-General Verma's resignation, the Indian Army still contained many officers like (then Major-General) Field Marshal Manekshaw and the vast majority of respondents who were opposed to Kaul for all his background, political and career factors listed above. Hangen himself quotes a 'Delhi editor who professes to know' as saying 'Kaul is a house-builder, not a military man. He couldn't pull a coup because the army wouldn't follow him'.[54] C.E. Welch, Jr. and A.K. Smith describe how militaries with 'high internal cohesion have a greater capacity to intervene in domestic politics than armed forces with lesser cohesion...'.[55] The Indian armed forces' officer corps in the months and years leading up to the 1962 Sino-Indian War was anything but internally united (see also chapter seven).

Despite the uproar caused by charges of politicizing the armed forces' officer corps, Menon could no wrong in Nehru's eyes. Indeed, that the DM was fast becoming the 'chief figure in the demonology of Indian politics', [56] only spurred PM's defence of him in the belief that criticism leveled against Menon was a disguised attack on his own performance. In the 1962 general election, Nehru's spirited support of Menon against Kripalani, the candidate supported by all the right-wing parties and even significant sections of Congress, resulted in the DM increasing his Bombay North majority by almost 100,000. Menon now had to be treated as one of the favourites to succeed Nehru as PM.

How far was Menon willing to go to ensure his succession to Nehru; might a military coup in India be led by a civilian? Air Chief Marshal 12 reports hearing from

> two brigadiers at the time that Menon deliberately wanted China to invade India and create chaos. Then he would take over with the aid of his loyal military officers....[Although] I can't believe it, I wouldn't put anything beyond Krishna Menon...he's a Rasputin.

Lieut.-General 17 also describes how Menon's 'aim seemed to be to place officers who he could trust in places of power and who were amenable to his dictates. My own suspicion was that it was being done to take over with the help of the military after Jawaharlal Nehru'. Brigadier 38 argues that Menon politicized the military because 'perhaps he thought he might succeed Nehru with the assistance and support of top brass in [the] defence services'.

Yet a more popular belief among those officers answering the questionnaires and/or interviewed is that Menon politicized the armed forces to *counter* any threat of a military coup. For Air Chief Marshal 12, the DM 'appointed his own military men partly to counter any possibility of a military coup'. Major-General 97 argues that Menon

> had a swollen head [and] harboured ambitions to become the next prime minister...[he] promoted his own favourites, his 'yes-men'...[and] went over the heads of senior officers to instruct their juniors...[because of] some lurking fear that the military would take over.

Others concur. Lieut.-General 56 writes:

> If it [politicisation] had a purpose other than to build his own self-esteem and importance, it was to cause a rift in the higher echelons, in the army especially. In this he succeeded. Possibly he suspected an internal threat from the military which didn't exist, and he ignored the external threats.

Menon politicized the army, adds Brigadier 29, 'by deliberately creating a cleavage among the higher echelons of senior officers with a view to minimise any chances of a military coup imaginary or otherwise'. Major-General 96 agrees the DM wanted 'to create dissension among senior officers so that any chance of a military take-over was obviated'.

While there were worries that turmoil might follow Nehru's exit from office, fears that Menon would use his ties with certain senior military officers to ensure his ascent to PM were unfounded. Air Chief Marshal 12 argues that any coup 'plot would have failed since Menon had too few personally loyal military officers to effect a takeover...'. Also, as described above, the DM's most ambitious ally, Lieut.-General Kaul, harboured his own hopes in this direction before the debacle of the Sino-Indian War intervened (see chapter seven). Finally, while an enemy of Congress' right-wing and unusually dependent on Nehru's patronage, Menon commanded respect among the left of the party and was considered a serious candidate to become PM by the normal democratic process.

Conclusion

Although Indian civil-military relations seemed poised for a fruitful era with the almost simultaneous elevation of Menon to DM and General Thimayya to army chief, it was not to be. Despite notable successes, his abrasive working style and disregard for normal civil-military decision-making procedure made him many enemies amongst both civilian bureaucrats and armed forces' officers. Menon found a ready partner in Lieut.-General Kaul. Highly ambitious, Kaul used his close relationship with Nehru, undoubted talent for administration, and willingness to obey Menon against the wishes of his superiors to surmount numerous professional liabilities in a quest to reach the office of CGS and beyond. Sycophantic Kaul-boys became a real threat to the careers of their brother officers openly critical of what appeared as a Menon-Kaul nexus. In the words of ex-ICS officer Vira,

> there was complete demoralisation in the ranks of our armed forces because Krishna Menon was functioning in the Defence Ministry according to his own whims and fancies. Even senior promotions and appointments were determined by his whims and fancies, with the result that there were a large number of disgruntled officers in the armed forces.[57]

Might such disgruntlement lead to a military coup?

No, for any number of factors, the most pertinent of which may be because the nature, if not extent, of the Menon-Kaul nexus' disregard for India's formal civil-military decision-making processes was not without precedent. Although many officers resented Lieut.-General Kaul's frequent and informal access to Nehru, a 'similar relationship'[58] existed between the PM and General Thimayya. Although the latter was in 'no way a "political" general....Nehru grew fond of him and "Timmy" did not scruple to exercise his presumed right of access to the PM'.[59] Lieut.-General Thorat agrees that Nehru, who had known Thimayya 'since 1947 when he was serving in the Boundary Force....had much respect for his ability....[and] treated Timmy as a friend'.[60] Major-

General Palit includes the PM in the blame for the Menon-Kaul nexus' politicisation of the armed forces:

> Menon was greatly in awe of the Prime Minister and it is unlikely that he would have dared breach military procedure so blatantly had he not had Nehru's precedent before him....Thus, if anyone was to blame for breaches of propriety and procedure that had crept into the Defence Ministry, it was Jawaharlal Nehru. Menon exploited the precedent for his own purposes.[61]

Other officers criticise Thimayya for not using his initially good relationship with Nehru to protect the army's corporate interests. This failure, combined with Thimayya's inability to stick to his resignation, reveals his weakness as an independent actor. As such, he was hardly likely to lead a military coup against the government.

Additional factors also continued to play their part in keeping India free from the threat of a military coup. However disgruntled, RMC and IMA graduates continued to adhere to the British notion of a professionalism based on perfecting management of violence expertise at the expense of political awareness and/or activity. Despite his intention to resign along with General Thimayya and his sadness at the extent of Nehru's subsequent castigation of the army chief in the Indian parliament, Admiral Katari acknowledges that the PM

> quite properly sought to emphasise the supremacy of the civil authority over the military. None of us in the armed force [sic] had the remotest doubts about this, nor was there even any thought of defying it...I can say with absolute honesty that any idea that they should take the law into their own hands, despite frustrating provocations sometimes, never entered their heads and, God willing, never will.[62]

Another factor was that, although the armed forces had performed creditably abroad and at home, their non-participation in the independence struggle continued to limit public respect for them as agents for positive change—especially when compared to the towering authority and popularity of Nehru. Finally, although now tarnished with the failures inevitable to governing, Congress' convincing victory in the 1962 general elections showed the party and its leader still commanded respect. For Welch and Smith, 'The ease with which the armed forces assume political power varies inversely with the legitimacy enjoyed by the existing civilian government'.[63] India's government, and the democratic process which kept it in power, continued to be seen as moral and effective.

---

[1] D. Vira, *Memories of a Civil Servant* (Delhi: Vikas Publishing House Pvt. Ltd., 1975), p. 82.

[2] Air Chief Marshal P.C. Lal, *My Years with the IAF,* Ela Lal, ed. (New Delhi: Lancer International, 1986), p. 75.

[3] Admiral K.D. Katari, *A Sailor Remembers* (New Delhi: Vikas Publishing House Pvt. Ltd., 1987), pp. 97, 99.

[4] Lieut.-General S.D. Verma, *To Serve with Honour: My Memoirs* (Dehradun: Natraj Publishers, 1988), p. 97.

[5] During the height of the Quit India movement, Lieut.-General Kaul met Valsa Mathai, a 19-year old 'revolutionary leader', who

> dared me to address a students' anti-British rally which I did and at which I spoke on the need of youngmen [sic] coming forward to join the war effort and its significance in the future free India....I expressed many nationalist sentiments publicly which amounted to 'sedition' from the British point of view.

After his (British) CO failed to punish him for speaking out, Kaul continued his nationalist activities 'in the underground movement and thoroughly enjoyed the experience'. He again breached military discipline during the Red Fort Three courts-martial by acceding to chief defence counsel Bhulabhbhai Desai's request to procure 'a document, in possession of the British intelligence authorities, which could prove valuable to the defence of these men'. Kaul also helped Colonel M.S. Himmatsinhji, a nominated military representative of the legislative assembly, to draft a speech defending the Indian national armies. See Lt. General B.M. Kaul, *The Untold Story* (Bombay: Allied Publishers, 1967), pp. 9-11, 62, 70-71, 74-75.

[6] Lieut.-General Kaul's official posts included military attaché in Washington DC, military advisor to India's delegation to the UN Security Council, commander of the J&K Militia, chief of staff to Neutral Nations Repatriation Commission (NNRC) Chairman (then Lieut.-General) General Thimayya, Uttar Pradesh area commander, quarter-master general (QMG), chief of the general staff (CGS), and general officer commanding (GoC) 4th Corps.

[7] Lieut.-General S.P.P. Thorat, *From Reveille to Retreat* (New Delhi: Allied Publishers Private Limited, 1986), p. 177. General Thimayya adds that when Lieut.-General Kaul returned from an official visit to China towards the end of his NNRC posting 'singing their praises....I sacked him. He offered me his

resignation. I refused and urged him to take long leave in India. We were all under pretty heavy strain in those days. The other officers thought I was a fool not to have accepted Kaul's resignation. Now I'm inclined to think they were right'. As cited in W. Hangen, *After Nehru, Who?* (London: Rupert Hart-Davis, 1963), p. 254. Kaul himself records both positive and negative impressions of China in his autobiography but omits any offer to resign.

[8] When Lieut.-General Kaul went ahead with his projects, he found himself the butt of a widespread and hurtful caricature of him as a 'house-builder'.

[9] Kaul, *The Untold Story,* p. 51.

[10] Kaul, *The Untold Story,* p. 50.

[11] Thorat, *From Reveille to Retreat,* p. 176.

[12] Kaul states his 'repeated requests' to be transferred back to an infantry outfit were always refused. See Kaul, *The Untold Story,* pp. 68-70, 87.

[13] Thorat, *From Reveille to Retreat,* p. 176.

[14] Verma, *To Serve with Honour,* pp. 100, 101.

[15] D.K. Palit, *War in High Himalaya: The Indian Army in Crisis, 1962* (London: C. Hurst, 1991), p. 72.

[16] Lal, *My Years with the IAF.,* p. 85.

[17] Verma, *To Serve with Honour,* p. 102.

[18] Neville Maxwell credits Field Marshal S.H.F.J. Manekshaw with originating the term. See N. Maxwell, *India's China War* (New York: Pantheon Books, 1970), p. 194.

[19] Palit, *War in High Himalaya,* p. 76.

[20] Maxwell, *India's China War,* pp. 189-190.

[21] Katari, *A Sailor Remembers,* pp. 102-103.

[22] Katari, *A Sailor Remembers,* p. 103.

[23] *The Statesman* (Calcutta) 1 September 1959.

[24] Katari, *A Sailor Remembers,* p. 103.

[25] Thorat, *From Reveille to Retreat,* p. 178.

[26] *The Statesman,* 3 September 1959.

[27] Thorat, *To Serve with Honour,* p. 178.

[28] Thorat, *To Serve with Honour,* p. 199.

[29] Katari, *A Sailor Remembers,* p. 105.

[30] Palit, *War in High Himalaya,* p. 73.

[31] V.I. Longer, *Red Coats to Olive Green: A History of the Indian Army 1600-1974* (Bombay: Allied Publishers, 1974), p. 99.

[32] As cited in Maxwell, *India's China War,* p. 193

[33] Lok Sabha Debates, LIV:41, col. 10577 as cited in Maxwell, *India's China War,* pp. 193-194.

[34] Palit, *War in High Himalaya,* p. 74.

[35] W.R. Thompson, *The Grievances of Military Coup-Makers* (Beverly Hills: Sage Publications, 1973), pp. 14-20.

[36] Longer, *Red Coats to Olive Green,* p. 99

[37] S.S. Khera, *India's Defence Problem* (Bombay: Orient Longmans, 1968), p. 74.

[38] I.M. Muthanna, *General Cariappa: The First Indian Commander-in-Chief* (Mysore City: Usha Press, 1964)), pp. 85-86.

[39] Muthanna, *General Cariappa*, p. 86

[40] *Vigil*, 21 November 1959, as cited in Muthanna, *General Cariappa*, p. 83.

[41] Verma, *To Serve with Honour*, p. 121.

[42] Khera, *India's Defence Problem*, p. 74.

[43] Verma, *To Serve with Honour*, p. 125

[44] Verma, *To Serve with Honour*, p. 121. General Thimayya was used to getting his way; his biography includes five separate instances where threatening to resign and/or refusing to follow conventional procedure resolved matters to his liking. See H. Evans, *Thimayya of India* (First published New York: Harcourt, Bruce & Co, 1960; Dehra Dun: Natraj Publishers, 1988).

[45] Thorat, *To Serve with Honour*, p. 204.

[46] Verma, *To Serve with Honour*, p. 125.

[47] Katari, *A Sailor Remembers*, p. 104.

[48] Hangen, *After Nehru, Who?*, pp. 245, 247.

[49] Kaul, *The Untold Story*, p. 286.

[50] Hangen, *After Nehru, Who?*, p. 246.

[51] Thorat, *From Reveille to Retreat*, p. 177.

[52] Kaul, *The Untold Story*, p. 462.

[53] Katari, *A Sailor Remembers*, pp. 101-102.

[54] Hangen, *After Nehru, Who?*, p. 270.

[55] C.E. Welch Jr., and A.K. Smith, *Military Role and Rule: Perspectives on Civil-Military Relations* (North Scituate: Duxbury Press, 1974) p. 14.

[56] S. Gopal, *Jawaharlal Nehru: A Biography: Volume III, 1956-1964* (Cambridge: Harvard University Press, 1984), p. 210.

[57] Vira, *Memories of a Civil Servant*, p. 82.

[58] Palit, *War in High Himalaya*, p. 74.

[59] Palit, *War in High Himalaya*, p. 74.

[60] Thorat, *From Reveille to Retreat*, p. 176.

[61] Palit, *War in High Himalaya*, p. 74.

[62] Katari, *A Sailor Remembers*, p. 104.

[63] Welch and Smith, *Military Role and Rule*, p. 30.

7. THE 1962 SINO-INDIAN WAR

The 1962 Sino-Indian War was the country's supreme test of civil supremacy-of-rule as Indians exposed for the first time to the psychological burden of defeat in battle openly called into question the competence of the ruling civilian regime. Whether the government would remain in power or be forcibly replaced depended in great part on who armed forces' officers—and the public—held responsible for the debacle. To help understand post-war attitudes, this chapter will examine how the civil-military hierarchy first countered the growing threat of Chinese aggression in the late 1950s and early 1960s, and then performed during the war, before looking at the factors which decided the future of civilian rule in India in the aftermath of defeat.

Formulation

The build-up to the 1962 Sino-Indian War was slow but steady. The 29 April 1954 agreement in which India recognized China's suzerainty of Tibet and bound Asia's two great powers to the *pancha sheela* (five principles) of mutual respect and peaceful coexistence ostensibly ushered in a mid-1950s period of co-operation characterized by Nehru's slogan *Hindi-Chini, bhai-bhai* (Indians and Chinese are brothers). But tensions over their shared borders as demarcated by the McMahon Line in northeast and northwest India, specifically in the areas known as the Northeast Frontier Agency (NEFA) and Ladakh, respectively, continued to grow (see **Map 1** and **Map 2**). In early 1959, the Dalai Lama fled Tibet for India after his country's Kampa Rebellion was brutally suppressed by the Chinese. In November, news that the NEFA frontier post of Longju had fallen to the Chinese on 25 August and that fighting 40 miles inside Indian territory at Leh, Ladakh, on 20-21 October had claimed the lives of nine members of the paramilitary Central Reserve Police Force (CRPF) forced Nehru to transfer responsibility for the defence of the northern borders from the home office to the ministry of

MAP 1: India's northwest border

Source: N. Maxwell, *India's China War* (New York: Pantheon Books, 1970). Used with the permission of the author.

MAP 2: India's northeast border

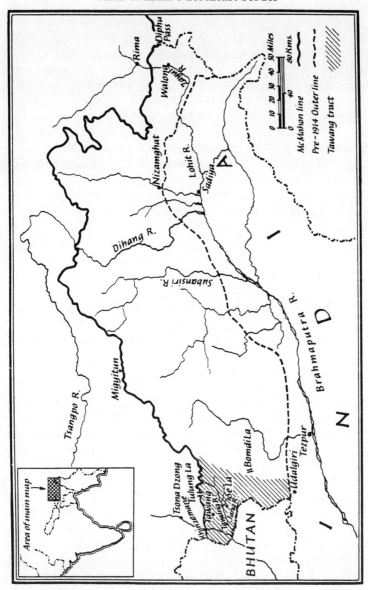

Source: N. Maxwell, *India's China War* (New York: Pantheon Books, 1970). Used with the permission of the author.

defence, and thus to the army. Despite this step, Sino-Indian relations continued to deteriorate and border skirmishes continued through 1961.

While welcoming the Indian Army's responsibility for the defence of NEFA and Ladakh (although the paramilitary Assam Rifles in the former and the CRPF in the latter remained deployed in some advanced positions), senior officers effectively disregarded the government's chosen defensive strategy. Local commanders repeatedly complained about the poor tactics of a policy which may be described as 'non-confrontational containment'—in NEFA patrols were ordered not to enter a self-imposed, three-kilometre buffer zone behind the McMahon Line; while in Ladakh, small outposts were to be established as far forward as possible without confronting Chinese encampments—and their lack of resources to implement it. For GoC 15th Corps Lieut.-General Verma, governmental instructions ordering him to add the defence of Ladakh from China to his existing commitment of protecting J&K against Pakistan were

> almost comic....Firstly, where exactly was the Indian territorial boundary? The small maps available were vague and inaccurate....Secondly, how were we to man this additional area? I already had approx. [sic] 750 miles of the cease-fire line with Pakistan to look after. Now this additional 450 miles of border with Tibet was given to me, but no additional troops or equipment, except one newly raised J&K militia battalion.[1]

Lieut.-General Thorat, appointed GoC Eastern Command in 1957 and now responsible for the defence of NEFA, had an 'unshakable conviction that if I were to listen to the Defence Minister [Menon]...and send troops to the McMahon Line without adequate maintenance cover, I would be sending them to certain defeat and death'.[2] Agreeing that the army was logistically unable to support anything but the smallest 'penny-packets'[3] of troops in forward positions, army chief General Thimayya deliberately toned down operational instructions to his commanders in the field.

Although the army could not meet the essentially defensive commitments of non-confrontational containment, Nehru's worsening relations with the Chinese leadership and the discovery of further enemy encroachments in 1961 led to the adoption of a more offensive strategy in NEFA and Ladakh which became known as the 'forward policy'. At a 2 November 1961 meeting,[4] Nehru laid out his strategy:

(a) So far as Ladakh is concerned, we are to patrol as far forward as possible from our present positions towards the international border. This will be done with a view to establishing our posts which should prevent the Chinese from advancing further and also dominating any posts which they may have already established in our territory. This must be done without getting involved in a clash with the Chinese, unless this becomes necessary in self-defence.

(b) As regards UP [Uttar Pradesh] and other northern areas [i.e., NEFA], there are not the same difficulties as in Ladakh. We should therefore, as far practicable, go forward and be in effective occupation of the whole frontier. Where there are any gaps, they must be covered either by patrolling or by posts.

(c) In view of numerous operational and administrative difficulties, efforts should be made to position major concentrations of forces along our borders in places conveniently situated behind the forward posts from where they could be maintained logistically and from where they can restore a border situation at short notice.[5]

While this forward policy might appear perfectly reasonable (how could any country be said to have a 'forward' policy on its own territory?), it effectively changed Indian military strategy in Ladakh and NEFA from one of non-confrontational containment to one of confrontational advance-and-hold. With respected KCIOs like General Thimayya and Lieut.-Generals Verma and Thorat deliberately neglecting to carry out the former strategy, how did India's civil-military decision-making hierarchy come up with the more demanding forward policy?

To a large extent, numerous mistakes made in the build-up to the 1962 Sino-Indian War may be ascribed to Nehru's towering authority. While democracy had flourished, collective cabinet decision-making had not and it was left to the PM and a few trusted advisors to decide India's approach to international issues. Nehru's belief that Pakistan remained the chief threat led the former to dismiss President Ayub

Khan's 1959 proposal of a joint Indo-Pak defence of the subcontinent with the question: 'Joint defence—against whom?'[6] In contrast, writes Lieut.-General Thorat, the PM and Menon 'refused to believe that China would make any inimical move against us, and, therefore, saw no reason why they should make warlike preparations...which, they feared, might annoy China'.[7] Nehru appeared to believe that in the unlikely eventuality of attack, his success on the world stage would bring protection for India. That he never assessed the Chinese threat in proper military terms also was due to his continued abhorrence of violence as a means of settling international disputes. The political leadership's belief that negotiation was superior to violence reached absurd heights: Menon, recalls Thorat, 'said that...in the most unlikely event of there being one [a Sino-Indian War], he was quite capable of fighting it himself on the diplomatic level'.[8]

To the political leadership's dismissive attitude towards the Chinese threat was added the parsimony of the treasury. For example, while a 1960 study of Italian alpine troops had led General Thimayya to recommend raising some lightly equipped and mobile mountain divisions which would have proved vital in the 1962 Sino-Indian War, his proposal was refused on grounds of expense and the unlikeliness of such formations ever being used. Replacing non-confrontational containment with the forward policy only compounded the army's shortfall in resources. Moreover, adds Lieut.-General Kaul, when any army representations for additional resources along the northern borders did get the backing of the defence ministry, a 'clash of personalities'[9] between Menon and the parsimonious Finance Minister Morarji Desai (on the Congress right and in competition with the DM as a possible successor to Nehru) produced an 'impasse...at this critical juncture. The Finance Ministry, therefore, must also bear responsibility for the Army remaining unprepared for war'.[10]

At this crucial juncture, Operation Vijay's successful liberation of the Portuguese territories of Goa, Daman and Diu in December 1961 stilled many claims that the armed forces were being mismanaged and/or under-resourced. Despite the limited scale of the operation, the political leadership's repeated assurances that the army was in top condition combined with the public's delight with the defeat of the Portuguese to create a popular demand that Chinese forces be forcibly expelled from Indian territory.

The civil-military hierarchy's unpreparedness also stemmed from a lack of comprehensive intelligence gathering.[11] The political and military leadership became over-dependent on the civilian IB, an unenviable situation compounded by the long and close relationship of its director, B.N. Mullik, and Nehru. As with Menon and Lieut.-General Kaul, Mullik's special access to the PM gave him a disproportionate say in formulating Indian defence policy. At the crucial 2 November 1961 meeting, his assurances (or 'divination')[12] that the Chinese would not encroach on land nominally held by Indian units of 'even a dozen soldiers'[13] led directly to Nehru's adoption of the forward policy. In the final build-up to the 1962 Sino-Indian War, Menon, Kaul and other senior officers all came to predicate their strategy on Mullik's assurances that China would never attack in force.

The responsibility for India's unpreparedness is also shared by senior military officers. Though he retired 18 months before the war, General Thimayya's 'defeatist'[14] attitude may be argued to have been at the root of India's military unpreparedness: at a ministry of external affairs (MEA) meeting he is reputed to have said that he could not envisage 'taking on China in open conflict...it must be left to the politicians and diplomats to ensure our security'.[15] Thimayya's retirement did not end army HQ's unprofessional strategic planning. At a July 1961 meeting on the state of its equipment reserves, Indian Army Deputy Chief Lieut.-General M.S. Wadalia stated how, 'if we ever found ourselves at war with China which might predictably be prolonged beyond six months, we could safely assume "foreign intervention"'.[16] Even Lieut.-General Kaul, the youthful arch-nationalist, appears to share this 'wishful assumption'[17] that former colonial powers inevitably would come to India's aid.[18] Many senior officers were content to follow rather than question Nehru's own judgment that a Sino-Indian conflict would inevitably expand into a worldwide confrontation in which the West would side with democratic India against communist China.

However, in the formulation of the forward policy, it is Lieut.-General Kaul, long the most influential officer in India's civil-military decision-making hierarchy, who must take much of the blame for the inadequate defence of the northern borders. Before the fighting started, he was not reticent in taking the credit: 'As late as October 1962...Kaul...told the writer [Neville Maxwell] that the forward policy had been his own conception, "sold to Nehru over the head of Krishna Menon"'.[19] Yet Kaul himself writes that, at the crucial 2 November 1961 meeting, it was Nehru who said that whoever succeeded in establishing (even a symbolic) post, would establish a claim to that territory, as possession was nine-tenths of the law. If the Chinese could set up posts why couldn't we?....A discussion then followed, the upshot of which I understood to be that (since China was unlikely to wage a war with India,) there was no reason why we should not play a game of chess and a battle of wits with them, so far as the question of establishing posts was concerned. If they advanced in one place we should advance in another....This was how, I think, this new policy on our borders was evolved (which was referred to by some as 'forward' policy).[20]

Kaul's adds that he added his weight to General Thapar and DMO Major-General Palit's point that the logistical difficulties of establishing, supporting and reinforcing outposts in forward areas would render them highly vulnerable. Palit recalls him as having remained silent. If Kaul cannot not be blamed for thinking up the forward policy, neither can he take credit for trying to forestall it.

While the top civil-military decision-makers decided upon the forward policy, it was the armed forces' field officers whose units would bear the brunt of the civil-military leadership's strategy for the defence of the northern borders. In 1962, most of the officers answering the questionnaires and/or interviewed were at or around field rank. Of these, a fifth say their relatively junior rank at the time meant they could offer no opinion as to the (de)merits of strategic thinking. Another fifth describe the forward policy itself as generally a good idea, but fault the civil-military leadership for compromising its implementation by under-resourcing and insufficiently training the military. Yet a two-thirds majority of this group of officers describe the forward policy as wrong, using such descriptions as 'ill-conceived and miscalculated', 'rank bravado', and 'premature and stupid'. Specifically cited are failures in diplomacy, intelligence, and strategic thinking. The popular notion that 'not an inch of Indian soil will be surrendered' was seen as foolish and inflammatory but left unchallenged by the civil-military leadership. In the final analysis, argues Brigadier 73, 'there was no immediate danger to the country. We forced the Chinese to enter India'.

Implementation

One of the 'more compelling'[21] accounts of how the forward policy came to be implemented blames Lieut.-General Kaul for sending small units of troops into wholly indefensible, advanced positions. Major-General Palit reveals that the policy's crucial third directive described above ('to position major concentrations of forces along our borders... behind the forward posts') was not mentioned by Nehru at the 2 November 1961 meeting but *later inserted into the official minutes of the meeting by Foreign Ministry officials seeking to create an alibi* in case the Chinese did attack in force. When Palit protested to Kaul that this 'brazen ploy at alibi-making' added logistical commitments which the army could not then fulfill, the latter 'somewhat sheepishly confessed that he had been shown a draft of the Foreign Ministry minutes before their issue and....had already accorded his approval'. Nor, continues Palit, did Kaul agree the third directive logically should be given priority over the first two; that is, that forward posts be established only after the provision of adequate logistical support. Acting on Kaul's advice, on 5 December 1961 army chief General Thapar ordered both Western and Eastern Commands to patrol as near to the border as possible, to establish posts blocking any further Chinese advances, and only then to make a fresh appraisal of the logistic requirements they might need.

The pattern of the forward policy was soon set (see **Map 3**). Whereas concern for the logistical shortcomings had led General Thimayya to water down the government's deployment orders regarding non-confrontational containment, similar worries now did not prevent General Thapar and Lieut.-General Kaul from wholeheartedly embracing the forward policy. When two minor Indian Army units in the Aksai Chin, Ladakh, faced down far superior enemy forces in the spring/summer of 1962, the press and public became convinced that the Chinese would not force their claim to border territories occupied by Indian personnel and the civil-military leadership was lulled into believing that the forward policy provided real security on the northern borders. More could be tried. In Ladakh, orders were given for penny-packets of Indian forces in to push ever forward, and their orders of engagement modified from 'fire only if fired upon' to 'fire if the Chinese press dangerously close to your positions'.[22] In NEFA, 'Operation Onkar', the establishment of up to 35 outposts along the McMahon Line to be occupied by Assam Rifles' personnel,

MAP 3: The forward policy along the northwest border

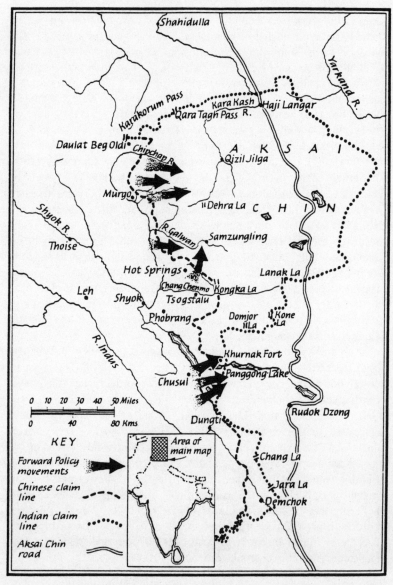

Source: N. Maxwell, *India's China War* (New York: Pantheon Books, 1970). Used with the permission of the author.

commenced. All this forward activity came in spite of local commanders' objections who saw the civil-military leadership in New Delhi making decisions based on what it wanted to believe was true rather than on what they advised was the reality on the ground.

The beginning of the end of Indian civil-military overconfidence came on 8 September 1962 when an Assam Rifles' outpost near the Dhola pass in eastern NEFA sent out a 'frantic'[23] signal reporting its encirclement by 600 Chinese troops and asking for immediate reinforcements. In response, GoC 4th Division Major-General Niranjan Prasad sent a company on the five-day march to the outpost and ordered the rest of the battalion to prepare to move to Lumpu, within easier reach of the pass. The next day, 7th Infantry Brigade CO Brigadier J.P. Dalvi and his battalion commanders, all with first-hand experience of the local terrain, advised that unfavourable geography and the Chinese forces' superiority of arms and ease of supply made the Dhola pass position 'completely indefensible'.[24]

The response of local commanders contrasts with the decision-making of India's civil-military leadership. On 10 September, GoC Eastern Command, Lieut.-General Sen, the officer with ultimate responsibility for NEFA, conferred telephonically with army chief General Thapar before ordering 9th Punjab to move immediately to Lumpu and 7th Brigade to prepare to leave in 48 hours to confront the Chinese at the Dhola pass. Thus, despite their lack of any first-hand knowledge of NEFA, and without consulting local commanders on the ground, CGS Lieut.-General Kaul or DMO Major-General Palit, all of whom knew the area from current/previous personal/command experience, Thapar and Sen changed army strategy in the northeast from one of backing forward patrols to one of direct confrontation by a significant military force.

On 11 September, the civil-military leadership went further, effectively changing the forward policy from aggressive self-defence to outright offence by ordering 'Operation Leghorn', the forcible eviction of the Chinese menacing the Dhola pass outpost and the capture of the local high ground, the Thagla ridge. Such was the poor state of India's civil-military decision-making that this momentous decision was taken in the absence of Nehru (since 8 September at the London conference of Commonwealth prime ministers), Finance Minister Desai (normally cabinet chair in the PM's absence but also in London) and Home Minister L.B. Shastri (the remaining senior member of the cabinet defence committee). Instead, at a New Delhi meeting attended by seemingly whoever remained of the government's defence decision-making hierarchy,[25] Menon accepted Lieut.-General Sen's assurance that within ten days an infantry brigade could be concentrated below the Thagla ridge to expel all Chinese forces in the area.

NEFA commanders were incredulous at their senior officers' unprofessional advice to the political leadership. What on a map seemed perfectly plausible to politicians and senior officers in New Delhi and to Eastern Command HQ in Lucknow was unattainable in the extreme mountain conditions of NEFA. When Lieut.-General Sen personally passed on the new deployment orders to Major-General Prasad and GoC 33rd Corps Lieut.-General Umrao Singh on 12 September, both protested at the impossibility of evicting a Chinese force they now estimated as a full division and a half. Yet Sen remained adamant. Nothing seemed to be thought impossible by senior commanders eager to please their civilian masters.

Four years into the reign of the Menon-Kaul nexus, such unprofessional behaviour had become the norm at army HQ. For a number of months, no proper records of vital decisions had been kept at headquarters; now Operation Leghorn saw orders increasingly issued telephonically instead of in writing. On 16 September, Major-General Palit returned from leave to find the military operations directorate in

a state of confusion....merely relaying orders on behalf of the officiating CGS [(then Major-General) Lieut.-General J.S. Dhillon, who]....focused on the political decision [to evict the Chinese from Thagla ridge]...rather than on the logistical and tactical factors that clearly denied the feasibility of that option.[26]

Even more unprofessional and dangerous to the corporate cohesion of the Indian Army was HQ's interference in the tactical deployment of troops in NEFA. Brigadier Dalvi states the obvious: 'In well regulated armies it is not the statutory function of superior commanders to order the moves of units, or to evict junior commanders from their HQs. A formation is given a task, and the formation commander executes it'.[27] Yet his brigade's deployment south of the Thagla ridge was orchestrated down to the smallest detail by his superiors.

Also now typical of army HQ was senior officers' servility to government civilians. On 22 September, General Thapar, worried that a fatal exchange of fire across the *de facto* border of the Namka Chu river two days earlier presaged a attack on vulnerable Indian outposts in NEFA and/or Ladakh, sought written confirmation of the 'eviction' order given at the 11 September New Delhi meeting. In the absence of Nehru (still in London), Menon (at a UN Security Council session in New York), Finance Minister Desai (in Washington, DC), and Home Minister Shastri (in Kerala), it was reportedly left to Joint Secretary (Defence) Harish C. Sarin to sign an order confirming the government's directive that the army expel the Chinese from Dhola and the Thagla ridge. Thapar accepted this confirmation and the same day issued the relevant orders to his commanders in NEFA.

Many officers saw General Thapar's acceptance of Sarin's authority as a failure of leadership. Lieut.-General Kaul, an exception to the majority of his comrades who believed the Lieut.-General Thorat had been the best candidate to succeed General Thimayya as army chief, felt Thapar 'had the courage of his convictions and was not afraid of expressing his opinions, even though unpalatable, in the presence of those above him'.[28] But for Major-General Palit, the fact that Thapar asked for a written order from Sarin showed

> that he was not wholly in agreement with the content of the verbal one....clearly he was alarmed about a possible riposte in both Ladakh and NEFA, and he must have known that in either event our forward posts stood no chance of a coordinated attack....why did he not resist the pressure on him to amount [sic] a reckless offensive at Thag-la [sic]?[29]

Brigadier Dalvi also found it 'unbelievable' that Thapar accepted the expulsion order: 'To be right and overruled is not forgiven to persons in responsible positions!'[30]

Yet, as before, those in responsible positions who contradicted the Menon-Kaul nexus soon found themselves in trouble. The latest victim was Lieut.-General Umrao Singh who had repeatedly protested against army HQ's thoughtless deployment of forward posts. Simply sacking him would have raised suspicions that sections of the army were either incompetent and/or displeased at government policy in NEFA (and left his successor with a potentially hostile staff). Instead, after meetings on 2-3 October between Nehru, Menon, General Thapar and Lieut.-Generals Sen and Kaul, it was announced that Umrao's 33rd Corps would be given exclusive responsibility for the Sikkim, Nagaland and East Pakistan fronts, while Kaul would be made GoC of a 'new' 4th

Corps headquartered in Tezpur with orders to carry out the eviction order in the Thagla ridge forthwith.

Replacing the respected Lieut.-General Umrao Singh and his experienced 33rd Corps with Lieut.-General Kaul and a new 4th Corps stunned the armed forces. Not only was Kaul the one senior officer derided for having no combat experience, he had been on leave in J&K since 3 September and was out of touch with recent developments. Major-General Palit was 'as surprised as aghast at the news. What new corps? Why him? Who would do the CGS's job when he left?' Kaul himself describes the enormity of his task:

> [4th Corps] was to consist at the moment of only...two (5th and 7th) Infantry Brigades, (with the possibility of a third Brigade joining me later) whereas normally there are six to twelve Infantry Brigades in a Corps....There was also another Division to be formed which would be given to me, apart from other reinforcements, later....Normally it takes between six months and a year to raise and train and a Corps Headquarters in its operational and administrative functions. It takes another six months to a year...after units and formations have been made available, to make a Corps battle-worthy....I, on the other hand, was given command of a Corps which was practically non-existent on the ground and the headquarters of which had yet to be raised. I was, thus, expected to perform a miracle and begin to operate immediately.[31]

General Chaudhuri disparages Kaul's complaints by pointing out that 'whatever the acts of omission and commission, he was himself to blame, being the Chief of the General Staff'.[32]

Notwithstanding his record of complaints after the event, Lieut.-General Kaul was keen to take charge. In discussion with the new GoC 4th Corps on the night before his departure for NEFA on 4 October, Major-General Palit perceived Kaul as 'greatly pleased....going to war at last, and at the top level. Here was his chance to make up for the past, to fill in the blanks in his credentials and to give lie to his detractors'.[33] A commander inexperienced in battle but desperately eager to prove himself, flying to the front with a staff of 'yes-men'[34] to take over a severely under-resourced corps was never going to give India's civil-military leadership the quick victory they believed still possible. Yet such was Nehru's belief in the abilities of his favourite officer that Kaul left for NEFA bearing just such expectations.

Despite his hopes, Lieut.-General Kaul committed an error of judgement on the evening of 11 October which was to prove the undoing of Indian Army defences in NEFA. The day before, he had been shocked at the force of an enemy attack on several Indian positions along the Namka Chu river, seeing with his 'own eyes the superior resources of the Chinese...and the untenability [sic] of our position....I thought we should reconsider the whole of our position in this theatre'.[35] Kaul agreed with local commanders Major-General Prasad and Brigadier Dalvi that their forces should pull back to more defensible and easily supplied positions, but refused to authorize this move until he could present the hopelessness of their present situation to his superiors in New Delhi. Yet, at a meeting the next night attended by top civil-military decision-makers including Nehru, Menon, IB Director Mullik, General Thapar and Lieut.-General Sen, Kaul offered the PM three choices: launch an attack despite the overwhelming odds; hold present positions; or retreat to more defensible locations. While accounts vary, it is apparent that when both Thapar and Sen, neither with any first-hand knowledge of the relevant terrain, scoffed at Kaul's assessment of the precariousness of the Indian positions and advised that the troops along the Namka Chu river hold their present positions, he did not protest. Nehru agreed and allowed the troops to remain overexposed to the enemy. In giving the civil-military leadership three choices where only one—retreat—was reasonable, Kaul ignored a commander's first duty to do what is best for his men.

Nehru also seemed unable to admit to Indian frailties on the northern borders. On 13 September, he told reporters that 'Our instructions [to the military] are to free our territory'.[36] Although he went on to discuss aspects of the situation which favoured China—their forces were more numerous and held the higher ground, their main supply base was closer to the disputed border, and wintry conditions limited Indian mobility— he made no mention of his decision to temporarily suspend Operation Leghorn because of Indian Army deficiencies. How could he, after years of asserting the opposite? While Nehru's statement may have been meant as an innocuous, if naively worded, reiteration of government policy, the international, Chinese and Indian press and people took it as a virtual declaration of war.

The civil-military leadership continued to stumble from one bad judgment to another, the most notable being the 19 September decision to retain Lieut.-General Kaul as GoC 4th Corps even though he had just been diagnosed as suffering from pulmonary oedema and flown back to New Delhi for 'complete rest'.[37] Following procedure would have seen him replaced by the NEFA theatre's next-ranking officer, Major-General Prasad. Why, too, when his illness had been diagnosed as too serious to be treated at the army hospital in Tezpur, was Kaul allowed to recuperate at home? Nonetheless, urged on by the cream of India's civil-military decision-makers constantly in attendance at his sickbed, Kaul continued to order his commanders in NEFA to remain in what he knew were untenable positions. It was in his bed that he heard news of a major Chinese invasion along the northern borders.

War

Just how critical the situation had become became apparent on 20 October when Chinese forces attacked Indian positions all along the northern borders and 'most of the troops deployed in penny packets in pursuance of the so-called "forward policy"….[were] swept away like driftwood before a torrent'.[38] In eastern NEFA, 7th Brigade 'virtually ceased to exist',[39] and within days Major-General Prasad was forced to abandon Tawang, over 20 miles inside Indian-claimed territory (see **Map 4**). Fierce fighting also broke out around Walong in the previously quiet western end of NEFA. Although isolated Indian Army and J&K Militia outposts offered stiff resistance in Ladakh, they were eventually overwhelmed by the enemy's superior numbers. By 24 October, the Chinese were secure enough in their gains to offer peace if India respected a 7 November 1959 'line of actual control' which effectively ceded the former 12,000 square miles of northern border land. Although India refused this offer, there occurred a brief lull in hostilities.

The Chinese attacks shocked both India and its PM. Nehru declared a state of national emergency, labelled the Chinese offensive a 'major invasion'[40] in which the fate of Asia and the world was at stake, appealed for foreign military aid and, under severe pressure from parliament and the press, took over the defence portfolio from Menon (now demoted to the new post of minister for defence production). Nehru also handed back to army HQ responsibility for military tactics and deployment: 'It is a matter *now* for the military to decide—where and how they should fight' [My italics].[41] From 24 October, he began to chair the daily defence meetings introduced by Menon a month earlier.

MAP 4: The Chinese advance in NEFA

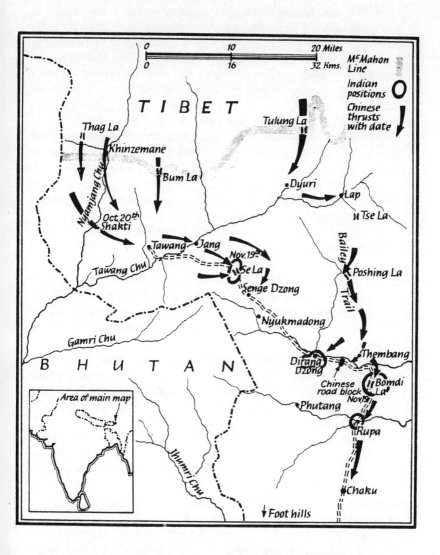

Source: N. Maxwell, *India's China War* (New York: Pantheon Books, 1970). Used with the permission of the author.

Despite these changes, the lull allowed the political leadership to convince itself that only the surprise of, and overwhelming numbers involved in the Chinese attacks were to blame for Indian reverses. If the army was allowed sufficient time to regroup, civil-military decision-making could remain unchanged. Tactics continued to be decided by small groups of senior civil-military leaders—mainly Nehru, Menon (decreasingly until the acceptance of his letter of resignation on 7 November), Foreign Secretary Desai (increasingly), Minister of Economic and Defence Coordination T.T. Krishnamachari (increasingly), General Thapar, Lieut.-Generals Sen and Kaul, and Major-General Palit—with little mutual consultation and/or regard for formal procedure. Perhaps the most glaring example of 'business as usual' came when Kaul, who had been formally replaced as GoC 4th Corps on 24 October, returned to his post on 29 October. That Kaul's reinstatement in place of the capable and respected Lieut.-General Harbakhsh Singh was likely to harm India's fighting efficiency and morale as front-line troops openly scoffed at their commander's 'timely' evacuation and 'political' rehabilitation did not deter Nehru from foisting upon the army his favourite commander.

The disastrous effect of the civil-military leadership's over-reliance on informal procedure, uninformed opinion and personality is perfectly illustrated in Major-General Palit's record of the 'nightmarish'[42] days of 17-18 November at 4th Corps HQ, Tezpur, eastern NEFA.[43] On 17 November, Indian Army HQ received a signal from Walong in which Lieut.-General Kaul 'sounded so desperate as to be almost demented'.[44] General Thapar and Palit, as DMO, responded by proceeding to 4th Corps HQ to join GoC Eastern Command Lieut.-General Sen and await Kaul so as to bolster his confidence.[45] None suspected they were about to fight the crucial battle of the 1962 Sino-Indian War.

The lull in fighting had allowed the Indian Army to quickly reconstitute a 4th Division of ten battalions to defend eastern NEFA. While deficient in high-altitude training and reserves, these battalions could draw upon artillery and other heavy weaponry, and the military leadership was confident of checking the Chinese at the high ground of Se La Pass held by the 62nd Brigade with the 65th in close attendance at Senge Dzong. Further defensive insurance was provided by the 48th Brigade, stationed 60 miles back at the other end of the Se La-Senge Dzong-(Nyukmadong)-Dirang Dzong-(Thembang)-Bomdila road.

Yet, within hours of General Thapar and Major-General Palit's appearance in Tezpur, the army's planned defence of eastern NEFA began to collapse. Immediately upon their arrival, Lieut.-General Sen informed them that 4th Division Major-General Anant Pathania, who had replaced Major-General Prasad on Sen's orders and was now in Bomdila, had ordered the 4th Garhwali Rifles to withdraw from the outer defences of Se La despite their just having repulsed successfully four attacks by 'motley'[46] Chinese forces. Soon afterwards came information that GoC 48th Brigade Gurbax Singh had okayed the retreat of 5th Guards, positioned at Thembang, after it had been encircled by Chinese troops. Thapar and Palit also learnt that Lieut.-General Kaul had already allowed Pathania to move 4th Division HQ, accompanied by 65th Brigade, down from Senge Dzong to the camp of the paramilitary Border Roads Organisation (BRO) at Dhirang Dzong, ostensibly so as to alleviate his high altitude headaches. Palit 'could scarcely believe what we were told. None of the commanders seemed to have the stomach for a fight'.[47]

Matters did not improve when Lieut.-General Kaul arrived from Walong to complete, with General Thapar and Lieut.-General Sen, the ruling triumvirate of India's military leadership. Already, Major-General Palit had taken a telephone call from Major-General Pathania asking for permission to now retreat from Dhirang Dzong because he feared the Chinese taking the Se La-Bomdila road and cutting off his escape route. Sen pleaded for Pathania's request to be granted:

> 'If 4th Infantry Division can make a clean break now...it will have a clear chance of getting away intact'. Before Thapar could be influenced by this specious argument I [Palit] asked the Army Commander what the Division's operational role was: to fight the enemy at Se-la or to keep itself intact?[48]

It was becoming obvious India's top three military decision-makers and assorted field commanders were not up to battle command. Soon after Kaul's arrival, Palit discovered that a signal had been issued granting Pathania's request to retreat. Imploring Thapar that 'we could never face the nation if 12,000 [Indian] troops..."ran away" without even facing the enemy',[49] he persuaded the chief to cancel the message and Kaul ordered 4th Division 'to remain at Se-la and to fight it out to the best of its ability and withdraw only if its position became untenable'.[50] Yet just over an hour later, Pathania was on the line again demanding permission to withdraw. Palit, who had answered the telephone, made

Pathania confirm there had been no frontal assault on Se La, just various minor activities in the Dhirang Dzong-Bomdila area. Yet Kaul,

> in words which will surely remain a classic double entendre in our military history books....[then told Pathania] 'For tonight you hang on to your defences. Have another chat with me in the morning'. How far that unconventional enjoyment would stand up as an imperative to a jittery subordinate to stay and fight, I need not comment upon...[51].

In any case nothing was done and, as India's top military leaders slept that night in Tezpur, Pathania acted as if he understood Kaul's words to mean he could begin pulling out.

The next morning exposed the consequences of the previous night's irresolution. Lieut.-General Kaul informed Major-General Palit that in the night 62nd Brigade CO Brigadier Hoshiar Singh had ordered his troops to pull out of their prepared defences around Se La, and that at 06:30 Major-General Pathania had telephoned to say that 'he was closing down his headquarters at Dhirang Dzong, because of the Chinese threat, and was moving—though he could not state what his destination would be'.[52] Discovering that all communication links with the forces defending the Se La-Bomdila Road silent, Palit was now in 'no doubt that everybody was on the run. 4th Infantry Division had ceased to exist'. Informed of these developments, General Thapar and Lieut.-General Sen 'looked stunned'.[53] With the Chinese seemingly advancing at will, Palit advised preparing for the defence of Assam. But the top triumvirate of India's military leadership again failed to seize control, discussing options instead of acting. At mid-afternoon, with no effective orders yet issued, Sen scraped the bottom of India's military decision-making barrel, saying to Thapar,

> 'Sir, there is no option left for us but to ask for a cease-fire!'
> 'What!' I [Palit] blurted out, 'Surrender?'
> 'If it comes to that, I suppose, yes,' he [Sen] replied.
> 'Never! What are you talking about....If the Chinese come down into to the plains, that's the time to get our own back on them—not to put out hands up!'
> I looked at Thapar and thought I sensed support, but he said nothing.[54]

This conversation immediately was followed by news that Bomdila was under attack. Leaving Sen and Kaul to organise what was left of the 4th Infantry Division's defence of eastern NEFA, Thapar and Palit left for New Delhi to brief the political leadership on the prospects of protecting Assam from a Chinese invasion.

The humiliation heaped on India's civil-military leadership seemed limitless. Already, Nehru had had to ask for Western military aid and been forced to accept Menon's resignation from the government (see below). Now, on 19 November, a day after the collapse of the Se La-Bomdila defences, he wrote to US President John F. Kennedy requesting American aircraft and pilots provide air cover for Indian cities. With little news of any effective armed resistance, the senior military leadership came close to recommending the evacuation of Assam, and the home ministry signalled its personnel in Tezpur and other northeast cities to prepare for a scorched earth policy of defence. General Thapar then resigned on grounds of ill-health to make way for (then GoC Southern Command Lieut.-General) General Chaudhuri. (Nehru had been dissuaded from his original intention of replacing Thapar with Lieut.-General Kaul only after some forceful persuasion by President S. Radhakrishnan.) In a national broadcast that evening, the PM seemed to be preparing the people of Assam for imminent invasion, giving rise to public panic. But Chaudhuri's first act as chief, a 20 November order that his commanders must stand and defend Assam, became redundant the very next day when the Chinese added the final humiliation of declaring a unilateral cease-fire on all fronts and a withdrawal, to begin on 1 December, to positions behind the same line of actual control which Nehru had refused to accept earlier. To reach this ignominious end had cost the Indian Army 1,423 killed, 3,078 wounded, 1,655 missing believed dead.[55]

Aftermath

India's political leadership was not keen to expose its decision-making failures to public scrutiny. The only official inquiry into the debacle of the 1962 Sino-Indian War, a wholly military affair instigated by General Chaudhuri and compiled by GoC 11th Corps Major-General Henderson-Brooks and IMA Commandant (then Brigadier) Lieut.-General P.S. Bhagat, was severely restricted in its access to both officers and documents. Nonetheless, the 'Henderson-Brooks Report' proved so disagreeable to the government that its findings remain secret to this day. The only official reaction came on 2 September 1963 when new Defence Minister Y.B. Chavan (sworn in on 21 November), stating that the purpose of the inquiry had never been 'in any way [to] undertake a witch-hunt into the capabilities of those who were concerned with or took part in these operations',[56] gave parliament a general description of its findings, including:

> (i) the need for more realistic battle training, especially in mountain warfare; (ii) the urgency of eliminating shortages of equipment; (iii) the need for curbing the tendency among senior officers to interfere in the tactical handling of troops at lower levels; (iv) the requirement of preparing troops adequately before committing them to a theatre of operations; (v) the requirement of better communications (signals and equipment); and (vi) the need for a better intelligence set-up.[57]

Although Chavan stated that the report recommended political directives be more closely related to the army's size and equipment, he neglected to add that Henderson-Brooks had apparently traced the roots of India's defeat to the 'higher direction of war'.[58] For the political leadership, the sooner the 1962 Sino-Indian War was forgotten, the better.

It was not so easy for the armed forces to forget. Those senior officers who had fallen foul of the Menon-Kaul nexus were quick to apportion blame and, while the poor performance of Indian intelligence and Lieut.-General Kaul's leaving the battlefield for reasons of ill-health come in for particular criticism, the entire top layer of civil-military leadership is also held responsible. Admiral Katari speaks for many of his fellow officers when he describes how the political leadership failed because of 'a lack of probity....One cannot play favourites and still expect to command universal loyalty or provide purposeful control...in war, it can be disastrous, as indeed it proved to be'.[59] More difficult for Katari to understand is the failure of the military leadership since 'at least [some] of the senior officers had proved themselves as good fighting leaders in the past. My only conclusion is that they were a demoralized lot, an extension to the individual level of the general demoralization that had been creeping into the army'.[60] Yet officers who had their differences with the Menon-Kaul nexus may be expected to be over-critical of the civil-military leadership's performance during the

1962 Sino-Indian War. What of those officers who had risen to top under this regime?

Of the three main military protagonists—General Thapar, Lieut.-Generals Sen and Kaul—in the debacle at NEFA, only the last has put his thoughts into writing. While Thapar himself has remained silent, Sen is quoted as to why, as army commander, he did not sack Kaul for incompetence:

> It is all very well for you to say this...but do you know what his stature was then? He never talked to me; he would just pick up the phone and talk to the Prime Minister. He never even consulted...[Thapar]. I would have got no support from anyone. Krishna Menon and...Kaul were running the armed forces of the country.[61]

Kaul blames all manner of factors, including the political leadership's continued faith in non-violence which stifled military spending, failure to provide 'clear policy directions'[62] to the army, and extraordinary concern with public opinion *vis-à-vis* border incursions. Particular civilians faulted include Nehru for formulating the forward policy and issuing inflammatory remarks, Menon and his civil servants for promoting indigenous defence production tomorrow at the expense of importing weaponry today, and Finance Minister Desai for providing insufficient funds when military resource requests were approved. Kaul also censures fellow officers Sen for a poor grasp of tactics, Major-General Pathania for misleading him about the strength of the Chinese attack on 17-18 November and for not putting up enough resistance, Brigadier Dalvi for insufficient preparation of his unit's defences, and assorted field commanders for not fighting the enemy with 'greater determination'.[63] While all of Kaul's criticisms may be correct, he refuses to accept any personal responsibility for the debacle, admitting only to that '*collective* responsibility'[64] which, as a member of the general staff, he shares for the troops' lack of training, acclimatisation, and resources. But then Kaul, opines Major-General Palit, 'seemed to spend a large part of his life in disguise, even from himself'.[65]

As DMO, Major-General Palit was at the heart of India's senior military leadership. He places responsibility for the defeat on the nature of India's civil-military decision-making hierarchy. Because meetings were *ad hoc*, policy decisions were made with little or no staff analysis. Decisions based on false or misguided assumptions were then compounded by the tendency, as the crisis on the northern borders developed, for the 'the decision-making cell in the government...[to grow] not larger but smaller and, consequently, not more but less accountable....Few authoritarian systems could have spawned a more exclusive policy-making apparatus'.[66] For all these faults, continues Palit, chief responsibility for defeat in war

> lies squarely on the shoulders of the high command and their staffs, for their unawareness or disregard of operational and logistical constraints on the Himalayan front, for their failure to impress on the politicos the impossibility of the operational tasks demanded of them, and, above all, for their insensitivity to the plight of the officers and men in the battalions witlessly pushed up into the high mountains— insufficiently armed, clothed or provisioned—at the mercy of an enemy well-prepared for war.[67]

Palit could hardly be more damning: 'If the fighting had continued on 20 November, I feel sure that there would have been few left among the top ranks who could, or would, have effectively directed the army in war or led army corps in battle'.[68]

What was the view of India's defeat further down the ranks? In 1962, the armed forces' field grade officers who experienced first-hand the bloody battle results of poor civil-military leadership decisions were those who answered the questionnaires and/or were interviewed. Given their position, it is unsurprising that they single out the lack of suitable equipment and training as the single most important factor contributing to the military's defeat in battle. Otherwise, their responses mirror those of their superiors as described above. Lieut.-General 10 makes an evocative comparison regarding India's poor political leadership:

> Compare Churchill in 1940 to Nehru in 1962. In 1940 the British Field Army had been destroyed in Dunkirk and Great Britain had no allies. But Churchill was moved to make his speech: 'I've nothing but blood, sweat and tears to offer. We'll fight on the beaches, we'll fight on the streets...'. In 1962 Nehru had lost only 25-30,000 [sic] men. India still had an army of 500,000 and allies in the US and UK. Yet he made a radio address which practically resigned Assam to the Chinese. He should have and could have fought back.

Despite such sentiments, most respondents naming a particular individual as a poor performer point not to Nehru, but to his defence minister, Menon. The military leadership is blamed for allowing the political leadership to dictate both strategic and tactical deployments, and for the poor individual performances of top commanders. While Brigadier 76 feels 'military honour dictated that, rather than jeopardise the safety of his troops and the prestige of his country....General Thapar should have at the time threatened to resign', it is Lieut.-General Kaul who comes in for the severest criticism. His lack of combat experience and overriding political ambitions meant, writes Major-General 20, that 'no one was surprised when he failed'. Finally, like their seniors, these officers include poor intelligence as contributing to defeat in the 1962 Sino-Indian War. Only the field officers themselves and the jawans escape blame.

Recriminations in the aftermath of the 1962 Sino-Indian War made civil supremacy-of-rule in India appear vulnerable for the first time. While various coup prediction theories believe a government's failure to meet the challenges of modernisation will pull or push armed forces' officers into taking over, such failings are usually described in the context of socioeconomic and internal political development. Yet the first duty of any competent regime is to protect its territory and citizenry from external aggression and this the Indian government signally failed to do. Other theories which see military takeovers of government as the result of officers' corporate grievances are much more specific when predicting the effect of defeat in war. Here, coup precipitants include instances of 'psychological violence'[69] when civilian governments blame the armed forces for defeat or when officers feel that an administration's 'incompetence has made the nation—and thus its standard bearer, the military—a standing joke to the outside world'.[70] Such grievances are magnified if officers feel that the performance of the armed forces was hampered by insufficient resources and/or support.[71]

Note that the question of continued civilian rule in the aftermath of defeat in war depends more on the attitudes of the armed forces' field officers—majors, lieut.-colonels, colonels, and brigadiers—than on their superiors. The latter are more likely to have been spared the trauma of the battlefield, be content with their positions and perks and, at least while working at military headquarters, command less personal loyalty among the men of the fighting arms. In contrast, field officers are more likely to be at the sharp end of any failures in civil-military decision-making, be envious of their superiors' position and perks, and command the personal loyalty of their men. Perhaps most importantly, disgruntled field officers are more likely to see the military leadership as part of the problem rather than the solution.

As field-grade officers in 1962, the post-cease-fire perspectives on the Sino-Indian War of those officers answering the questionnaires and/or interviewed would be crucial in determining whether civil supremacy-of rule continued in India. These officers appear to blame everything and everyone but themselves and their men for performing poorly during wartime. How did this affect their perceptions of civilian rule? If blame centred on the political leadership, if the respondents felt distanced from their superiors, if they perceived public support for the armed forces and anger at the political leadership, a military coup in India was not unthinkable.

TABLE 4: Post-Sino-Indian War attitudes towards the political leadership.*

	Field Officers		The Public	
	Per cent (Number)			
Negative	60.66	(37)	96.55	(58)
No Change	9.84	(6)	1.71	(1)
Positive	29.51	(18)	1.71	(1)
Total	100.01	(61)	99.99	(58)

* Percentages have been adjusted after subtracting those officers (35 and 11, respectively) giving 'No Answer' in each column.

Unsurprisingly, a large majority of the Indian armed forces' field officers recall a negative attitude towards the political leadership in the aftermath of defeat (see **Table 4**). Without repeating the list of failures committed by the government administration, it is worth noting the depth of anger felt by these officers; for instance, Brigadier 73 who recalls how 'the army felt that Menon and IAS officers should be drowned in the dirty nallahs [ditches] of Delhi....All in all, if China would not have acted in 1962, Menon would have ruined the armed forces and the country. We must thank the Chinese for getting rid of Menon'. It is also notable that, despite the humiliation of defeat, a third of this group of officers remember a positive post-war attitude towards the political leadership, mainly due to the administration's improved appreciation of the importance of respecting the military's corporate sphere of decision-making. Finally, a small number of these officers understand there to have been no change in post-war attitudes. The military, says Lieut.-General 49, 'were earlier and continued to be neutral in politics'.

In contrast, Table 4 also shows that this group of officers were in no doubt that the overwhelming majority of Indian people had a negative post-Sino-Indian War attitude towards the political leadership. The administration was in 'total disgrace' with the public, argues Major-General 34; they felt 'disgust' and 'anger' add Brigadier (Dr.) 55 and Major-General 32, respectively. Despite the prewar machinations of the Menon-Kaul nexus, the Nehru government never had been under serious threat by the military because he and Congress remained demonstrably popular. Now, however, India's field officers perceived that their civilian rulers were almost universally unpopular with the public. If, as one coup prediction theory has it, officers act like any other political actor and push their way into power when they detect a weakness at the centre, this perception of the public's marked disapproval of the political leadership, combined with the government's unpopularity with officers themselves, may well endanger civil supremacy-of-rule in India.

TABLE 5: Post-Sino-Indian War attitudes towards the military.

	The Public		Field Officers*		Political Leadership	
	Per cent	(Number)				
Positive	51.04	(49)	11.46	(11)	60.42	(58)
No Change	7.29	(7)	9.38	(9)	0.00	(0)
Negative	36.46	(35)	75.00	(72)	26.04	(25)
Total	100.00	(96)	100.01	(96)	100.00	(96)

* Field officers asked for their attitude towards the 'military leadership'.

Yet, after 15 years of uninterrupted democratic rule, the political leadership's unpopularity with both the public and the armed forces was insufficient motive for a coup. Such a momentous step also depended on military officers' understanding of the post-war (un)popularity of the armed forces (see **Table 5**). If field officers perceived themselves as enjoying public support, even after the humiliation of defeat in war, the chances of a military takeover of government would increase. If their characterisation of the senior military leadership's performance as poor distanced field officers from their superiors, the odds of a group of officers acting as a clique also would rise. So, too, would the chances of a coup increase if field officers viewed the political leadership as blaming them for failure in war.

Those officers answering the questionnaires and/or were interviewed recall the public's attitude towards the armed forces as being mixed. Almost half describe it as negative due to the military's obvious rout on the northeast frontier, or having not changed. Is class the key? Brigadier 70 divides the Indian public

> into two broad segments—the multitude of ignorants [sic]...and the few who [are] comprised of newspaper readers and are thus aware of what is happening. The latter sympathised with the dilemma of the services having to contend with the ignorant political leadership whose credibility had dwindled considerably.

The influence of 'newspaper readers' is shown by the slim majority of officers who believe the public displayed a positive attitude towards the military, even in defeat. For Lieut.-General 10, the Indian people understood the 'military had been let down by the political leadership'.

Might the Indian armed forces use this perceived public support to act as one against the government? In an Indian Army of huge numbers, nationally representative personnel and, in 1962, three commands, it was always unlikely that any small group of officers united by personal/clientelist ties would be capable of acting alone to end civil supremacy-of-rule. Only an entire class of officers, thinking and acting together, might be able to threaten the government. Did such a class now exist in the form of the army's field officers?

The poor state of corporate unity in the post-war Indian armed forces is shown by the three-quarters majority of field officers in Table 5 who recall a negative attitude towards their superiors. Brigadier 83's attitude towards his seniors was 'one of revulsion because the military chiefs were more concerned with personal grandiosement [sic] and ambitions rather than serious training and soldiering'. Brigadier 31 recalls field officers as

> generally bitter....They considered that the chiefs did not provide proper leadership...failed to highlight problems faced by field commanders and at no time cautioned the government of the unpreparedness of the forces from the point of view of logistics, training and equipment.

The average field officer, concludes Lieut.-General 88, 'felt sorry for his weak chief [General Thapar] and cursed [Lieut.-General] Kaul'.

The field officers' post-cease-fire resentment with the military leadership signalled danger for both the army's corporate cohesiveness and civil supremacy-of-rule. Relatively junior officers are more likely than their superiors to stage a coup. The majority perception that senior officers contributed to the debacle could allow Indian field officers to unite, not as a small personal/clientelist group, but as an entire class against both the civil and military leadership in a coup to save both the army and the country. If senior officers, asks Lieut.-General 95, 'knew of China's probability of acting and their recommendations to prepare for this were not heeded, why didn't they do the honourable thing and resign? Younger officers like myself felt to hell with the top field, let us do our own thing to rectify the situation'.

What other motivation did they need? Over a quarter of officers in Table 5 perceive the political leadership as having held a negative post-cease-fire attitude towards the armed forces. The government was 'suspicious' recalls Lieut.-General 19, 'sceptical' continues Wing Commander 26, and displayed a 'lack of confidence' in the military adds Brigadier 43. Politicians, adds Brigadier 61, 'kept blaming the armed forces for this debacle'. In 1962, might this perception combine with military and public anger with the government, public support of the armed forces, and field officers' disillusionment with their seniors to create an unprecedented challenge to civil supremacy-of-rule?

No; that civil supremacy-of-rule in India was not in danger is shown by the three-fifths majority of officers who remember the political leadership as having a positive post-war attitude towards the military. They argue that defeat provoked any number of beneficial changes for Indian civil-military relations. To begin with, recalls Major-General 96 and Air Chief Marshal 12, respectively, 'the politicians generally felt guilty' about their role in the debacle and had 'an awareness that they themselves were to blame'. In defeat, argues Brigadier 30, the political leadership finally 'realized that [the] country's might is not only democratic socialism but also its military potential'. This new understanding, adds Lieut.-General 94, made for 'a sea change' in the political leadership's attitude in terms of 'greater attention and respect' for officers' advice on military matters and 'the allocation of sufficient funds for the modernisation of the armed forces'. Lieut.-General 10 gives thanks that 'the era of overbearing bureaucrats matching arrogance with ignorance and of a non-professional intelligence agency was over'.

This group of officers also highlights the welcome changes made to heal the rift between field officers and military leaders when vilified superiors resigned and were replaced by respected commanders. Within months of China's unilateral cease-fire, General Thapar, Lieut.-General Kaul and Major-General Pathania resigned from the army. Although Major-General Palit recommended to the new chief that Lieut.-General Sen also be forced to retire, he continued in this post for some time until also resigning for unrelated matters. In contrast, Major-General Prasad appealed his dismissal by Sen to President Radhakrishnan and was reinstated as a division commander.[72] The real improvement in the Indian Army's morale and corporate cohesiveness came with the respective appointments of (then Lieut.-General) Field Marshal Manekshaw as GoC 4th Corps, and General Chaudhuri as army chief.

That many officers had been unfit was obvious. Although the 40 per cent casualty rate of those fighting in the north let many believe that the military had defended stoutly, only 24,000 of the Indian Army's approximately 550,000 personnel took part in the war, and thus few officers could know of their comrades' mixed performance. In the northwest, isolated officers and men often had performed heroically. In other places, admits Brigadier 69, 'the military ran away...so the military blamed itself for defeat'. Civil supremacy-of-rule was helped by many officers' sense of having shared responsibility for the defeat tempering some of their more negative attitudes towards the military and political leadership. Any lingering resentment, says Major-General 89, was 'by and large confined to those troops and officers who fought in NEFA and Ladakh'.

That defeat in war had become 'real' helped both sides of the civil-military 'divide' to improve themselves and to strengthen civil supremacy-of-rule. The likelihood of a military coup is less if there exists a 'clear-cut, external focus for national defence'.[73] China's arrival as a threat to national security made Indian officers focus their attention on developing and deepening their professional expertise and corporateness. The war also forced Indian politicians and bureaucrats to reappraise national defence with a new understanding of the military's importance as a deterrent to potential enemies.

The political leadership's improved understanding of the armed forced as a vital component of national defence brought changes to the civil-military decision-making hierarchy as well. An improved rapport between civilian politicians and bureaucrats and military officers began when Chavan replaced Menon as defence minister. Joint Secretary (Defence) Sarin was also transferred, and Defence Secretary Pulla Reddy replaced by P.V.R. Rao, one of whose first acts was to take personal charge of general staff matters. To prevent poor civil-military communications, the service chiefs were now given a greater voice in defence policy, and were henceforth allowed to attend the defence committee of the cabinet whenever necessary. The administration also created an advisory national defence committee composed of the PM, the emergency committee of the cabinet, the service chiefs, assorted retired officers, state chief ministers, and prominent citizens. Hopefully, Indian civil-military decision-making would never again be so blinkered.

If only the seniormost officers appreciated the decision-making modifications, field officers and the public could understand the other post-cease-fire changes in civil-military relations: money and size. Broadcasting over All-India Radio, the minister for planning stated: 'We can safeguard peace only when we have the strength to make aggression a costly and profitless adventure....From now on, defence and development must be regarded as integral and related parts of the national economic plan'.[74] In 1964-65, a five-year defence plan was for the first time formulated and implemented, while immediately the defence budget leapt from 17 to 32.4 per cent of total central expenditure and military personnel increased by over half, from around 550,000 in 1962-63 to over 850,000 in 1964-65.[75]

To all of the above anti-coup factors must be added the continued respect shown Nehru and the availability of Menon as a foil for post-cease-fire resentment. Despite defeat in war, the PM was still seen as the father of the country and remained almost above reproach. In contrast, the DM was blamed by the public, military officers and civil servants for misreading Chinese intentions, misleading Nehru, and politicizing and neglecting the training and equipping of the armed forces. So great was the feeling against Menon that when Nehru fought to keep his long-time colleague and friend in office, he himself was threatened with removal by Congress. When Menon went, anger with the political leadership dissipated, civil-military relations improved, and civil supremacy-of-rule was safe.

Or was it? Nine of those officers answering the questionnaires and/or interviewed say civilians and/or military officers spoke of a coup in the immediate aftermath of the 1962 Sino-Indian War (see **Table 6**). Of these, four, three and two, respectively, recall civilians only, officers only, and civilians and officers indulging in such discussions. Most were nothing more than idle gossip. Yet, points out Brigadier 73, among military officers even those few rumblings of discontent lasted 'only up to the time when the Prime Minister refused to remove his Defence Minister. Once that happened all dissidence against the government disappeared'. That just nine of 96 officers recall civilians and/or military officers talking of moving against the government, despite defeat in war, indicates just how strong civil supremacy-of-rule was embedded in India. Comparing Tables 3 and 6 shows officers recall less talk of a military coup in the aftermath of the Sino-Indian War than after Ayub Khan's 1958 coup in Pakistan. Both the public and armed forces' officers appear to have felt that the proper response to the gravity of defeat was not a revolution but reform. Thus, huge majorities of officers can remember no sector of society as desirous of an armed forces' coup. The stability of civil supremacy-of-rule in India is most accurately indicated by Brigadier 9's response to the question posed on Table 6: 'No! No! No!'

Conclusion

In shattering any number of myths—the PM always knew best, *Hindi-Chini bhai-bhai,* negotiation and not military might could settle all international differences, national defence policy could be decided by a tiny coterie of civil-military decision-makers operating *ad hoc,* China would never attack isolated forward outposts, the armed forces did not need additional resources, the Indian professional officer and his troops were the equal of any in the world—previously believed by the Nehru administration, the 1962 Sino-Indian War tested civil-supremacy-of-rule in India to the full. After China's unilateral and humiliating declaration of cease-fire, military field officers, that segment of any officer corps most likely to instigate a coup, held a negative opinion of the forward policy and felt their superiors had performed abysmally. They also perceived the public to be sympathetic towards the military and resentful of the political leadership. Yet, hardly any respondent can recall talk of moving against the government.

Civil supremacy-of-rule remained intact mainly because field officers' grievances were directly addressed. Disgraced senior officers were replaced. The government embraced the armed forces as an integral part of national defence, showering them with money and men.

The civil-military hierarchy was modified to include the opinion of senior officers and their staff, and the whole nation focused their attention not on internal revolution but external vigilance. In time, the army also admitted to some responsibility for not meeting the enemy with as much conviction as indicated by its previously outstanding combat record. In the eyes of field officers—and the public—the chief 'villain of the piece', DM Menon was removed. With him, Nehru had been seen as part of the problem. Without him, the PM was free to, if not regain his prewar stature, then at least remain as the uncontested head of a civilian administration.

TABLE 6: Post-Sino-Indian War, should the Indian armed forces move against the government?

	Civilians		Field Officers	
	Per cent (Number)			
No	91.67	(88)	92.71	(89)
Yes	5.21	(5)	4.17	(4)
No Answer	3.13	(3)	3.13	(3)
Total	100.01	(96)	100.01	(96)

The 1962 Sino-Indian War may be argued to have benefited India. The political leadership realized that the strength and numbers of the armed forces are an essential measurement of national defence, that professional merit and not personal connections should be the criteria for advancement, and that civil-military decision-making is best done in a formal structure and with proper staff support. For Ambassador T.N. Kaul (no relation to the lieut.-general), the 'Chinese invasion proved indeed to be a blessing in disguise. India woke up to the need to mend her defences, unite the people and harness her resources. India had lost a battle but not the war'.[76] Victory in the 1965 Indo-Pak War would show the Indian Army 'professional enough to reconstruct itself'[77] after the humiliation of defeat by China. But that lay in the future. For now, it was enough that those fateful months in the autumn of 1962, characterised by Major-General Palit as 'a time out of reality',[78] were over.

---

[1] Lieut.-General S.D. Verma, *To Serve with Honour: My Memoirs* (Dehradun: Natraj Publishers, 1988), p. 115.

[2] Lieut.-General Thorat, *From Reveille to Retreat* (New Delhi: Allied Publishers Private Limited, 1986), p. 202.

[3] D.K. Palit, *War in High Himalaya: The Indian Army in Crisis, 1962* (London: C. Hurst, 1991), p. 165.

[4] In attendance was India's top civil-military decision-making hierarchy: Nehru, Menon, Foreign Secretary M.J. Desai, Joint Secretary (Defence) Harish C. Sarin, IB Director B.N. Mullik, IB Joint Director Dave, Indian Army Chief General Thapar, CGS Kaul, DMO Palit, and Director of Military Intelligence Brigadier Bim Batra.

[5] See N. Maxwell, *India's China War* (New York: Pantheon Books, 1970), pp. 221-222; and Palit, *War in High Himalaya*, p. 107.

[6] Rajya Sabha 4/5/59; P.M.S.I.R. I i, p. 42 as cited in Maxwell, *India's China War*, p. 206.

[7] Thorat, *From Reveille to Retreat*, p. 196. China's numerous and pressing domestic and international problems also conspired against Nehru and his administration taking the Chinese threat seriously.

[8] Thorat, *From Reveille to Retreat*, p. 191.

[9] Lt. General B.M. Kaul, *The Untold Story* (Bombay: Allied Publishers, 1967), p. 332.

[10] Kaul, *The Untold Story*, p. 332.

[11] In 1951, internal and external intelligence duties had been transferred from Military Intelligence (MI) to the civilian IB. By 1962, writes Major-General Palit, MI Director Brigadier Batra 'deployed no agent, inside or outside the country; his sources of information were all second-hand'. Even in the Joint Intelligence Committee (JIC), chaired by a ministry of external affairs (MEA) joint secretary and including defence and home ministry representatives, the respective directors of intelligence of the three armed services, and a senior IB officer), the IB representative 'was the only member who could make an original contribution....[He] had taken to presenting...reports as conclusions rather than as items presented for...assessment'. See Maxwell, *India's China War*, p. 310; B.N. Mullik, *The Chinese Betrayal* (Bombay: Allied Publishers, 1972), p. 305; Palit, *War in High Himalaya*, p. 84-85; and A.L. Venkateswaran, *Defence Organisation in India: A Study of Major Developments in Organisation and Administration since Independence* (Government of India Ministry of Information and Broadcasting, 1967), p. 96.

[12] Maxwell, *India's China War*, p. 310.

[13] Palit, *War in High Himalaya*, p. 105.

[14] Palit, *War in High Himalaya*, p. 80.

[15] Palit, *War in High Himalaya*, p. 80. General Thimayya made a similar statement after retiring. See *Seminar,* July 1962, as cited in T.J.S. George, *Krishna Menon: A Biography* (London: Jonathan Cape, 1964), 249.

[16] Palit, *War in High Himalaya*, p. 88.

[17] Palit, *War in High Himalaya*, p. 88.

[18] In March 1962, Lieut.-General Kaul told President Kennedy's Special Representative, Chester Bowles, that in the now 'likely...clash [with China]...in the summer or autumn of 1962....powers-that-be in our country would...work out....with some friends a basis of mutual co-operation to meet such a (serious) contingency in advance rather than too late or after the event'. See Kaul, *The Untold Story*, p. 341.

[19] Maxwell, *India's China War*, p. 174.

[20] Kaul, *The Untold Story*, p. 280.

[21] S.A. Hoffmann, *India and the China Crisis* (Berkeley: University of California Press, 1990), p. 98.

[22] Maxwell, *India's China War*, p. 239.

[23] V.I. Longer, *Red Coats to Olive Green: A History of the Indian Army 1600-1974* (Bombay: Allied Publishers, 1974), p. 370.

[24] Brigadier J.P. Dalvi, *Himalayan Blunder,* pbk. ed. (Hind Pocket Books Pvt. Ltd., n.d., in arrangement with Thacker & Company Ltd., Bombay), pp. 157-158.

[25] In addition to Menon, the 11 September 1962 meeting included IB Director Mullik, Foreign Secretary M.J. Desai, Cabinet Secretary S.S. Khera, Joint Secretary (Defence) Sarin, General Thapar and, with Lieut.-General Kaul on holiday, Deputy CGS (then Major-General) Lieut.-General J.S. Dhillon.

[26] Palit, *War in High Himalaya*, pp. 195, 199.

[27] Dalvi, *Himalayan Blunder*, p. 176.

[28] Kaul, *The Untold Story.*, p. 271.

[29] Palit, *War in High Himalaya*, p. 214.

[30] Dalvi, *Himalayan Blunder*, p. 203.

[31] Kaul, *The Untold Story*, pp. 336-367.

[32] General J.N. Chaudhuri, *General J.N. Chaudhuri: An Autobiography*, as narrated to B.K. Narayan (New Delhi: Vikas Publishing House, 1978), p. 173.

[33] Palit, *War in High Himalaya*, p. 222.

[34] Palit, *War in High Himalaya*, p. 222.

[35] Kaul, *The Untold Story,* pp. 383-384. Brigadier Dalvi writes that the Chinese attack caused Lieut.-General Kaul to exclaim 'Oh my God....You are right, they mean business'. See Dalvi, *Himalayan Blunder*, p. 255.

[36] See *The Statesman*, 13 October 1962.

[37] Kaul, *The Untold Story*, p. 391.

[38] Verma, *To Serve with Honour*, p. 120.

[39] Palit, *War in High Himalaya*, p. 242.

[40] L.J. Kavic, *India's Quest for Security: Defence Policies, 1947-1965* (Berkeley: University of California Press, 1967), p. 178.

[41] Palit, *War in High Himalaya*, p. 246.

[42] Palit, *War in High Himalaya*, p. 324.

[43] Of the two published narratives which describe the events of 17/18 November 1962, Major-General Palit's *War in High Himalaya* is far more

authoritative than Lieut.-General Kaul's *The Untold Story.* While the latter often appears a self-serving justification of the reasons for India's defeat, the former draws upon Palit's 'Summary of Events and Policies' (his official general staff report compiled after the war from his daily notes), files of the directorate of military operations, and TOPSEC (top secret) documents. From private correspondence between myself and Major-General Palit, 1995; and Palit, *War in High Himalaya.*

[44] Palit, *War in High Himalaya*, p. 301.

[45] Just how ill-suited the 'frail and distraught' General Thapar was for this task became evident on the flight up when he intimated he was pondering his resignation/dismissal. See Palit, *War in High Himalaya,* p. 304.

[46] Palit, *War in High Himalaya*, p. 308

[47] Palit, *War in High Himalaya*, p. 309.

[48] Palit, *War in High Himalaya*, p. 311.

[49] Palit, *War in High Himalaya*, p. 315.

[50] Palit, *War in High Himalaya*, p. 315.

[51] Palit, *War in High Himalaya*, pp. 317-318.

[52] Palit, *War in High Himalaya*, p. 319.

[53] Palit, *War in High Himalaya*, p. 321.

[54] Palit, *War in High Himalaya*, p. 327.

[55] Longer, *Red Coats to Olive Green*, p. 397.

[56] Statement in Lok Sabha, 29.9.63 as cited in Maxwell, *India's China War.*, p. 437.

[57] As cited in Major K.C. Praval, *Indian Army After Independence* (New Delhi: Lancer International, 1987), pp. 326-327.

[58] Maxwell, *India's China War.*, p. 438.

[59] Admiral K.D. Katari, *A Sailor Remembers* (New Delhi: Vikas Publishing House Pvt. Ltd., 1982), pp. 116-117.

[60] Katari, *A Sailor Remembers*, pp. 116-117.

[61] Praval, *Indian Army After Independence*, p. 325.

[62] Kaul, *The Untold Story*, p. 327.

[63] Kaul, *The Untold Story*, p. 406.

[64] Kaul, *The Untold Story*, p. 425.

[65] Palit, *War in High Himalaya*, p. 77.

[66] Palit, *War in High Himalaya*, pp. 124, 275-276.

[67] Palit, *War in High Himalaya*, pp. 354-355.

[68] Palit, *War in High Himalaya*, p. 352.

[69] W.R. Thompson, *The Grievance of Military Coup-Makers* (Beverly Hills: Sage Publications, 1973), p. 16.

[70] Thompson, *The Grievance of Military Coup-Makers*, p. 16.

[71] See Thompson, *The Grievance of Military Coup-Makers*, p. 25; and C.E. Welch, Jr. and A.K. Smith, *Military Role and Rule: Perspectives on Civil-Military Relations*, (North Scituate: Duxbury Press, 1974), p. 22.

[72] In one of Nehru's last acts before his death, General Thapar was appointed India's ambassador to Afghanistan. General Chaudhuri apparently offered to 'rehabilitate' Lieut.-General Kaul in some unspecified post in the civil-military hierarchy but was refused. In the 1965 Indo-Pak War, Major-General Prasad allowed to fall into enemy hands some of his papers which were sharply critical of his superiors and the government, and was forced to leave the army. In 1966, Brigadier Dalvi was superseded in promotion to major-general and resigned.

[73] Welch and Smith, *Military Role and Rule*, p. 11.

[74] As quoted in R.G.C. Thomas, 'The Armed Services and the Indian Defence Budget', *Asian Survey*, XX:3, 1980.

[75] See Y. Lakshmi, *Trends in India's Defence Expenditure* (New Delhi: ABC Publishing House, 1988), pp. 69, 144; Major-General K.S. Pendse, 'India's Defence Budget: A Case for Better Planning', *Indian Defence Review*, July 1989; and Praval, *Indian Army After Independence*, p. 321.

[76] T.N. Kaul, *Reminiscences Discreet and Indiscreet* (New Delhi: Lancers Publishers, 1982), p. 172.

[77] S. Cohen, 'The Military and Indian Democracy' in A. Kohli, ed., *India's Democracy: An Analysis of Changing State-Society Relations* (Princeton: Princeton University Press, 1988), p. 112.

[78] Palit, *War in High Himalaya*, p. 200.

8. INDIRA GANDHI'S EMERGENCY RULE

From 1975-77, PM Indira Gandhi (henceforth referred to by surname only)[1] instituted a state of national emergency in the country, ostensibly to preserve internal order but in reality to evade legal proceedings and consolidate her grip on power.[2] None of the previous tests of the Indian armed forces' ability to respect civil supremacy-of-rule involved questioning the very legitimacy of the civilian government. If, like many of their countrymen, military officers perceived the imposition of Gandhi's 'Emergency' and/or the excesses committed in its name as an unjustified and illegitimate attempt to end India's democracy, might they act to overthrow the government? If, on the other hand, officers admired the discipline and order imposed by the Emergency, might they forcibly act to keep Gandhi in office after electoral defeat in 1977?

Imposition

Indian civil-military relations in the decade after the humiliation of the 1962 Sino-Indian War were characterised by a string of successes. There had been no crisis of leadership succession after the death of Nehru, and the political and military leadership, as well as the field officers and their men, had worked together creditably in the 1965 Indo-Pak War and notably in the 1971 Bangladesh Liberation War. Indeed, in the latter engagement, the efficiency and effectiveness of coordination in the top echelon of politicians, bureaucrats and military officers in planning, orchestrating and carrying out the lighting campaign which transformed East Pakistan into the new nation of Bangladesh stunned their Pakistani counterparts.

Yet, for Gandhi and the Indian people, the euphoria of victory over Pakistan in 1971 soon faded as the huge economic cost of the campaign and the up to ten million refugees which had streamed into the country from former East Pakistan became apparent. India also faced severe crop failures in 1972 and 1973 in the wake of poor monsoons, a quadrupling of its energy import bill after the steep oil price hikes of 1973-74, and a subsequent drop in overall industrial output. Not even a substantial loan from the International Monetary Fund stemmed the general perception of a country in deep economic trouble. By 1975, widespread economic hardship and charges of rampant political corruption by Congress administrations at the centre and in the states of Gujarat and Bihar, especially, combined to produce daily strikes and protests nationwide demanding a change of government.

The political battle to oust Gandhi came to a head in the summer of 1975. On 12 June, the Allahabad High Court found the PM guilty of two charges of corrupt election practices in her 1971 parliamentary campaign. Despite calls for her immediate resignation, Gandhi appealed the decision to India's Supreme Court where, on 24 June, the one sitting justice granted her a 'conditional stay' until the full court's reconvening at the end of summer. Although this decision allowed her to remain in office, it forbade Gandhi from voting and/or participating in parliament, and calls for her resignation grew. In addition to the two court decisions, Congress suffered an overwhelming defeat in the Gujarat state elections in the face of a challenge from the Janata Morcha (People's Front) alliance. Led by the charismatic hero of the nationalist movement and founder of the Socialist Party Jayaprakash Narayan and the former Finance and Deputy Prime Minister Morarji Desai, this popular movement was dedicated to ousting Gandhi and Congress by all non-violent means possible. At a mass rally in New Delhi on 25 June, Narayan urged his audience to resist the government and repeated his plea for the police and armed forces to refuse to obey its 'illegal and immoral'[3] orders and uphold the constitution against all usurpers.

In an All-India Radio broadcast the very next day, Gandhi announced that President Fakhruddin Ali Ahmed, a staunch supporter of the PM, that morning had invoked Article 352 of the constitution which allows the president, if 'satisfied that a grave emergency exists whereby the security of India or any part of its territory is threatened, whether by war or external aggression or internal disturbance...(to) make a declaration of Emergency'.[4] Although Gandhi also stated that the imposition of Emergency would allow her to carry out a 'Twenty-point Programme' of comprehensive economic and social reform to revitalise the country, it more immediately entailed strict press censorship, the banning of most opposition parties as well as other organisations, and the jailing of hundreds of her political opponents. The numbers of those incarcerated under the draconian Defence of India regulations and Maintenance of Internal Security Act would eventually total over 100,000. Basic civil liberties were further abused, especially by the forced sterilisation and 'beautification', or slum clearance, programmes of Gandhi's second son and political heir apparent, Sanjay. She also set about prolonging her rule by extending parliament's term in office and expanding the PM's executive powers through a series of laws and constitutional amendments which retroactively exonerated her from any and all charges now pending and/or placed in the future, and disallowed any judicial challenges to the declaration of Emergency and/or the measures which followed from it. 'My eyes were set on my country. I have done no wrong for I have not done anything for myself', [5] declared Gandhi. The lie appeared obvious, and abroad and at home people were lamenting the end of India's 'experiment' with democracy.

As described above, civil supremacy-of-rule in India had never had to endure popular doubt as to the very legitimacy of the national government. The military officer's professional responsibility to deploy his expertise only at the discretion of his client, society's legitimate ruler, last came under question when discussing whether Indian officers during the interwar years and the Second World War would remain loyal to the king-emperor or shift their allegiance to the leaders of the nationalist movement. Now, almost 30 years later, the question was whether officers would remain loyal to the Gandhi administration or act out of a higher loyalty to the 'nation' and move against the government to restore democracy.

Logistically, the portents for a successful military intervention were increasingly favourable. In Table 1, those officers answering the questionnaires and/or interviewed rank 'logistics unfavourable: five regional army commands, troops dispersed nationally, etc.', as the joint eleventh most important factor in having prevented a coup in India. Yet never before had political power been so concentrated at the centre as during the Emergency. Lieut.-General 4 recalls how 'the reins of power were already neatly and effectively controlled by one person. The states were also used to receiving orders directly from one source at the centre. All one had to do was get her [the PM] out of the way'. Would any officer be so bold as to think of replacing Gandhi with himself?

Of those officers answering the questionnaires and/or interviewed, 76 were on active service during the Emergency. These officers are no longer the junior officers of the Menon-Kaul era; by the mid-1970s, they had risen to the higher echelons of the armed forces and their responses to the imposition of Emergency and its excesses would be crucial in determining whether or not the Indian military would remain in their barracks or attempt to move into politics.

This group of officers is divided as to whether or not the declaration of Emergency was justified. Over a third support the move, many because of their perception that general political unrest was sweeping the country and adversely affecting day-to-day administration. Others, pointing to contemporary political instability in Chile and Bangladesh, saw the imposition of Emergency as a justifiable reaction to 'foreign hands' intent on destabilizing India. In the end, concludes Brigadier 90, 'everyone was relieved to have some order in the country'. The almost two-thirds who record their opposition to Gandhi's declaration of Emergency disagree. Instead, the PM's action was seen as a naked attempt to stifle democracy so as to keep Gandhi and Congress in power. Others argue that the internal political disturbances did not threaten the country, were not anti-national and included no foreign component. As such, says Major-General 72, the imposition of Emergency was 'a perversion of the constitution'.

That a large majority of questionnaire respondents and/or interviewees report feeling that the imposition of Emergency was incorrect does not mean they were prepared to act unilaterally. Several make the point that, however strong their disapproval of Gandhi's act, the officer corps as a whole was very reluctant to heed Narayan's call to disobey what he perceived to be the government's illegal and immoral orders. Major-General 105 and Colonel 24 dismiss his appeal as 'absolutely silly' and 'ridiculous', respectively. Whatever their personal feelings regarding the declaration of Emergency, military officers were willing to wait and see how the country was governed under this 'new' regime.

Duration

The difficulty of commissioned military officers acting together against the government is further illustrated by the mixed responses of those answering the questionnaires and/or interviewed when asked if the Indian armed forces as whole approved or disapproved of Emergency rule itself. Just over a third say that their fellow officers approved, mainly because officers are trained to value discipline and efficiency, qualities which many perceived to be the highlights of Emergency rule.

Just under a third characterise their comrades as 'apolitical', able to ignore the excesses of Emergency because its imposition and subsequent acts passed by the government were technically legal. A fifth perceive that their comrades disapproved, feeling Emergency to be unnecessary overkill. Half this percentage again say that officers had mixed feelings. The then director of military intelligence, Lieut.-General 10, recounts a change over time in the armed forces from being 'impressed by the talk and show of discipline' at the beginning of Emergency rule to becoming 'gradually...disillusioned as the reality of the situation began to dawn'.

The reckless behaviour of a number of politicians during the period of Emergency rule showed that military officers were not the only ones with the potential to damage India's tradition of civil supremacy-of-rule. Lieut.-General 10 reports that on more than one occasion he had to repulse Congress officials seeking military support and/or materials for party functions. Lieut.-General 56 adds that 'attempts were made to involve my command in politics (quite subtly); these attempts were repulsed by me (not so subtly)'. The danger to Indian civil supremacy-of-rule was that if politicians could interfere in the military's corporate sphere of decision-making, officers might be able to justify interfering with decisions and institutions normally the preserve of other professionals; that is, politicians and the civilian government of India.

Several officers reveal that some of their comrades were getting overly cosy with Gandhi and her regime. Lieut.-General 23 states that his very pro-government predecessor as director-general (signals) was appointed to a 'very prestigious and lucrative post' in a state-owned industry soon after Emergency was announced. Air Marshal 5 recalls how 'the normal process of promotions and appointments tended to be bypassed'; for example, in the case of two 'very pro-government' officers elevated in rapid succession and over the heads of more senior officers to the post of IAF air chief marshal. These supercessions seemed to follow a pattern established less than one month before the imposition of Emergency when Gandhi had appointed General T.N. Raina as army chief over the heads of more senior officers. Some officers feel this move signalled the beginning of the military leadership's servility to government excesses during the subsequent months, and speculated as to what the top brass knew and when. Lieut.-General 108 thinks Gandhi must have consulted the three service chiefs to see if they would stand by her if she declared Emergency. They all said no but she went ahead anyway. I know that she consulted both Western Command Commander [Lieut.-General] Gill and Eastern Command Commander [Lieut.-General] J.F.R. Jacob who both said no.

The widespread belief that a conversation occurred between Raina and Gandhi before the imposition of Emergency can now be confirmed by (then) Adjutant-General Lieut.-General 17 who reveals that, although the PM 'called him in just before declaring Emergency to put him in the picture, Raina took no steps to warn anybody. I think he had just a damn good night's sleep'. As during the Menon-Kaul nexus, the danger was that any interference in the military corporate sphere of decision-making, in this case promoting officers sympathetic to the ruling regime, might create a backlash against the government in the form of a military coup.

Yet suspicions that General Raina might act as the government's 'poodle' were soon allayed by his impeccably professional behaviour. Major-General 68, in 'daily' contact with the chief and 'in [regular] touch with all area commanders and principle staff officers [PSOs]' characterises 'the behaviour of all [these officers] and especially Raina as very correct'. Lieut.-General 49 describes how the army chief

refused to deploy soldiers in support of the Emergency['s] objectives. He informed the PM that the army could not be relied on for such a commitment and offered to replace the Border Security Force [BSF] at their posts if more paramilitary forces were needed for maintenance of public order. The army made no public or government/private commitment in support of what was patently a political move.

Vice Admiral 2 goes further when recalling how Raina told Gandhi 'very bluntly' that the army would not be used to 'further her ends' but obey only those orders of a 'legally constituted government'. This was the most crucial factor in keeping the military out of politics during this time. The (just) technical legality of the imposition of Emergency and subsequent actions taken in its name gave Gandhi's 1975-77 regime a legitimacy which allowed the military leadership to continue their apolitical tradition.

Being able to remain apolitical while tens of thousands of their fellow citizens were being jailed also stemmed from the government's decision never to involve large numbers of armed forces' personnel at the sharp end of Emergency rule. Instead, it was the police and, especially, paramilitary forces such as the BSF which were deployed in aid-to-the-civil authority actions against Indian civilians, quelling internal disturbances and carrying out excesses committed in the name of government policy. Not assigning military officers and men to such unpopular duties prevented them from witnessing the worst side of Emergency for themselves, thus keeping many from questioning and perhaps even abandoning their apolitical stance. Avoiding internal policing duties also allowed officers to concentrate on their usual routines of practicing and perfecting their professional expertise in the military's primary role of defending the national borders.

An Electoral End

Having concluded that Indian democracy was dead, many observers at home and abroad were stunned when Gandhi announced on 18 January 1977 that parliamentary elections were to be held in March and Emergency measures would be relaxed to allow oppositions parties to campaign against her. Although given only six weeks from their release from jail to the date of the elections, opposition leaders quickly united and, aided by the defection of a number of prominent Congress politicians, organised a national political campaign to unseat Gandhi. The result was spectacular as, for the first time in the history of independent India, Congress and even its sitting PM herself suffered electoral defeat. While Gandhi remained unrepentant about the Emergency, she accepted the people's verdict and left office in favour of the victorious Janata coalition. On 21 March, India's new PM, Morarji Desai, ordered the end of Emergency rule and his administration set about rescinding the more excessive laws and constitutional amendments passed in the previous 21 months.

According to those officers answering the questionnaires and/or interviewed, the armed forces were virtually certain that Gandhi would step down after defeat in the 1977 elections. Although a small minority express doubts, especially given her imposition of Emergency in the first place, the vast majority feel that she had no choice in the matter. In the words of Lieut.-General 49, 'no dictator can survive a free election and no rigging is possible on a national scale'. If she had resisted, warns Brigadier 43, 'there would have been a rebellion in the party, in the services and in the country'.

These officers are even more certain that the armed forces would not have acted to keep Gandhi in office if she had tried to remain in power after the general election results of 1977 (see **Table 7**). Such a move is described as 'far-fetched' by Vice Admiral 2, a 'fantasy' by Lieut.-General 49, and 'wild conjecture' by Lieut.-General 94. Again, many point to the legality of the declaration of Emergency and its subsequent measures. They add that in the unlikely case of Gandhi now attempting an illegal action to remain in office, the armed forces would have taken orders from the constitutional head of state, the president of India.

TABLE 7 If so ordered, would the Indian armed forces have acted to keep Indira Gandhi in office?

	Per cent	(Number)
No	87.14	(61)
Yes	5.71	(4)
No Answer	7.14	(5)
Total	100.00	(70)

Nonetheless, four officers argue that the armed forces would have acted to keep Gandhi in office if asked. Major-General 32 'would have counselled her [to remain in office]'. Major-General 96, admitting that 'it is difficult to say what a service chief would have done if given an order by the PM which was unlawful', wonders if 'he [the service chief] would perhaps comply'. Brigadier 61 believes 'there may have been direct/indirect soundings taken from some senior officers at that time...[although] the army leadership I feel stood very firm in remaining professional to the last'. Lieut.-General 54 argues that 'the army would have obeyed the order of the government. That is what they are supposed to do at all times'. However, Lieut.-General 54 does not venture an opinion as to whether the government at the moment of Gandhi's electoral defeat constituted of herself and Congress or Desai and Janata.

The one officer named by several sources, including himself, as a possible executor of military action to keep Gandhi in office is Air Chief Marshal 12. Highly critical of democracy as 'bogus in this country....India needs a benevolent dictatorship', and personally close to

'Madam [Gandhi]', he describes the Emergency as a 'desirable…and normal way of life' for India. While Air Chief Marshal 12 admits that General Raina would never have sanctioned military action in the wake of the 1977 election result, he himself was 'extremely upset' and boasts of 'fears' that he might 'get together…[with] some army men…[to] rig up something'. Lieut.-General 10 points out that Air Chief Marshal 12 'came a cropper' with the Shah Commission, charged with examining the excesses of Emergency rule, because 'he was always willing to bend the rules' to provide planes and other support to Gandhi and her government. Although Lieut.-General 10 does not believe him to have posed a serious threat to the peaceful change-over of government in 1977, Air Marshal 5 is less sure, admitting that Air Chief Marshal 12 'could' have been plotting against the new Janata government. Whatever the truth of the matter, it is certain that Air Chief Marshal 12 could not have taken any action to keep Gandhi in office without the cooperation of both the army and the PM herself, both doubtful occurrences.

Conclusion

Gandhi's imposition of Emergency rule divided the officers of the Indian armed forces. Many were opposed, others supportive. As time wore on, the excesses committed its name by the Gandhi administration and its supporters changed some opinions. Yet officers remained constant in their determination to keep their views of Emergency rule private and to maintain their professional responsibility to obey their client, society's legitimate ruler, at all times. Lieut.-General 16 re-states the case:

If the declaration of Emergency were not provided for in the Constitution or were this declaration to be successfully challenged in [the] courts, the question of using the armed forces could have arisen. As it is, it was not challenged and the question of using the military did not arise.

Neither President Ahmed's formal imposition of Emergency rule, parliament's passing of acts infringing traditional Indian civil liberties, nor Gandhi's defeat in the 1977 elections caused their attention to their professional role and responsibilities to waver.

A number of additional factors also contributed to preserving officers' respect for civil supremacy-of-rule in India. Political interference in their corporate sphere of decision-making was relatively minor, especially compared to the excesses of the Menon-Kaul years. Avoiding internal policing duties kept military personnel from becoming embroiled in the seamy side of domestic politics. More generally, a number of factors listed in Table 1, including a 'widely held belief in democracy', the 'political awareness of the masses' and a 'decades-old habit of democracy' also figure prominently as contributing to the peaceful, ordered end to Emergency rule.

One additional socioeconomic factor also may have played a part in keeping at least some military officers from moving against Gandhi's Emergency regime. Huntington postulates that in societies where the 'mass society looms on the horizon...[the military officer] becomes the conservative guardian of the existing order'.[6] As such, Gandhi's ambitious Twenty-point Programme of comprehensive economic and social reform may have antagonised those senior Indian officers grown used to the perks and privileges of bourgeois lifestyles and supportive of Emergency because it stopped the leftist threat posed by Narayan and Desai. Yet the programme was never implemented and the lives of this section of the armed forces remained untouched.

Whatever the possibilities, Gandhi's period of Emergency rule again proved that Indian armed forces officers as a whole were keen to refrain from interfering in government when not directly affected by political decisions. How would the country's long tradition of civil supremacy-of-rule be affected if government policy did impact on a certain segment of officers united by the more primordial bonds of ethnicity or religion?

---

[1] Despite their surnames, Indira Gandhi is unrelated to Mahatma Gandhi.

[2] Indira Gandhi's Emergency rule is unusual for the lack of works dedicated to this period of Indian politics. Books worth perusing include P. Bhushan, *The Case that Shook India*, pbk., (New Delhi: Bell Books, 1978); M. Henderson, *Experiment with Untruth: India Under Emergency*, pbk., (The Macmillan Company of India Limited, 1977); K. Lal, *Emergency: Its Needs and Gains* (New Delhi: Hittashi Publishers, 1976); D.R. Mankekar & K. Mankekar, *Decline and Fall of Indira Gandhi: 19 Months of Emergency*, pbk., (New Delhi: Orient Paperbacks, 1977); and K. Nayar, *The Judgement: Inside Story of the Emergency in India*, pbk. (New Delhi: Bell Books, 1978).

[3] R.L. Hardgrave, Jr., and S.A. Kochanek, *India: Government and Politics in a Developing Nation,* pbk. ed. (Fifth edition; Fort Worth: Harcourt Brace Jovanovich College Publishers, 1993), p. 244.

[4] G.N. Joshi, *The Constitution of India* (London: Macmillan & Co Ltd, 1954), p. 351.

[5] V. Mehta, *The New India* (Harmondsworth: Penguin Books, 1971), p. 36.

[6] S. Huntington, *Political Order in Changing Societies* (New Haven: Yale University Press, 1968), p. 221.

9. OPERATION BLUE STAR

While Indira Gandhi had been careful to keep the armed forces from the sharp edge of enforcing internal order during Emergency rule, she was unable to resist using them when attempting to quell growing separatist unrest in Punjab. Although 'Operation Blue Star', a military operation to flush out Sikh militants in and around their religion's most holy Golden Temple in Amritsar, was successful in its immediate aims, its aftereffects were disastrous for the armed forces, civilian Sikhs living outside Punjab, and Gandhi herself. This chapter focusses on the post-Operation Blue Star mutinies of thousands of Sikh military personnel and their impact on the army's continued recruitment of Sikh men and officers in numbers disproportionate to their share community's of their national population, civil-military relations and civil supremacy-of-rule.

Sikh Military Personnel

The Great Mutiny of 1857 caused the British to re-examine the recruitment of Indian soldiers into the Honourable East India Company's three respective presidency armies of Bengal, Bombay and Madras. Despite repeated recommendations that these forces henceforth be composed of 'different nationalities and castes...mixed promiscuously through each regiment'[1] as a classic *divide et impera* precaution, regimental commanders soon began favouring the recruitment of men from north and northwest India. Here were communities which, for any number of reasons, British officers identified as having greater war-like characteristics than the central and southern peoples who had made up the bulk of pre-1857 troops. The communal character of the unified Indian Army became entrenched with the introduction of class and class company regiments.

Despite an official post-Independence policy of recruitment open to all,[2] many 'die-hard'[3] senior officers remained believers in the 'tribal'[4] *izzat* of the martial races and the Indian Army continued to enlist men from the north and northwest in numbers disproportionate to their respective communities' share of the national population. The immediate post-Independence conflict in J&K followed by years of Indo-Pakistani and Sino-Indian tension further inhibited successive administrations from enforcing 'radical changes in the organisation of the fighting arms'.[5] Thus, while most 'tail' units and all post-independence raisings such as the Parachute Regiment have been constituted on an all-India basis, the majority of the army's 'teeth' arms remain the preserve of the martial races.

One of most numerous and successful of the Indian Army's recruited communities are the Sikhs of Punjab. Their high standing among British recruiters was reflected in the rise of Punjabi infantry units, which included Sikh and non-Sikh personnel, from a fifth to almost half of the army total from 1862 to 1914 By the turn of the century, Sikhs alone made up over a quarter of Punjab's contribution to the army, despite accounting for less than six per cent of the province's population in 1911. While recruiting difficulties during the interwar years lessened Punjabi enlistment, Sikhs still constituted a quarter of all army personnel during the Second World War.

Although the Indian government refuses to release the religious and/or ethnic origins of Indian military personnel, the army apparently continues to recruit and post Punjabi Sikh soldiers in much the same pre-1947 patterns. Sikhs and non-Sikhs from Punjab continue to account for 10-15 per cent of all ranks in the army, despite the state containing just 2.45 per cent of India's national population in 1981. Moreover, with the exception of Gurkhas (recruited in Nepal), Sikhs remain the only community to have infantry regiments drawn exclusively from their own numbers: the Sikh Regiment which consists of high caste Jat Sikh troops; and the Sikh Light Infantry, manned entirely by Mazhabi, or scheduled caste Sikhs.

Punjabi Sikhs continue to follow a tradition of being even more disproportionately represented in the Indian Army's officer corps. Over two-fifths of the first 85 Indians admitted by the British into the RMC from 1919-25 as prospective commissioned officers were from a Punjab which accounted for just 6.5 per cent of India's 1921 population. Although the IMA was created in part to admit a wider cross-section of Indian youth, its first ten regular courses saw a Punjab with less than seven per cent of the 1931 national population again contribute over two-fifths per cent of GCs. The preponderance of Sikhs among RMC and IMA cadets became more apparent after partition caused the vast majority of Punjabi Muslim officers to opt for Pakistan: in 1962 almost 40 per cent of the army's brigadiers and over 45 per cent of its major-generals were Sikhs. A Punjab with just 2.45 per cent of India's population in 1981 still accounted for over a tenth of all cadets attending the IMA's ten regular courses from 1978-82. A 1991 report estimates that Sikhs continue to constitute a fifth of all Indian Army officers. Sikhs also make up 'perhaps a quarter'[6] of IAF pilots (all officers) and 'substantial numbers'[7] of the IN.

Aid-to-the Civil Authority

The continued recruitment and posting together of men drawn from specific communities may endanger both the army's corporate cohesiveness and continued civilian supremacy-of-rule in India for any issue which strongly affects one member of a group united by ethnicity, community, religion and/or region may readily affect them all. If so motivated, the men and officers of one or more of the army's favoured communities may prove numerous enough to preserve, protect and/or enlarge their own group interests to the detriment of the military as a whole. Such related personnel may also provide a more fertile ground for spreading any existing anti-government grievances which, in the extreme case, can lead to a military. That those officers answering the questionnaires and/or interviewed place a great emphasis on recruiting all communities into the armed forces may be seen on Table 1 where 'nationally representative military personnel' is ranked as the fourth most important factor in India never having experienced a military coup.

Perhaps the easiest way to create a grievance of armed forces' personnel united by ethnicity, community, religion and/or region is to deploy them in aid-to-the civil authority duties directed against their own community. The nature of the military's deployment of maximum force often means that internal policing duties are short and swift. The loyalty of officers and men may hold firm during the immediate action of quelling disturbances to the point sufficient for paramilitary or police forces to resume responsibility for enforcing law-and-order. Yet such duties are unpopular at the best of times and an overwhelming majority of those officers answering the questionnaires and/or interviewed describe them as detrimental to the military's efficiency in its primary role of defending the national borders. When armed forces' personnel are used repeatedly against civilian members of their own community, they may question the civilian authorities' competence in finding a solution to the disturbance if not also their role in its creation. In extreme cases, such doubts will lead to officers moving against the government, either to protect their own community or to 'save the nation' as a whole.

To prevent such a result, successive Indian administrations have created an ever greater array of paramilitary organisations to act as an intermediate step between relying on the police and calling in the army. By the mid-1990s, close to 700,000 officers and men were serving in over 15 such forces assigned to the various aid-to-the-civil authority tasks of spurring national development (e.g., the Border Roads Organisation), backing up local police (Provincial Armed Constabulary), protecting essential services and industries (Central Industrial Security Force), combating terrorism (National Security Guards), and guarding the national borders in peace-time and assisting the military during war (Assam Rifles).[8] Although merging several paramilitary organisations into more coherent forces has been discussed, so too has creating additional units designed for ever more specific problems. Despite their proliferation, the centre has increasingly deployed the army in internal law-and-order actions; for instance, from just under 500 occasions between 1951 and 1970, to 64 times in the 18 months from June 1979 to December 1980.[9]

The dangers of such deployment were most evident in the aftermath of Operation Blue Star. Here, the army's disproportionate recruitment of Sikh men and officers in terms of their share of the national population combined with aid-to-the-civil authority actions against militants drawn from this very same community to challenge both internal military cohesion and external societal peace.

Build-up and Action

The military action codenamed Operation Blue Star was the central government's belated, if overwrought, response to the increasing militancy of Jarnail Singh, or Sant (Saint), Bhindranwale (henceforth referred to by surname only) and his followers.[10] Bhindranwale himself was plucked from the obscure position of Damdami Temple leader by Sanjay Gandhi and ex-Punjab Chief Minister Zail Singh in the hope that the post-1977 anti-Congress coalition in Punjab could be weakened by promoting a radical new Sikh leader to discredit the moderate Sikh religious party, the Akali Dal.[11] In his first public act, Bhindranwale incited an attack on the Amritsar congress of the 'heretical' Sikh sect of Nirankaris resulting in over a dozen deaths.[12] Yet the Congress publicity machine portrayed him as a hero and, in return, Bhindranwale openly campaigned for the party's candidates in the 1980 general elections, once even sharing a dais with Indira Gandhi.[13]

After Indira Gandhi's return as PM in 1980, Bhindranwale used the government's apparent protection of his increasingly militant activities to great effect. Twice suspected of involvement in the killings of prominent opponents to his increasing militancy, he was twice allowed to walk free after appeals from (now) Minister of Home Affairs Zail Singh.[14] Bhindranwale's second release was a turning point. He was now seen as the one militant Sikh leader capable of openly defying the government. His erstwhile political 'handlers' in New Delhi would no longer be able to influence his actions.

While the professedly non-violent Akali Dal had eventually allied itself with Bhindranwale as a means of pressuring Gandhi during their tortuous negotiations over the 1973 Anandpur Sahib Resolution and other issues,[15] it too became incapable of controlling his behaviour. Bhindranwale had sworn an oath of loyalty and obedience to Harchand Singh Longowal, the most powerful of the Akali Dal's leadership trio, during the party's successful *rasta roko* (block roads) campaign of April 1983. Yet it was Longowal himself who, fearful for his own safety, used the Sikh splinter group Babbar Khalsa to push Bhindranwale and his followers out of Amritsar's Golden Temple hostel and into the temple complex itself some six weeks later.

Bhindranwale's strategy of violence was meant to create communal tension sufficient both to drive Hindus from Punjab and to provoke a national backlash which would force the approximately 20 per cent of Sikhs living elsewhere in India to seek the safety of their 'home' state. In 1982, parliament had passed a special resolution expressing 'deep anguish and concern'[16] over the situation in Punjab. By 1983, the identity of many of the militants were known to the local population and police but there was no attempt to bring them to justice as 'Bhindranwale and his men were above the law'.[17] The level of violence escalated. On 23 April 1983, Punjab Police Deputy Inspector-General (DIG) A.S. Atwal was shot dead while on his way out of the Golden Temple complex; on 5 October Sikh militants hijacked a local bus, separated the Hindu and Sikh passengers and shot the former, killing six; on 18 November another bus was hijacked, the passengers again separated by religion, and four Hindus shot dead. Although Gandhi imposed president's (i.e., direct) rule in Punjab on 6 October, the killings spiralled out of control.

Finally, with Bhindranwale openly fortifying the Golden Temple complex and his followers firing on the paramilitary CRPF surrounding them, Gandhi sent the Indian Army into Punjab on 2 June 1984. By the next day it had surrounded 38 gurudwaras (Sikh temples) believed to be harbouring Sikh militants under the command of Bhindranwale, including the Golden Temple and hostel complex where he and a large number of his followers were sheltered.

Operation Blue Star commenced on 5 June. Eschewing a prolonged siege of the Golden Temple and hostel complex for fear of provoking a state-wide uprising, the commander of the army in Punjab, (then Lieut.-General) General K. Sundarji, ordered a night-time attack to flush out Bhindranwale and his followers. In the first move, the army's Para Commandos extricated a number of Sikh moderates from the hostel complex under heavy fire. Leading elements of 10th Guards then stormed the main entrance, only to encounter withering machine gun fire and grenades thrown from concealed positions. The Para Commandos and the paramilitary Special Frontier Force units which were simultaneously attacking the heavily fortified *Akal Takht* (Eternal Throne, the symbol of Sikhism's temporal power) met similar difficulties, as did personnel of 26th Madras when attempting to link up with the former two. (The militants demonstrated their fire-power by immobilizing an army armoured personnel carrier with a anti-tank weapon.) Nor did the inducement of units of 9th Garhwali Rifles and 15th Kumaon bring the operation back on schedule. Desperate to complete the action by daybreak, Sundarji sought and received the government's permission to use tank fire to neutralise the *Akal Takht* defences. Although sniper fire would continue throughout the next day, this move effectively ended the militants' defiance.

Operation Blue Star left many scars. The approximately 1000 army personnel involved in the unexpectedly ferocious fighting endured a very high one-third casualty rate of four officers and 79 men killed, 12 officers and 237 men wounded. The subsequent government White Paper also stated that the militants suffered 493 dead, including Bhindranwale, and 86 injured, figures still much disputed. While the Golden Temple itself (the *Hari Mandir*, or Temple of God) sustained little damage as army forces had been under strict orders to avoid damaging it, the *Akal Takht* was almost destroyed and the precious Golden Temple library set on fire. Both sides are reported to have committed atrocities during the battle, especially on the unarmed civilians caught in the middle of the fight for the Golden Temple hostel complex.

Those officers answering the questionnaires and/or interviewed are particularly well-suited representatives of the Indian armed forces' opinions on Operation Blue Star. They consist of a 1:5 mix of Sikh to non-Sikh officers, closely representative of the army's current ratio as described above. Of the 96 officers answering the questionnaires, 16 are Sikhs. The remaining non-Sikhs consist of 63 Hindus, six officers with 'no religion', five Christians, one Muslim, one Buddhist, one Zoroastrian, two who follow 'all religions', and one officer who gives no answer. The Sikh/non-Sikh officers are also closely matched by rank; consisting of 1/18 lieut.-generals, 6/11 major-generals, 4/34 brigadiers, 0/2 colonels, 2/3 lieut.-colonels, 0/1 admiral and 0/3 vice admirals, 1/2 air chief marshals, 1/3 air marshals, 1/1 group captains, and 0/1 wing commander. One non-Sikh officer does not give his rank. This group of officers also moved through the military together and over half were serving at the top of their profession during the 1980s.

The responses of this group show that Indian armed forces' Sikh and non-Sikh officers markedly differ in their opinion of the central government's responsibility for the situation which led to Operation Blue Star. The latter group are themselves divided, with virtually equal numbers saying that the Gandhi administration's level of culpability for the escalating violence in Punjab ranged from 'a little'—the government was somewhat negligent—to 'a fair bit'—its mismanagement of events helped fuel the crisis—to 'a lot'—its bad decisions were to a great extent directly responsible for the deterioration of law and order. A small number of non-Sikh officers suggest that the administration was 'not responsible at all' for the events which led to Operation Blue Star, but merely responding to events outside its control. The non-Sikh Lieut.-General 19 describes the situation as a 'totally terrorist movement' made up of 'uneducated, unemployed, landless youth' who had become 'basically smugglers'.

No Sikh officer shares Lieut.-General 19's view of the situation in Punjab. Instead, almost two-fifths say the government's level of responsibility for the situation which led to Operation Blue Star was 'a fair bit', while over half argue that it was 'a lot'. The Sikh Brigadier 60 holds the central government 'entirely responsible' for the Punjab crisis, arguing that it 'encouraged and set up Bhindranwale with a view to destroy the Akali [Dal] party and create a rift between Hindus and Sikh so that they could get all the Hindu votes for the Congress'.

The differences between non-Sikh and Sikh officers' respective opinions as to actual need for Operation Blue Star are even more marked. Whereas over two-thirds of non-Sikhs say the government was justified in ordering the army into the Golden Temple, only one Sikh officers agrees. For the non-Sikh Major-General 34, the situation could not have been more grave:

> The Sikh militancy had gathered a vast quantity of arms and ammunition through the connivance of the Sikh police and Sikh civil service in Punjab. Further they had let loose a reign of terror and were on the verge of committing genocide of the Hindu population in Punjab.

In contrast, even the one Sikh officer, Major-General 96, who agrees with the necessity of Operation Blue Star thinks 'the amount of force used was excessive'.

This uncertainly over the force used is reflected in the responses of those officers who feel Operation Blue Star was not absolutely necessary. Over a third of the non-Sikh officers say other actions short of calling in the army should have been pursued, including using the police and paramilitary forces to flush out the militants. The non-Sikh Brigadier (Dr.) 55 argues that any overt use of force simply 'could have been avoided by judicial cutting off of electricity, water and food' to those ensconced in the Golden Temple complex. The Sikh officers, almost unanimous in their condemnation of the necessity of Operation Blue Star, could not agree more. In addition to the above alternatives is Sikh Brigadier 60's suggestion that the 'Sikh community should have been asked to get Bhindranwale out of the Golden Temple complex. If the Akali [Dal] party was not prepared to do so, other prominent Sikh citizens of Punjab should have asked to do it'. Whatever the alternatives, Sikh officers like Air Marshal 3 are sure that the 'villain of the piece was the central government—Indira Gandhi, her advisors and the Congress, which in effect created Bhindranwale'.

The above responses reveal Sikh and non-Sikh officers to be sharply divided over the responsibility for, and necessity of Operation Blue Star. While just under a third of the latter think the central government was relatively blameless for the deterioration of law and order in Punjab, every Sikh officer offering an opinion holds the Gandhi administration largely responsible. Moreover, whereas a majority of non-Sikh officers think Operation Blue Star was necessary, every Sikh officer offering an opinion bar one disagrees with the need for the army's storming of the Golden Temple complex. Would the stark differences between Sikh and non-Sikh over the responsibility for, and necessity of Operation Blue Star affect internal military discipline?

Mutinies

Two years before Operation Blue Star, the government had been 'thoroughly alarmed'[18] to learn that several thousand Sikh ex-servicemen, including senior officers, had answered Longowal's call to attend a Golden Temple complex meeting on 23 January 1982 to discuss ways of remedying the government's failure to address Akali Dal demands. Many of these men had been greatly upset when security measures imposed for the 1982 Asian Games resulted in the arrest of over 1500 Sikhs and the brutal stop and search on the Punjab/Haryana border of countless others, including retired officers Air Chief Marshal Arjan Singh, Lieut.-General Jagjit Singh Aurora and Major-General Shahbeg Singh, on their way to New Delhi. Although non-violent options were debated, Bhindranwale's argument that only force would achieve success persuaded Major-General Jaswant Singh Bhullar and Shahbeg Singh to join him. Bhullar played a relatively minor role, leaving the Golden Temple complex just before Operation Blue Star.[19] Shahbeg Singh, an expert on insurgency warfare hailed as a hero for training the Mukhti Bahini, the underground force instrumental in winning the 1971 Bangladesh Liberation War, was a more valuable recruit and soon became Bhindranwale's chief military advisor, expertly organizing the fortification of the Golden Temple.[20] While few other Sikh ex-servicemen openly joined the militants,[21] the government—and Indian military commanders—had to wonder how many present at Longowal's Golden Temple gathering were covertly sympathetic to Bhindranwale and, if so, were prepared to influence their relatives in the armed forces against the policies of the national political leadership.

Many believed that such influence had indeed taken place when over 2000 Sikh Indian Army personnel deserted/mutinied upon learning of Operation Blue Star. On 7 June 1984, 600 soldiers of the Sikh Regiment's 9th Battalion broke into the regimental armoury, drove through the Punjabi cantonment town of Ganganagar shouting 'long live Sant Jarnail Singh Bhindranwale'[22] and firing indiscriminately. One policeman was killed, another wounded. While some fled into nearby Pakistan, the rest were apprehended by the Rajputana Rifles before they could proceed to Delhi as planned. Two days later, having learnt of the 9th Battalion mutiny from BBC radio reports, almost 1500 soldiers of the Sikh Regimental Centre in Ramgarh, Bihar, attacked the armoury, killing their CO, Brigadier S.C. Puri, and wounding two other senior officers when the three approached. They then commandeered civilian vehicles and set off for Amritsar, 840 miles distant. After dividing into two groups just before Varanasi to avoid a rumoured roadblock, half were engaged by an army artillery unit(s?) at Shakteshgarh railway station and the remnants rounded up by the 21st Mechanised Infantry Brigade. The other half, confronted by artillery and troops of the 20th Infantry Brigade, stopped to fight and 35 were killed. Six, more minor cases of indiscipline are believed to have occurred, including one involving another Sikh Regiment battalion stationed in J&K, a second of Sikhs serving in the Punjab Regiment in Pune, and a third of Sikhs deployed in units guarding Bombay's Santa Cruz airport.

How to punish the post-Operation Blue Star indiscipline initially vexed the authorities. Whereas the defence ministry first appeared to soft-pedal the incidents, describing the men as 'misguided...We understand the feelings of the Sikh jawans',[23] GoC South Lieut.-General T.S. Oberoi, a Sikh himself, declared that the 'deserters who have surrendered will be court-martialled and punished'.[24] In an unprecedented all-India broadcast one month later, Indian Army Chief General A.S Vaidya made the first public acknowledgment that the indiscipline had included mutinies (open revolt against superiors' orders) rather than desertions (leaving their posts), and laid out the authorities' final position:

> I would like to give an assurance that those who acted in a mutinous manner will be dealt with severely under the law as enacted for the army, so that those who remain with us in the army and have the honour of bearing arms for the country, would [sic] be a proud and disciplined body of soldiers.[25]

In September 1985, the now retired Vaidya explained his reasons for punishing the mutineers: 'I do not see any difference in taking up arms against a foreign enemy or an enemy from within...one who takes up arms against his own Constitution and legally-constituted government is enemy enough, deserving the most ruthless punishment'.[26]

Yet Sikh and non-Sikh opinion on the post-Operation Blue Star indiscipline remained divided. A group of five retired Sikh lieut.-generals protested to (now) President Zail Singh that the mutineers were a special case. All Indian army regiments induct their personnel with a religious as well as civil oath thus, as Sikhs, these soldiers had sworn their allegiance on the Guru Grant Sahib (Sikh holy book). In addition, they had been let down by military superiors who had kept them uninformed of the situation leading up to and including Operation Blue Star.[27] Although the president reportedly sympathized with their demand that the mutineers be reinstated to their units, he declared himself lacking the power to do so. Subsequent government statements about the mutineers' attempts to 'spread disaffection in the ranks of the armed forces'[28] were seen as counter-attacks on those who had sympathized with the indiscipline and were now protesting about the mutineers' brutal treatment at the hands of the army.

Sikh and non-Sikh opinion was also divided as to whether the post-Operation Blue Star indiscipline affected ethnic relations within the military. Among those answering the questionnaires, two-fifths *versus* one-fifth of Sikh and non-Sikh officers, respectively, perceive ethnic relations changed for the worse in the aftermath of Operation Blue Star. While the latter stress that any resultant discrimination against, and/or loss of confidence in Sikh personnel is covert and individual, the former believe such prejudice is more overt and widespread, if not officially endorsed. Not so, says the small minority of non-Sikh officers who perceive ethnic relations to have changed for the *better* after Operation Blue Star since, according to the non-Sikh Vice Admiral 2, 'there is more attention paid to understanding each other'. Not one Sikh officer agrees with this view.

The views of those officers answering the questionnaires and/or interviewed as to ethnic relations within the military could not help but be influenced by events in the wider Indian society. A number of Sikh officers describe how they, their family and/or Sikh friends were directly caught up in the anti-Sikh riots which followed Gandhi's assassination by two of her Sikh bodyguards just over four months after Operation Blue Star. New Delhi was particularly badly hit by violence, and estimates of those Sikh men, women and children who died range from two to six thousand. Unsurprisingly, Sikh officers affected by the rioting were slow to credit the army with improved ethnic relations in the aftermath of Operation Blue Star.

The sharp differences of Sikh and non-Sikh officers' opinions on the responsibility, necessity and after-effects of Operation Blue Star beg the question of whether the Indian Army should terminate its disproportionate recruitment and posting together of personnel drawn from specific communities of the north and northwest, particularly Sikhs from Punjab. If the above mutinies are taken as a demonstration that personnel closely related by ethnicity, religion and/or region may act in a unified manner detrimental to military discipline at the least and civil-supremacy-of-rule at the most, the answer must be affirmative. As stated above, Sikhs continue to account for large percentages of both officers and soldiers in the army. Surely, suspicions about this community's loyalty in the aftermath of the post-Operation Blue Star mutinies must have weakened the army's fighting effectiveness, at least for a time, and given rise to fears that Sikhs may have become politicised to the extent of plotting against the government.

In its defence, the pro-Sikh recruitment lobby makes several telling points. As shown by the haphazard nature of the post-Operation Blue Star indiscipline, the mutinous Sikh military personnel appear to have had no premeditated plan of action in the eventuality of army action in Punjab. Nor did the Sikh Regimental Centre Court of Inquiry find any evidence of systematic attempts to influence the loyalty of Sikh military personnel by ex-army relatives or foreign powers. Instead, it blamed the post-Operation Blue Star indiscipline on the regimental centre's junior and senior officers' ignorance of the need to keep their men informed of the specific motives, objectives and/or results of army actions in Punjab. This failure of leadership left inexperienced soldiers—1,050 of the Sikh Regimental Centre's 1,461 mutineers were raw recruits, untrained and with no experience of army *izzat*—open to the mutinous exhortations of their more religiously fervent comrades. Even so, the court of inquiry found that many of these men had been forced to desert at gunpoint.

Where Sikh soldiers were experienced and well led, there was no indiscipline. Although unhappy with the short period of preparation allowed him, 9th Division CO Major-General Kuldip Singh Brar found time to visit his Sikh and non-Sikh troops, explain the rationale behind the forthcoming Operation Blue Star and, in a move without precedent in the history of the Indian Army, offer them the chance to refuse to participate with no repercussions. Not one took up this offer and they fought under Brar in the assault on the Golden Temple complex with perfect discipline.

Even more importantly, the sharp differences between the Sikh and non-Sikh officers over the responsibility for, and necessity of army action in Punjab and the military indiscipline which followed was not reflected in the behaviour of serving Sikh officers either during or after Operation Blue Star. While the non-Sikh (then Lieut.-General) General Sundarji was in charge of the army in Punjab, his Sikh chief-of-staff, Lieut.-General Ranjit Singh Dayal, planned Operation Blue Star, the Sikh Major-General Brar commanded 9th Division's liberation of the Golden Temple and hostel complex, and the Sikh Major-General Gurdial Singh led the army operation against pro-Bhindranwale militants encountered in Patiala's Gurudwara Dukhniwaran.

Although most Sikh armed forces' personnel must have been deeply upset with Operation Blue Star, they did not react as a self-interested corporate group or clique. Indeed, that no mutineers came from among the Mazhabis of the Sikh Light Infantry suggests that Sikhs remain more divided by caste than united by ethnicity, religion and region. In the end, just three per cent of the army's Sikh soldiers and *not one* Sikh commissioned officer joined in the post-Operation Blue Star indiscipline.

In light of the above, it is not surprising that almost half of both Sikh and non-Sikh officers as represented by those answering the questionnaires say the post-Operation Blue Star mutinies made no change in the Indian armed forces' ethnic relations. Although this could be understood as 'things are as bad as ever', the comments of this group reveal this choice to mean 'things are as good as ever'. These officers agree wholeheartedly with the findings of the Sikh Regimental Centre Court of Inquiry and blame not those troops who mutinied but the officers who failed to lead them properly.

Conclusion

The mutinies by several thousand Sikh troops in the aftermath of Operation Blue Star reveals the danger of deploying military personnel in sensitive aid-to-the-civil authority duties directed against representatives of a particular community, especially when that group is one of those recruited in numbers disproportionate to their share of the national population and posted together in army units. Questions as to the professional corporateness and responsibility of Sikh commissioned officers as a group distinct from their comrades are highlighted by the marked differences in the responses of Sikh and non-Sikh officers as to the responsibility for, and necessity of Operation Blue Star, as well as the anti-Sikh violence in the wider Indian society which followed Gandhi's assassination. Yet, given the number of Sikh officers and men in the Indian armed forces and the strength of the pro-military recruitment lobby of this and other traditional martial races, summarily ending their preferential enlistment on the basis of their 'questionable' loyalty risked damaging both the efficiency of the armed forces and wider, societal relations.

Externally, at least, the loyalty of Sikh commissioned officers was never in doubt. Despite their differences, Sikh and non-Sikh officers tend to agree that the post-Operation Blue Star mutinies were isolated cases of inexperienced personnel being poorly led in extreme circumstances. 'In the ultimate analysis the [mutinous] actions of certain individuals turned out to be an emotional reaction rather than a deliberate premeditated action', argues the non-Sikh Brigadier 90. That Sikh commissioned officers were intimately involved in the planning and execution of Operation Blue Star, and that not one joined the mutineers ensured that they and other traditionally recruited communities would continue to join and serve in the armed forces in all capacities. Once again, a severe challenge to civil supremacy-of-rule in India revealed the remarkable strength of its commissioned officers' professional responsibility to the legitimate government.

As with the potentially disastrous 1962 Sino-Indian War, lessons learned from Operation Blue Star and its subsequent mutinies bettered Indian civil-military relations. In an attempt to assuage Sikh feelings, 900 of the 2,606 military mutineers were rehabilitated by August 1985 as part of the Rajiv-Longowal Accord[29] signed one month previously. Those guilty of perpetrating the anti-Sikh rioting in New Delhi are slowly being brought to trial. The authorities also placed a greater reliance on swift police responses. When 200 Sikh militants took refuge in a fortified Golden Temple complex in 1988, they were forced to surrender in a police-led operation which resulted in the comparatively low casualty rate of three security forces' personnel and 30 militants killed. The authorities also used armed police to surround the Golden Temple complex and evict the approximately 300 Sikhs inside protesting the October 1992 execution of those found guilty of assassinating General Vaidya on 10 August 1986. Finally, although the government found it necessary to re-deploy Indian Army units in Punjab during the abortive June 1991 elections and the February 1992 elections, there were no reported instances of military indiscipline.

[1] Great Britain, *Report of the Commissioners Appointed to Inquire into the Organisation of the Indian Army; together with the Minutes of Evidence and Appendix*, CND. 2515, 1859, as cited in S. Cohen, *The Indian Army: Its Contribution to the Development of a Nation* (Berkeley: University of California Press, 1971), p. 38.

[2] As the Indian government refuses to give the specific ethnic or religious origins of its military personnel, the exact numbers of martial versus non-martial men and officers cannot be completely known. However, from independence onwards new Indian Army units such as the Parachute Regiment have been constituted on an all-India basis. In 1949, C-in-C Field Marshal Cariappa formally scrapped the concept of martial and non-martial races. In 1954, a policy (further modified in 1963 by the cabinet's Military Affairs Committee) began which disallowed any one Indian state from having a dominant position in military recruitment. During Indira Gandhi's Emergency rule a circular was issued undertaking to enlist armed forces' personnel in proportion to their state's share of the national population. Most recently, it has become common knowledge that the Indian Army is making efforts to ensure that all units reflect a completely mixed and all-India character.

[3] D.K. Palit, *War in High Himalaya: The Indian Army in Crisis, 1962* (London C. Hurst, 1991), p. 12.

[4] Palit, *War in High Himalaya*, p. 12.

[5] Palit, *War in High Himalaya*, p. 12.

[6] S. Cohen, 'The Military and Indian Democracy' in A. Kohli, ed., *India's Democracy: An Analysis of Changing State-Society Relations* (Princeton: Princeton University Press, 1988), p. 132.

[7] Cohen, 'The Military and Indian Democracy', p. 132.

[8] Other paramilitary forces include the Border Security Force, Central Reserve Police Force, Coast Guard, Defence Security Force, Home Guards, Indo-Tibetan Border Police, Ladakh Scouts, Railway Protection Force, Rapid Action Force, Rashtriya Rifles, Special Frontier Force, State Armed Police, and Uttar Pradesh Special Police Force. With the exception of the RR which is under the command of the ministry of defence, these paramilitary forces are the remit of the ministry of home affairs. See Lt.Gen. M.L. Chibber, *Para Military Forces*, USI Papers (Number Four), (New Delhi: United Services Institution of India, September 1979); S. Gupta, 'Paramilitary Forces: The Tired Trouble Shooters', *India Today*, 15 February 1988; and R. Menon and W.P.S. Sidhu, 'The Trust Breaks: Partisan police forces during the riots cause fear and exacerbate the divide', *India Today*, 31 January 1993.

[9] Cohen, 'The Military and Indian Democracy', p. 123.

[10] Operation Blue Star may also be seen as the government's cumulative reaction to a long history of political, socioeconomic and religious agitation by the Sikh of Punjab. See, for instance, J.J.M. Pettigrew, *The Sikhs of the Punjab: Unheard Voices of State and Guerrilla Violence* (London: Zed Books, 1995);

and R.A. Kapur, *Sikh Separatism: The Politics of Faith,* pbk. ed. (First published London: Allen & Unwin; New Delhi: Vikas Publishing House Pvt Ltd, 1987).

[11] Sanjay Gandhi and Zail Singh conspired to promote Bhindranwale by forming a new Sikh political party, the Dal Khalsa, which from its inception advocated transforming Punjab into an independent Sikh state of Khalistan. While the Dal Khalsa became known as Bhindranwale's party, he himself never formally joined any political organisation.

[12] Accounts of the exact number killed vary. See K. Nayar and K. Singh, *Tragedy of Punjab: Operation Bluestar & After,* pbk. ed. (New Delhi: Vision Books Pvt Ltd. incorporating Orient Paperbacks, 1984), pp. 26, 32; and M. Tully and S. Jacob, *Amritsar: Mrs. Gandhi's Last Battle,* pbk. ed. (Calcutta: Rupa & Co. by arrangement with Pan Books Ltd., London, 1985), p. 59.

[13] See Nayar and Singh, *Tragedy of Punjab,* pp. 36-37; and Tully and Jacob, *Amritsar,* p. 59, 61-62.

[14] Named by police as a suspect in the shooting to death of the Nirankari Guru, Baba Gurbachan Singh, in April 1980, Bhindranwale took refuge in the Golden Temple hostel until Zail Singh assured parliament of his innocence. Five months later, when the police named Bhindranwale as a conspirator in the killing of newspaper proprietor Lala Jagat Narain, he was allowed to flee from Haryana to a Punjab gurudwara, allegedly with the connivance of Haryana chief minister and Congress member, Bhajan Lal. Although Bhindranwale surrendered to police five days later, Zail Singh again told parliament he was innocent and he was freed without benefit of a court order. Apparently, Zail Singh wanted to release Bhindranwale because he thought he could use him to bring about the downfall of his rival, the Punjab chief minister while Gandhi wanted Bhindranwale freed in an attempt to maintain influence over Sikhs in Delhi.

[15] Akali Dal demands included restricting the central government's powers over Punjab's defence, foreign policy, currency and communications, guaranteeing the state's river water rights, granting it sole possession of Chandigarh as the state capital, and amending Article 25 of the constitution to recognize Sikh religious institutions as separate from those of Hindus. In August 1982, after yet another round of negotiations with New Delhi had broken down, the Akali Dal joined with Bhindranwale in a *morcha* (movement) which led PM Indira Gandhi to release all jailed Akali agitators and reopen talks. For a variety of reasons for which neither party is blameless, these and three subsequent negotiations failed.

[16] Tully and Jacob, *Amritsar,* p. 79.

[17] Tully and Jacob, *Amritsar,* pp. 94-95.

[18] Cohen, *The Military and Indian Democracy,* p. 89.

[19] Although Major-General Bhullar went on to organize pro-Khalistan propaganda efforts in the USA, many overseas Sikh leaders are reported to

believe he was deliberately used by the Indian government to hinder their pro-Khalistan activities.

[20] Bitter about his dismissal from the Indian Army on three corruption charges one day before due to retire (he subsequently won two civil court cases in an effort to clear his name), and humiliated by his treatment on the Punjab/Haryana border as described above, Major-General Shahbeg Singh had increasingly turned to religion for solace.

[21] Tully and Jacob describe how 'People living in the bazaars surrounding the [Golden] temple...had been told that some of the ex-servicemen were giving weapons training to young Sikhs'. See Tully and Jacob, *Amritsar*, p. 103.

[22] Tully and Jacob, *Amritsar*, p. 194.

[23] Tully and Jacob, *Amritsar*, p. 198.

[24] Tully and Jacob, *Amritsar*, pp. 198-199.

[25] Tully and Jacob, *Amritsar*, p. 199.

[26] M. Rahman, 'A.S. Vaidya The Killing of a General', *India Today*, 31 August 1986, p. 21.

[27] The protesting officers were Lieut.-Generals M.S. Wadalia, Harbaksh Singh, J.S. Dhillon, J.S. Aurora and Sartaj Singh.

[28] See 'Forces Being Denigrated' and 'Leave the Army Alone', *The Times of India*, 28 November 1984, as cited in Cohen, *The Military and Indian Democracy*, p. 137.

[29] The accord was brokered between PM Rajiv Gandhi and Harchand Singh Longowal in an attempt to bring peace to Punjab. Both parties would be later assassinated; Gandhi allegedly by Tamil separatists for his part in sending the Indian armed forces' contingent known as Indian Peace Keeping Force (IPKF) to Sri Lanka in 1987 and Longowal by Sikh separatists for negotiating with New Delhi.

CONCLUSION

In the history of independent India, there has never been any serious threat that armed forces' officers would instigate a coup against the government. A brief review of the evidence provided confirms this.

Selected from the best of backgrounds, educated and trained to British standards of an officer and gentleman, commissioned Indian officers' loyalty to the Raj came from both their identification with the ruling elite and desire, especially as pioneers in this profession, to perfect their professional expertise and corporate *izzat*. A trickier notion was that of professional responsibility for, if not internalized as an explicit principle, it may encourage a military coup by leading officers to understand their duty as loyalty to the nation rather than the legal government.

This confusion of loyalties was potentially explosive with the rise of the independence movement's challenge to British rule. Just who would commissioned Indian officers' perceive as the legitimate voice of the subcontinent? This question proved somewhat irrelevant as, except for some youthful involvement in nationalist activities, the struggle for *swaraj* barely touched commissioned Indian officers. The non-violent nature of the independence movement, the indifference of public and nationalist leaders to military matters, and the privileged backgrounds and physical separation of commissioned Indian officers all contributed to ensuring their loyalty to the Raj throughout the interwar years.

The creation of various Indian national armies from Indian military POWs and civilians during the Second World War appeared to offer another potent challenge to the professional responsibility of commissioned Indian officers. Yet these forces proved both militarily ineffectual and professionally irrelevant to those officers—and jawans—on active service in all theatres of the war. Although the post-war trial of the Red Fort Three created some sympathy for Indian national armies' personnel, commissioned Indian officers of the British-led Indian armed forces remained free from (overt) doubt as to their ultimate loyalty to the legitimate government of the day.

When independence arrived, Nehru's seemingly naive assumption that with political control would come civil supremacy-of-rule proved true. That this astonishingly smooth transference of professional responsibility took place despite the multiple challenges of the transfer of power and partition was due to commissioned officers' demonstrated confidence in their own professional competence and in the skills of the new political and administrative elite, all of which continued to be practiced largely according to British norms. India would not flounder on the path to modernisation. Politicians continued to lead, bureaucrats to administer and the country to develop. That, for the most part, officers, politicians and bureaucrats continued to be drawn from the same socioeconomic strata and believe in the same values of democracy, secularism and development further ensured the security of civil supremacy-of-rule in India.

These shared backgrounds and beliefs manifested itself in Indian officers' indulgent attitude towards the government in the first decade of independence. Corporate grievances over pay, share of the national budget, downgrading in the warrant of precedence, and perception of political and bureaucratic indifference to their organisational worth did not lead officers out of their barracks and into politics. Even the example of their former comrades in Pakistan taking over power failed to stir their ire. Although the reference-group theory of military intervention may have applied to Pakistani officers' involvement with the American armed forces, it had limited resonance with Indian officers overtly conscious of their superior professionalism and serving a government which practiced international non-alignment.

During the rise of the Menon-Kaul nexus, any number of personal and corporate grievances were generated as the expertise of senior officers was disputed, their institutional sphere of decision-making invaded, and the civil-military decision-making process ignored and/or manipulated for personal ambition. Yet, even as officers began to be identified as being for or against the Menon-Kaul nexus, the possibility of a coup remained small. Opponents of Menon-Kaul also had circumvented formal civil-military decision-making procedures and their champion, General Thimayya, had meekly withdrawn his resignation. Any officers thinking of offering themselves as popular alternatives to the Nehru government continued to be hampered by their non-participation in the nationalist movement and, especially, Congress' continued electoral strength.

Defeat in the 1962 Sino-Indian War challenged all these notions by openly exposing governmental ineptitude. The Indian Army's field officers, potentially the group most likely to stage a coup, blamed the political leadership's forward policy and its craven implementation by their military superiors, while perceiving the public as sympathetic towards them and resentful of the administration. Yet, in this ultimate test of the strength of civil supremacy-of-rule in India, hardly any officers can recall talk of moving against the government. Civil supremacy-of-rule remained intact because of quick and decisive decisions by the political leadership. The grievances of field officers were assuaged by replacing disgraced senior officers and civil servants, most notably Menon, modifying the civil-military hierarchy to reflect the importance of the military as a instrument of policy, and re-invigorating the armed forces with additional money and men.

Indira Gandhi's imposition of Emergency rule raised the stakes from a question of governmental ineptitude to one of legitimacy. Yet, however distasteful many officers found the excesses committed during this period, they understood Emergency and its actions designed to keep Gandhi in power as strictly legitimate. There was never any suggestion that they deviate from their professional responsibility to their client, society's legitimate ruler. Even less plausible was any idea that officers might act to retain Gandhi in power after her electoral defeat. The rule of law existed for all to obey.

The mutinous actions of several thousand Sikh jawans in the aftermath of Operation Blue Star highlighted the danger posed to civil supremacy-of-rule by military personnel united by primordial ties acting against specific government policies directed at the community from which they are recruited. Yet, despite sharply differing opinions as to the responsibility for, and necessity of the army action in the Golden Temple complex, Sikh and non-Sikh officers generally agreed that the mutinies were isolated instances of poorly led, inexperienced recruits acting on the spur of the moment. That not one commissioned officer participated in any indiscipline meant the corporate cohesiveness and fighting effectiveness of the armed forces was never seriously undermined, nor civil supremacy-of-rule endangered. The recruitment and posting together of certain communities in numbers disproportionate to their share of the national population continues, as does the use of the military in aid-to-the-civil duties.

Underpinning the relative ease with which all of the above tests to Indian civil supremacy-of-rule were dealt with is the ingrained professionalism and long tradition of commissioned Indian officers. As

Ruth First wrote many years ago: 'The virginity of an army is like that of a woman....once assailed, it is never again intact'.[1] From independence to today, Indian officers have been content—and even proud—spinsters.

The sureness of civil supremacy-of-rule in India during that period in which civilian regimes are most vulnerable, the transition to an independent state and the first years of self-government, suggests there are measures applicable to civil-military relations in throughout the third world. In Table 1, four of the 17 factors which the questionnaire respondents rank as having contributed to India never having experienced a military coup may be true of many other developing countries:

7th	•	Widely held belief in democracy.
Joint 8th	•	Wisdom and stature of national leaders.
Joint 14th	•	Example of ineffectiveness of military rule in Pakistan and Bangladesh.
17th	•	Political unawareness of the masses.

Another five factors, including three of the top four, are found in a number of third world countries:

1st	•	Professionalism of the armed forces.
3rd	•	Initial political stability, quality, and/or democratic rule.
4th	•	Nationally representative military personnel.
Joint 11th	•	Institutionalisation of diverse centres of power.
Joint 11th	•	Logistics unfavourable: five regional army commands, troops dispersed nationally, etc.

The apparent commonality of these anti-coup factors is, however, misleading. Take the crucial first-, third- and fourth-place factors described above. Other than India, which third world state can be argued to have a professional officer corps, stable democratic rule at independence and armed forces containing a representative mix of personnel? Many may enjoy the first two qualities, but most fail to have the third. Similarly, few developing countries have managed to institutionalise political, social, administrative and/or economic power in cities or regions outside the national capital area.

Moreover, the remaining factors ranked by respondents in Table 1 are unique and/or virtually unique to India. Two apply to India alone:

   6th • Dominant Hindu culture.
Joint 14th • Independence struggle's non-violent nature.

Another three, applicable individually to other developing countries, are not found together elsewhere:

Joint 8th • Administrative efficiency.
Joint 8th • Political awareness of the masses.
Joint 11th • Decades-old habit of democracy.

Leaving out '16th: Other', the two remaining factors, both in the top five, further illustrate the uniqueness of the Indian experience:

   2nd • Diversity of peoples, cultures, languages.
   5th • Sheer size of India.

These two factors have hitherto not been specifically highlighted in this book since the unparalleled scale and complexity of India's social mix and size is obvious. Indian military officers are well aware of the immensity of the task of governing such a state as well, if not better, than any civilian regime.

Of course, those armed forces' officers answering the questionnaires and/or interviewed are by no means the only judges of which factors have contributed to India never having experienced a military coup. Nonetheless, as the ultimate arbiters of any such action, their understanding of coup inhibitors must be respected. And their particular list of factors in its entirety seems inapplicable to all other third world countries. Is it?

While the particular mix of coup-inhibiting factors on Table 1 may suggest that India has remained free from a military coup by chance, this is not so. Granted, the country is large, diverse, predominantly Hindu and had the 'father of the country' Nehru and other nationally respected and able politicians live long into its initial years as an independent state. Yet the remaining factors are the result of deliberate choices by the civil-military leadership, either of the Raj or independent India or both. Of these, professionalism is undoubtedly the most important, and the British ideal of an officer and gentleman welded by *izzat* to his regiment and by professional training to his barracks remains the model taught even today. The British practices of recruiting officers, if not troops, from all over the country (even though some communities like the Sikhs of Punjab are over-represented) and having separate regional army commands has also continued. Other factors such as the country's initial political stability, quality and tradition of democracy, its relative administrative efficiency, and institutionalisation of diverse centres of power also were the result of imported policies which Indians consciously embraced as their own. Their great improvement on the Raj pattern of governance was in the enrollment of the masses in a unique non-violent independence movement which raised their political awareness and instilled in them the idea that votes counted. These choices were all deliberately made, and all have contributed to India's decades-old habit of democracy which its officers are so reticent to threaten.

Although this examination of Indian civil-military relations does not suggest a general theory of the conditions which preclude a military coup, other third world countries wishing to ensure civil supremacy-of-rule would be wise to take the following steps (in no particular order):

- Maximize their officer corps' professionalism.
- Recruit military personnel from all societal groups.
- Disperse concentrations of military force.
- Raise the political awareness of their people.
- Preach and practice democracy.
- Allow political power to flourish outside the capital.
- Increase the efficiency of administrators.

Perhaps taking all of the above steps will keep the 'man on horseback'[2] from (re)appearing on the political scene.

What this book does reveal is that a military coup is ultimately the result of commissioned officers' perceptions—of their personal and institutional role in society, the abilities of the civilian political and bureaucratic elite, and the will of the people. At the transfer of power, Indian officers may have perceived themselves as altruistic citizens most qualified to lead the modernisation of their country. During the first decade of independence, they may have wanted to behave as any other political actors to further their institutional concerns. In the early 1960s, they may have used a host of grievances to move against the government. The Emergency rule of the mid-1970s may have caused them to question the administration's legitimacy and therefore act to save the nation. After Operation Blue Star, a section of officers may have moved against the political leadership because of policies perceived as threatening to the community from which they were recruited. At any time during the history of independent India, commissioned armed forces' officers may have formed self-interested personal/clientelist associations with ambitions to overthrow the ruling civilian administration.

That Indian armed forces' officers have never attempted a coup is partly because civilian politicians and bureaucrats have been more qualified and motivated to rule, because no such opportunity ever arose, because military grievances were never enough to force this momentous step, and/or because their numbers and diversity thwarted the primacy of any one internal group. Other factors, including officers' remoteness to the people, their antagonistic relationship with civil servants, and a popular public belief in democracy, also mitigated against the success of an attempted coup, much less a military regime.

Nonetheless, their virtual monopoly of weaponry and organisational size and efficiency may still have led Indian officers to attempt to intervene against the government. That they did not was their decision; whether based on professional conditioning, respect for the political leadership and civil service, understanding of the government's budgetary priorities, pride in their difference from their former comrades in Pakistan, professional and psychological inability to challenge Nehru, and/or satisfaction with their corporate rewards.

Will commissioned Indian officers remain out of politics during the challenges to come? While the variation of the tests to civil-military relations examined in this work may appear exhaustive, current issues such as the increasing recruitment of GCs from lower socioeconomic classes, increasing opportunities for corruption in the awarding of defence contracts, and the growing communalism in Indian society need to be studied for their potential effects on officers' understanding of their personal and professional role in, and responsibility to society. An especially close eye needs to be kept on the civilian authorities' continued over-dependence on the armed forces as enforcers of internal order. At the height of this practice in 1992, nearly one-third of all Indian Army personnel were reported to be deployed in combating internal insurgencies in Assam, Punjab and J&K. Nonetheless, the worst-case scenario of the entire army moving against the government because of prolonged exposure to the domestic fallout of political mismanagement seems extremely unlikely. Such duties make officers reflect on the tremendous complexity of political management in India, not its ease, and many end up admiring efforts of politicians rather than thinking they could do better.

Barring extreme and unforeseen circumstances, commissioned Indian officers will *never* instigate a coup against the civilian government. Their professional training and historical traditions demand they remain in their barracks. Officers also realize that to move successfully against the government demands a representative mix of coup executors from the diverse ethnic, regional and religious groups in the armed forces, as well as the cooperation of all army commands—hardly likely. They further recognize that to govern effectively as a military regime would demand the collaboration of the civil service and the general acquiescence of the people—even more improbable. Officers also concede the unlikelihood of tackling the challenges of administering a state as large and diverse as India better than a civilian administration. Finally, commissioned Indian officers take great pride in the contrasts between themselves and the officer corps of neighbouring Pakistan. They have, and will never wish their self-perceived high military professionalism and record of respect for democracy to be tarnished by entering the 'dirty' world of politics.

---

[1] R. First, *The Barrel of a Gun: Political Power in Africa and the Coup d'État* (London: Allen Lane The Penguin Press, 1970), p. 20.

[2] A phrase coined by S.E. Finer in his seminal work, *The Man on Horseback: The Role of the Military in Politics* (London: Pall Mall Press, 1962).

ABBREVIATIONS

AG	Adjutant-General
BRO	Border Roads Organisation
BSF	Border Security Force
C-in-C	Commander-in-Chief
CGS	Chief of the General Staff
CMLA	Chief Martial Law Administrator
CO	Commanding Officer
CRPF	Central Reserve Police Force
DIG	Deputy Inspector-General
DM	Defence Minister
DMO	Director of Military Operations
ECO	Emergency commissioned officer
FPSC	Federal Public Service Commission
GoC	General officer commanding
HQ	Headquarters
IAF	Indian Air Force
IAS	Indian Administrative Service
IB	Intelligence Bureau
ICO	Indian commissioned officer
ICS	Indian Civil Service
IDF	Indian Defence Force
IMA	Indian Military Academy
IMS	Indian Medical Service
IN	Indian Navy
IPKF	Indian Peace Keeping Force
ISC	Indian Sandhurst Committee
ISF	Indian State Forces
J&K	Jammu & Kashmir
JCO	Junior commissioned officer
JIC	Joint Intelligence Committee
KCIO	King's commissioned Indian officer

KCO	King's commissioned officer
MDO	Minister of Defence Organisation
MEA	Ministry for External Affairs
MI	Military Intelligence
ML	Muslim League
NAM	Non-aligned Movement
NCC	National Cadet College
NCO	Non-commissioned officer
NEFA	Northeast Frontier Area
NNRC	Neutral Nations Repatriation Committee
OTC	Officer Training Corps
PMA	Pakistan Military Academy
POW	Prisoner-of-war
PRG	Punjab Research Group
PSO	Principal Staff Officer
QMG	Quarter-Master General
R&D	Research and Development
RAF	Royal Air Force
RAFC	Royal Air Force College
RFC	Royal Flying Corps
RIAF	Royal Indian Air Force
RIN	Royal Indian Navy
RIM	Royal Indian Marine
RMA	Royal Military Academy
RMC	Royal Military College
SEATO	Southeast Asia Treaty Organisation
SES	Department of Social and Economic Studies
SOAS	School of Oriental and African Studies
UN	United Nations
VCO	Viceroy's commissioned officer
WO	Warrant officer

APPENDIX A

Military Officers: Questionnaire and Interview Details

Rank	Code	Answered Questionnaire I	Answered Questionnaire II	Were interviewed	Where and when interviewed	
Air Chief Marshal	1	●		●	New Delhi	1987
Vice Admiral	2	●		●	Bombay	1987
Air Marshal	3	●		●	New Delhi	1987
Lieut.-General	4	●		●	Pune	1987
Air Marshal	5	●		●	New Delhi	1989
Vice Admiral	6	●				
Air Marshal	7	●				
Vice Admiral	8	●				
Brigadier	9	●				
Lieut.-General	10	●		●	Patna	1989
Lieut.-Colonel	11	●				
Air Chief Marshal	12	●		●	Pune	1987
Major-General	13	●				
Lieut.-Colonel	14	●				
Lieut.-General	15	●				
Lieut.-General	16	●		●	New Delhi	1987
Lieut.-General	17	●		●	London	1988
Air Chief Marshal	18	●		●	New Delhi	1987

Lieut.-General	19	•		•	New Delhi	1987
Major-General	20	•				
Anonymous	21	•				
Brigadier	22	•		•	New Delhi	1987
Lieut.-General	23	•		•	New Delhi	1987
Colonel	24	•		•	New Delhi	1987
Lieut.-Colonel	25	•		•	Richmond	1987
Wing Commander	26	•				
Group Captain	27	•				
Brigadier	28		•			
Brigadier	29		•			
Brigadier	30		•			
Brigadier	31		•			
Major-General	32		•			
Major-General	33		•			
Major-General	34		•			
Lieut.-General	35		•			
Major-General	36		•			
Brigadier	37		•			
Brigadier	38		•			
Brigadier	39		•			
Brigadier	40		•			
Brigadier	41		•			
Brigadier	42		•			
Brigadier	43		•			
Brigadier	44		•			
Brigadier	45		•			
Brigadier	46		•			
Brigadier (Justice)	47		•	•	New Delhi	1989
Brigadier	48		•			
Lieut.-General	49		•			
Brigadier	50		•			
Brigadier	51		•			
Major-General	52		•			
Brigadier	53		•			
Lieut.-General	54		•			
Brigadier (Dr.)	55		•			
Lieut.-General	56		•			

Rank	No.			Place	Year
Brigadier (Dr.)	57	•			
Admiral	58	•	•	Gurgaon	1989
Major-General	59	•			
Brigadier	60	•			
Brigadier	61	•			
Brigadier	62	•			
Brigadier	63	•			
Brigadier	64	•			
Brigadier (Dr.)	65	•			
Lieut.-General	66	•			
Major-General	67	•			
Major-General	68	•			
Brigadier	69	•	•	Pune	1989
Brigadier	70	•			
Lieut.-General	71	•			
Major-General	72	•			
Brigadier	73	•			
Major-General	74	•	•	New Delhi	1989
Major-General	75	•	•	New Delhi	1989
Brigadier	76	•			
Group Captain	77	•			
Air Marshal	78	•			
Colonel	79	•			
Lieut.-Colonel	80	•			
Lieut.-Colonel	81	•			
Brigadier	82	•			
Brigadier	83	•			
Brigadier	84	•			
Major-General	85	•	•	New Delhi	1989
Major-General	86	•			
Lieut.-General	87	•			
Lieut.-General	88	•			
Major-General	89	•	•	New Delhi	1989
Brigadier	90	•			
Brigadier	91	•			
Lieut.-General	92	•			
Lieut.-General	93	•			
Lieut.-General	94	•	•	New Delhi	1989

Position	Code			Where and when interviewed	
Lieut.-General	95	•	•	New Delhi	1989
Major-General	96	•			
Major-General	97		•	Noida	1989
Brigadier	98		•	New Delhi	1989
Commodore	99		•	Bombay	1987
Lieut.-General	100		•	New Delhi	1989
Lieut.-General	101		•	New Delhi	1989
Lieut.-Colonel	102		•	New Delhi	1987
Vice Admiral	103		•	New Delhi	1987
Major-General	104		•	London	1988
Major-General	105		•	New Delhi	1987
Admiral	106		•	New Delhi	1987
Lieut.-General	107		•	New Delhi	1987
Lieut.-General	108		•	Meerut	1989

Totals:		
Answered Questionnaire I:	27	
Answered Questionnaire II:	69	
Were interviewed:		36
Answered a questionnaire only:		72
Answered a questionnaire and were interviewed:		24
Were interviewed only:		12
Grand total:		108

Civilians: Interview Details

Position	Title	Code	Where and when interviewed	
Defence journalist	Mr.	C1	New Delhi	1989
International affairs expert	Mr.	C2	New Delhi	1989
Professor	Prof.	C3	New Delhi	1989
Ex-principal defence secretary	Mr.	C4	New Delhi	1989
Ex-defence secretary	Mr.	C5	New Delhi	1989
Ex-military officer	Dr.	C6	Pune	1989
Ex-governor	Mr.	C7	New Delhi	1989
Defence expert	Mr.	C8	Cambridge	1988
Grand total:		8		

BIBLIOGRAPHY

Articles

Ali, S. 'In step with tradition' and 'The Raj is dead but the Sahibs live on'. *Far Eastern Economic Review*. 31 May 1984.

Antia, Major-General S.N. 'A Military Coup in India?' *Asiaweek*. 18 August 1978.

Arya, K.C. 'Defence Expenditure After 1960'. *Eastern Economist.* 70:19, May 1978.

Arya, K.C. 'Defence Production in India—Problems and Perspectives'. *Southern Economist*. 17:10, September 1978.

Badhwar, I. and D. Bobb. 'General K. Sundarji: Disputed Legacy'. *India Today*. 15 May 1988.

Bajwa, Major-General K.S. 'Military Leadership and the Changing Social Ethos'. *USI Journal*. 107A:453, July-September 1978.

Bajwa, Major-General K.S. 'Training in the Armed Forces—A Fresh Look'. *USI Journal*. 109:455, January-March 1979.

Baral, L.R. 'Nation Building and Region Building in South Asia'. *Asia Pacific Community*. Vol. 28, Spring 1985.

Barclay, C.N. 'The Indian Army'. *Army*. 17:7, July 1967.

Bhatia, H. 'Reorganisation of the Armed Forces'. *USI Journal*. 95:401, October-December 1965.

Bienen, H. 'Armed Forces and National Modernization Continuing the Debate'. *Comparative Politics*. 16:1, October 1983.

Bienen, H. 'Civil-Military Relations in the Third World'. *International Political Science Review*. 2:3, 1981.

Bopegamage, A. 'The Military as a Modernizing Agent in India'. *Economic Development and Cultural Change*. 20:1, October 1971.

Bose, A.C. 'Netaji and the Nazis: A Study in Their Relations'. *Journal of India History*. Vol. 50, 1972.

Candeth, K P. 'Rehabilitation of Defence Service Personnel'. *USI Journal*. 105:439, April-June 1975.

Chari, P.R. 'Civil-Military Relations in India'. *Armed Forces and Society*. 4:1, November 1977.

Chari, P.R. 'Indo-Soviet Military Cooperation: A Review'. *Asian Survey*. 19:3, March 1979.

Chopra, P.S. 'The Air Force Story'. *Illustrated Weekly of India*. 94:13, 1 April 1973.

Chowdhury, M. 'Military Coups and Military Rule in Bangladesh'. *European Journal of Sociology*. Vol. 17, June-December 1983.

Chowdhury, Z.A. 'Army trouble exposes diarchy in Bangladesh. *The Times of India*. 22 May 1996.

Cohen, S. 'India's China War and After'. *Journal of Asian Studies*. August 1971.

Cohen, S. 'Officer Tradition in the Indian Army'. *USI Journal*. Vol. 94, January 1964.

Cohen, S. 'The Untouchable Soldier: Caste, Politics and the Indian Army'. *Journal of Asian Studies*. 28:3, May 1969.

Davie, M. 'How Mr. Bose Came to Declare War on the Raj'. *The Observer*. 18 December 1983.

Decalo, S. 'Military Coups and Military Regimes in Africa'. *The Journal of Modern African Studies*. 2:1, 1973.

Dev, A. 'An Interview With General Sundarji'. *Gentleman*. April 1986.

Dogra, K.K. 'How Army Fosters Internal Cohesiveness and National Integration'. *USI Journal*. 110:461, July-September 1980.

Dowden, R. 'Coups blight Africa reform'. *The Independent on Sunday*. 24 October 1993.

D'Souza, Major-General E. 'Bombay: Riots, Serial Blasts and the Army's Role'. *Defence Today*. 1:1, August 1993.

Dupree, L. 'Democracy and the Military Base of Power'. *The Middle East Journal*. 22:1, Winter 1968.

Editorial. 'Cooking Kichiri—Army Style'. *The Sikh Review*. 41:2, No. 471 March 1993.

Editorial. *The Statesman*. 1 September 1959.

Elkin, J.F. and W.A. Ritezel. 'Military Role Expansion in India'. *Armed Forces and Society*. 11:4, Summer 1985.

Ewing, A. 'Administering India: The Indian Civil Service'. *History Today*. Vol. 32, June 1982.

Feit, E. 'Pen, Sword, and People: Military Regimes in the Formation of Political Institutions'. *World Politics*. 25:2, January 1973.

Finer, S.E. 'The Man on Horseback—1974'. *Armed Forces and Society*. 1:1, November 1974.

Fossum, E. 'Factors Influencing the Occurrence of Military Coups d'état in Latin America'. *Journal of Peace Research*. Vol. 3, 1967.

Gandhi, M.K. Editorial. *Harijan*. 10 February 1940.

Gandhi, M.K. 'Foreign Soldiers in India'. *Harijan*. 26 April 1942.

Gandhi, M.K. 'Notes'. *Young India*. 27 October 1921.

Gandhi, M.K. 'Outside His Field'. *Harijan*. 16 November 1947.

Gandhi, M.K. 'The Doctrine of the Sword'. *Young India*. 11 August 1920.

Germani, G. and K. Silvert. 'Politics, Social Structure and Military Intervention in Latin America'. *European Journal of Sociology*. 11:1, 1961.

Gupta, S. 'Paramilitary Forces: The Tired Trouble Shooters'. *India Today*. 15 February 1988.

Gupta, S. with P.G. Thakurta. 'Defence Forces Heading for a Crisis'. *India Today*. 28 February 1989.

Gutteridge, W. 'A Commonwealth Military Culture?' *Roundtable*. Vol. 239, July 1970.

Hanif, M. 'Foiling the Hawks: The arrest of senior army officers for plotting a coup reveals the threat Benazir Bhutto faces from the Right'. *India Today*. 15 November 1995.

Hauser, W.L. 'Careerism vs. Professionalism in the Military'. *Armed Forces and Society*. 10:3, Spring 1984.

Heeger, G.A. 'Politics in the Post-Military State: Some Reflections on the Pakistani Experience'. *World Politics*. 29:2, January 1977.

Hussain, S.A. 'Military in Politics: 1969 Coup d'État in Pakistan'. *Dacca University Studies*. 34:Part A, 1981.

Hill, K.M. 'Research Note: Military Role vs. Military Rule Allocations to Military Activities'. *Comparative Politics*. 11:3, April 1979.

Hopkins, K. 'Civil-Military Relations in Developing Countries'. *The British Journal of Sociology*. 17:2, 1966.

Jackman, R. 'Politicians in Uniform: Military Governments and Social Change in the Third World'. *American Political Science Review*. 70:4, December 1976.

Jahan, R. 'Ten Years of Ayub Khan and the Problem of National Integration'. *Journal of Comparative Administration*. 2:3, November 1980.

Jain, T.K. 'Role of the Bureaucracy in Political Development: A Comparative Study of India and Pakistan'. *South Asian Studies*. 16:2, 1981.

Janowitz, M. 'From Institutional to Occupational: The Need for Conceptual Continuity'. *Armed Forces and Society*. 4:1, November 1977.

Jeffery, K. 'The Eastern Arc of Empire: A Strategic View 1850-1950'. *Journal of Strategic Studies*. 5:4, December 1982.

Jennings, M.K. and G.B. Markus. 'The Effect of Military Service on Political Attitudes: A Panel Study'. *American Political Science Review*. 71:1, March 1977.

Joshi, M. 'The Army: Fighting Fit'. *Frontline*. 9-22 January 1988.

Kaul, Lt. General Hridaya. 'Whither the Army'. *Indian Defence Review*. January 1989.

Khan, M.M. 'Administrative Reforms in the Indian Civil Service'. *Dacca University Studies*. 25:Part A, December 1976.

Khondker, H.H. 'Bangladesh: Anatomy of an Unsuccessful Military Coup'. *Armed Forces and Society*. 13:1, Fall 1986.

Klieman, A.S. 'Confined to Barracks: Emergencies and the Military in Developing Societies'. *Comparative Politics*. 12:2, January 1980.

Kukreja, V. 'Civilian Control of the Military in India'. *The Indian Journal of Political Science.* 50:4, October-December 1989.

Kukreja, V. 'Military Intervention in Politics: Contrasting Cases of Pakistan and India'. *Indian Quarterly.* 37:3&4, July-December 1982.

Kundu, A. 'Civil-Military Relations in India: Why No Coup? *Asian Affairs.* 7:3, July-September 1985.

Kundu, A. 'Commissioned Indian Officers and the Indian National Armies of World War II'. *Defence Today.* 2:2, May 1994.

Kundu, A. 'Commissioned Indian Officers and the Independence Movement During the Interwar Years'. *Defence Today.* 2:1, February 1994.

Kundu, A. 'Operation Blue Star and Sikh and Non-Sikh Indian Military Officers'. *Pacific Affairs.* 67:1, Spring 1994.

Kundu, A. 'The Attitudes of Commissioned Indian Officers Towards Indira's Emergency Rule'. *Defence Today.* 4:2, April-June 1996.

Kundu, A. 'The Indian Army's Continued Dependence on Martial Races' Officers, *Indian Defence Review.* Summer 1991.

Lasswell, H.D. 'The Garrison State'. *American Journal of Sociology.* 46:4, January 1941.

Lin, C.C. 'The Sino-Soviet Rivalry on the Indian Subcontinent, 1960-1976'. *Asian Profile.* 9:5, October 1981.

Lissak, M. 'Center and Periphery in Developing Countries and Prototypes of Military Elites'. *Studies in Comparative International Development* 5:7, 1970.

Lissak, M. 'Modernization and Role Expansion of the Military in Developing Countries: A Comparative Analysis'. *Comparative Studies in Society and History.* 9:3, April 1967.

Lofchie, M.P. 'The Uganda Coup—Class Action by the Military'. *Journal of Modern African Studies.* 10:1, May 1972.

Luckham, A.R. 'A Comparative Typology of Civil-Military Relations'. *Government and Opposition.* 6:1, Winter 1971.

Mahmud, A. and S. Goldenberg. 'General defies political master: troops surround palace in Bangladesh capital'. *The Guardian.* 21 May 1996.

Makrig, D.A. 'War, No-War, and the India-Pakistan Negotiating Process'. *Pacific Affairs.* 60:2, Summer 1987.

Malik, Y.K. and S.M. Bhardwaj. 'Politics, Technology and Bureaucracies: An Overview'. *Journal of Asian and African Studies.* 17:1-2, 1982.

Martin, G. 'The Influence of Racial Attitude on British Policy Towards India during the First World War'. *Journal of Imperial and Commonwealth History.* 14:2, January 1986.

Maxwell, N. 'Towards India's Second China War?' *South.* May 1987.

McKinlay, R.D. and A.S. Cohan. 'A Comparative Analysis of the Political and Economic Performance of Military and Civilian Regimes: A Cross-National Aggregate Study'. *Comparative Politics.* 8:1, October 1975.

McKinlay, R.D. and A.S. Cohan. 'Performance and Instability in Military and Nonmilitary Regime Systems'. *American Political Science Review.* 70:3, September 1976.

Menon, R. and W.P.S. Sidhu. 'The Trust Breaks: Partisan police forces during the riots cause fear and exacerbate the divide'. *India Today,* 31 January 1993.

Moskos Jr., C.C. 'From Institution to Occupation Trends in Military Organization'. *Armed Forces and Society.* 4:1, November 1977.

N.a. 'Bangla army chief sacked, troops on alert'. *The Times of India.* 20 May 1996.

N.a. 'Battle of the Budgets'. *Gentleman.* April 1986.

N.a. 'Coup plotters aimed to hit Pak army chief too'. *Asian Age.* 15 November 1995.

N.a. 'Dicing with Democracy'. *The Economist.* 3 February 1990.

N.a. 'Ghana timetable for civilian rule'. *The Independent.* 7 March 1992.

N.a. 'Indian Navy Can't Match Pak'. *The Hindustan Times.* 31 August 1987.

N.a. 'London School's Survey Stirs Ire of Indian Left'. *The Washington Times Insight* section. 24 August 1987.

N.a. 'Officers for the Twenty-first Century'. *USI Journal.* Vol. 97, October-December 1966.

N.a. 'Pakistan: A troubled history'. *The Economist.* 23-39 November 1991.

N.a. 'Pakistan: The plot thickens'. *The Economist.* 21 October 1995.

N.a. 'Police Ministry suggested'. *The Tribune.* 18 August 1989.

N.a. 'Some Lessons from NEFA '62'. *Journal of the Institute for Defence Studies and Analyses.* March 1987.

N.a. 'The Indian Army: 1962 and After'. *Illustrated Weekly of India.* 91:3, 18 January 1970.

N.a. 'The Trouble at Singapore'. *India.* 26 February 1915.

N.a. 'Where Soldiering is Good Business'. *The Economist.* 3 September 1988.

Nagabhushan, Brigadier V. 'Waning Glamour of an Army Career'. *Indian Express.* 28 November 1985.

Needler, M.C. 'Political Development and Military Intervention in Latin America'. *American Political Science Review.* 60:3, September 1966.

Nehru, J. 'The Defence of India'. *Young India.* 1 October 1931.

Nordlinger, E.A. 'Soldiers in Mufti: The Impact of Military Rule Upon Economic and Social Change in the Non-Western States'. *American Political Science Review.* 64:4, December 1970.

Pendse, Major-General K.S. 'India's Defence Budget: A Case for Better Planning'. *Indian Defence Review.* July 1989.

Perlmutter, A. 'The Israeli Army in Politics: The Persistence of the Civilian Over the Military'. *World Politics.* 20:4, July 1968.

Perlmutter, A. 'The Praetorian State and the Praetorian Army: Toward a Taxonomy of Civil-Military Relations in Developing Politics'. *Comparative Politics.* 1:3, April 1969.

Price, R. 'A Theoretical Approach to Military Rule in New States: Reference Group Theory and the Ghanaian Case'. *World Politics*. 23:3, April 1971.

Proudfoot, C.L. 'The Indian Soldier: Cornerstone of Democracy'. *USI Journal*. Vol. 421, October-December 1970.

Putnam, R.D. 'Toward Explaining Military Intervention in Latin American Politics'. *World Politics*. 20:1, October 1967.

Rajurkar, N.G. 'The Partition of India in Perspective'. *Indian Journal of Politics and Sociology*. 43:2.

Rahman, M. 'A.S. Vaidya: The Killing of a General'. *India Today*. 31 August 1986.

Rahman, Major-General (Retd) M. K. 'How Army Law was Violated on May 18-20'. *The Daily Star*. 26 May 1996.

Rashid, M. 'Fundamental Problem: Islamic officers' coup plot shocks country'. *Far Eastern Economic Review*. 26 October 1995.

Rizvi, H. 'The Civilianization of Military Rule in Pakistan'. *Asian Survey*. 26:10, October 1986.

Rudolph, L.I. and S.H. Rudolph. 'Generals and Politicians in India'. *Pacific Affairs*. 38:1, Spring 1964.

Sadasivan, C. 'The Nehru-Menon Partnership'. *Roundtable*. Vol. 301, January 1987.

Sadasivan, S.N. 'Inequality in Indian Administration'. *Indian Political Science Review*. 25:1, January 1981.

Sahay, A.K. 'Supercessions Demoralise Armymen'. *The Times of India*. 24 August 1987.

Sandhu, K. 'The War Within: How does the Army see its Future?' *India Today*. 31 October 1992.

Sathyamurthy, T.V. 'Indian Nationalism and the "National Question"'. *Millennium*. 14:2, Summer 1985.

Sharp, A. 'The Indianisation of the Indian Army'. *History Today*. Vol. 36, March 1986.

Shukla, M.K. 'Blue-sky Naval Aspiration Expensive'. *The Hindustan Times*. 20 September 1987.

Sidhu, W.P.S. 'Quelling Sordid Affairs'. *India Today*. 31 October, 1990.

Sinha, Lt. Gen. S.K. 'Army and Politics in India'. *USI Journal*. 109:456, April-June 1979.

Sinha, Lt. Gen. S.K. 'Bofors and Army Morale'. *Indian Express*. 25 August 1987.

Sinha, Lt. Gen. S.K. 'Our Defence High Command'. *USI Journal*. Vol. 94, July 1964.

Sinha, V M. 'The Indian Administrative Service: A Comparative Review'. *Political Science Review*. 12:3-4, 1973.

Sodhi, Brigadier H.S. 'Punjab: The Trendsetter'. *India Today*. August 1993.

Tannahil, R.N. 'The Performance of Military and Civilian Governments in South America, 1948-1967'. *Journal of Political and Military Sociology*. Vol. 4, Fall 1976.

Tejpal, Tarun J. 'As long as the army is apolitical, it can hold its own': Lieutenant General S D Verma (retired) talks to Tarun J Tejpal'. *Indian Express* magazine section. 16 February 1986.

Tellis, A. 'Who Will Win the Next War ?' *Gentleman.* April 1986.

Terhal, P. 'Foreign Exchange Costs of the India Military, 1950-1972'. *Journal of Peace Research.* 19:3, 1982.

Thakur, R. 'Liberalism, Democracy, and Development: Philosophical Dilemmas in Third World Politics'. *Political Studies.* 33:3, September 1982.

Thomas, R.G.C. 'The Armed Services and the Indian Defence Budget'. *Asian Survey.* 20:3, 1980.

Thompson, W.R. 'Regime Vulnerability and the Military Coup'. *Comparative Politics.* 7:4, July 1975.

Tinker, H. 'The Contraction of Empire in Asia, 1945-48: The Military Dimension'. *Journal of Imperial and Commonwealth History.* 16:2, January 1988.

Toba, R. 'In Search of Stability on the Indian Subcontinent'. *Asia Pacific Community.* Vol. 28, Spring 1985.

Vanaik, A. 'The Pros'. *Asiaweek.* 18 August 1978.

Venkataraman, R. 'Krishna Menon: Architect of India's Defence Modernization'. *Link.* 34:42, 31 May 1992.

Verma, A.N. 'Shortcomings in the Staff Officers of Today: Their Causes and Remedial Measures'. *USI Journal.* 109:455, January-March 1979.

Vertzberger, Y. 'India's Strategic Posture and the Border War Defeat of 1962: A Case Study in Miscalculation'. *Journal of Strategic Studies.* 5:3, September 1982.

Welch, Jr., C.E. 'Civil-Military Relations: Perspectives From the Third World'. *Armed Forces and Society.* 11:2, Winter 1985.

Welch, Jr., C.E. 'Long Term Consequences of Military Rule: Breakdown and Extrication'. *Journal of Strategic Studies.* 1:2, September 1978.

Willner, R.A. 'Perspectives on Military Elites as Rulers and Wielders of Power'. *Journal of Comparative Administration.* 2:3, November 1970.

Wolpin, M. 'Marx and Radical Militarism in the Developing Nations'. *Armed Forces and Society.* 4:2, February 1978.

Wolpin, M. 'Sociopolitical Radicalism and Military Professionalism in the Third World'. *Comparative Studies.* 15:2, January 1983.

Zagorski, P.W. 'Civil-Military Relations and Argentine Democracy'. *Armed Forces and Society.* 14:3, Spring 1988.

Zaman, R. 'Dhaka alert amid coup rumours'. *The Times of India.* 21 May 1996.

Zinkin, T. 'Notes and Comment: India and Military Dictatorship'. *Pacific Affairs.* 32:1, March 1959.

Zolberg, A. 'The Military Decade in Africa'. *World Politics.* 25:2, January 1973.

Zolberg, A. 'The Structure of Political Conflict in the New States of Tropical Africa'. *American Political Science Review.* 62:1, 1968.

Books

Abrahamsson, B. *Military Professionalization and Political Power.* Beverly Hills: Sage Publications, 1972.

Adelman, I. and C.T. Morris. *Society, Politics and Economic Development: A Quantitative Approach.* Baltimore: The Johns Hopkins Press, 1967.

Afrifa, A.A. *The Ghana Coup: 24th February 1966.* London: Frank Cass & Co. Ltd., 1966.

Ahmad, Borhanuddin. *The Generals of Pakistan and Bangladesh.* New Delhi: Vikas Publishing House Pvt. Ltd., 1993.

Akbar, M.J. *Nehru: The Making of India.* London: Viking, 1988.

Ali, T. *The Nehrus and the Gandhis: An Indian Dynasty.* London: Picador published by Pan Books in association with Chatto and Windus, 1985.

Ashton, S.R. *British Policy Towards the Indian States, 1905-1939.* London: Curzon Press, 1982.

Baig, M.R.A. *In Different Saddles.* Bombay: Asia Publishing House, 1967.

Bhagat, Lt. Gen. P.S. *The Shield and the Sword.* 2nd ed., 1974. First published New Delhi: Vikas Publishing House, 1966.

Bhagat, Lt. Gen. P.S. *Wielding of Authority in Emerging Countries.* New Delhi: Lancer international, 1986.

Bhushan, P. *The Case that Shook India.* Pbk. New Delhi: Bell Books, 1978.

Bidwell, S. *Swords for Hire: European Mercenaries in Eighteenth-Century India.* London: Shelford Bidwell, 1971.

Bienen, H., ed. *The Military Intervenes: Case Studies in Political Development.* New York: The Russell Sage Foundation, 1968.

Blomfield-Smith, D., comp. *Fourth Indian Reflections: Memoirs of a Great Company.* Privately published by Brigadier D.C. Blomfield-Smith, 1987.

Bonarjee, N.B. *Under Two Masters.* London: Oxford University Press, 1970.

Bose, M. *The Lost Hero: A Biography of Subhas Bose.* Pbk. ed. First published London: Quartet Books, 1982.

Bose, S.C. *An Indian Pilgrim.* Bombay: Asia Publishing House, 1965.

Bowles, C. *Ambassador's Report.* New York: Harper & Brothers, 1954.

Brecher, M. *Nehru: A Political Biography.* London: Oxford University Press, 1959.

Brown, J.M. *Modern India: The Origins of an Asian Democracy.* Pbk. ed., 1988. First published Oxford: Oxford University Press, 1985.

Chaturvedi, Air Marshal M.S. *History of the Indian Air Force.* New Delhi: Vikas Publishing House Pvt. Ltd., 1978.

Chaudhuri, General J.N. *Arms Aims and Aspects.* Bombay: Manaktalas, 1966.

Chaudhuri, General J.N. *General J.N. Chaudhuri: An Autobiography.* As narrated to B.K. Narayan. New Delhi: Vikas Publishing House, 1978.

Chibber, Lieut.-General Dr. M.L. *Military Leadership to Prevent Military Coup.* New Delhi: Lancer International, 1986.

Chibber, Lieut.-General Dr. M.L. *Soldier's Role in National Integration (with Special Reference to Jammu & Kashmir)*. New Delhi: Lancer International, 1986.

Chopra, P.N., ed. *Towards Freedom 1937-47*. New Delhi: Indian Council of Historical Research, 1985.

Chopra, P. *Uncertain India: A Political Profile of Two Decades of Freedom*. Cambridge: The MIT Press, 1968.

Choudhury, G.W. *The Last Days of United Pakistan*. London: C. Hurst & Company, 1974.

Cohen, S. *The Indian Army: Its Contribution to the Development of a Nation*. Berkeley: University of California Press, 1971.

Cohen, S. *The Pakistan Army*. Berkeley: University of California Press, 1984.

Collins L. and D. Lapierre. *Freedom at Midnight*. London: Collins, 1975.

Connell, J. *Auchinlek: A Biography of Field-Marshal Sir Claude Auchinlek*. London: Cassell, 1959.

Conran, Major H. *Autobiography of an Indian Officer*. London: Morgan & Chase, 1871.

Corr, G.H. *The War of the Springing Tigers*. London: Osprey, 1975.

Daadler, H. *The Role of the Military in the Emerging Countries*. The Hague: Mouton & Co., 1962.

Dalvi, Brigadier J.P. *Himalayan Blunder*. Delhi: Hind Pocket Books Pvt. Ltd., n.d., in arrangement with Thacker & Company Ltd., Bombay.

Danopoulos, C.P., ed. *Military Disengagement from Politics*. London: Routledge, 1988.

Das, D. *India From Curzon to Nehru and After*. London: Collins, 1969.

Das, M.N. *The Political Philosophy of Jawaharlal Nehru*. London: George Allen & Unwin Ltd., 1961.

David, S.R. *Defending Third World Regimes from Coups d'État*. Lanham: University Press of America, 1985.

Davis, P. A. *Child at Arms*. London: Hutchinson & Co (Publishers) Ltd., 1970.

Davis, S.R. *Third World Coups d'État and International Security*. Baltimore: The Johns Hopkins University Press, 1987.

Decalo, S. *Coups and Army Rule in Africa: Studies in Military Style*. New Haven: Yale University Press, 1976.

Dutt, R.C. *Socialism of Jawaharlal Nehru*. New Delhi: Abhinar Publications, 1981.

Evans, H. *Thimayya of India*. Dehra Dun: Natraj Publishers, 1988. First published New York: Harcourt, Bruce & Co, 1960.

Edmonds, M. *Armed Services and Society*. Leicester: Leicester University Press, 1988.

Edwardes, M. *Nehru: A Political Biography*. London: Allen Lane The Penguin Press, 1971.

Farwell, B. *Armies of the Raj: From the Mutiny to Independence, 1858-1947*. New York: W.W. Norton & Company, 1990.

Fay, M.W. *The Forgotten Army: India's Armed Struggle for Independence 1942-1945*. Ann Arbor: University of Michigan, 1993.

Finer, S.E. *The Man on Horseback: The Role of the Military in Politics*. London: Pall Mall Press, 1962.

First, R. *The Barrel of a Gun: Political Power in Africa and the Coup d'État*. London: Allen Lane The Penguin Press, 1970.

Gaitonde, P.D. *The Liberation of Goa: A Participant's View of History*. London: C. Hurst & Company, 1987.

Galbraith, J.K. *Ambassador's Journal: An American View of India*. Pbk. ed. Bombay: Jaico Publishing House, 1972. Published by arrangement with Hamish Hamilton Ltd., London, 1969.

Gandhi, M.K. *Gandhi: An Autobiography: The Story of my Experiment with Truth*. Translated from the Gujarati by Mahadev Desai. London: Phoenix Press, 1949.

George, T.J.S. *Krishna Menon: A Biography*. London: Jonathan Cape, 1964.

Ghosh, K.K. *The Indian National Army: Second Front of the Indian Independence Movement*. Meerut: Meenakshi Prakashan, 1969.

Gopal, S. *Jawaharlal Nehru: A Biography: Volume I, 1889-1947*. Cambridge: Harvard University Press, 1976.

Gopal, S. *Jawaharlal Nehru: A Biography: Volume II, 1947-1956*. London: Cape, 1979.

Gopal, S. *Jawaharlal Nehru: A Biography: Volume III, 1956-1964*. Cambridge: Harvard University Press, 1984.

Gopal, S., ed. *Selected Works of Jawaharlal Nehru: Volume 1*. Second series. New Delhi: Jawaharlal Nehru Memorial Fund, 1984-.

Gopal, S., ed. *Selected Works of Jawaharlal Nehru: Volume 2*. Second series. New Delhi: Jawaharlal Nehru Memorial Fund, 1984-.

Gopal, S., ed. *Selected Works of Jawaharlal Nehru: Volume 3*. Second series. New Delhi: Jawaharlal Nehru Memorial Fund, 1984-.

Gopal, S., ed. *Selected Works of Jawaharlal Nehru: Volume 4*. Second series. New Delhi: Jawaharlal Nehru Memorial Fund, 1984-.

Gordon, L.A. *Brothers Against the Raj: A Biography of Indian Nationalists, Sarat and Subhas Chandra Bose*. New York: Columbia University Press, 1990.

Gutteridge, W. *Military Institutions and Power in the New States*. London: Pall Mall Press, 1964.

Halpern, M. *The Politics of Social Change in the Middle East and North Africa*. Princeton: Princeton University Press, 1963.

Hangen, W. *After Nehru, Who?* London: Rupert Hart-Davis, 1963.

Hardgrave Jr., R.L. *India Under Pressure: Prospects for Political Stability*. Boulder: Westview Press, 1984.

Hardgrave, Jr., R.L. and S.A. Kochanek, *India: Government and Politics in a Developing Nation*. Pbk. ed., fifth edition. Fort Worth: Harcourt Brace Jovanovich College Publishers, 1993.

Hastings, Commander D.J., ed. *'Bombay Buccaneers': Memories and Reminiscences of the Royal Indian Navy.* London: BASCA, 1986.

Hastings, Commander D.J. *The Royal Indian Navy, 1612-1950.* Jefferson: McFarland & Company, Inc. 1988.

Haswell, J. *The British Army: A Concise History.* London: Thames and Hudson, 1975.

Heathcote, T.A. *The Indian Army: The Garrison of British Imperial India 1822-1922.* Vancouver: David and Charles, 1974.

Heathcote, T.A. *The Military in British India: The Development of British Land Forces in South Asia, 1600-1947.* Manchester: Manchester University Press, 1995.

Henderson, M. *Experiment with Untruth: India Under Emergency.* Pbk. New Delhi: The Macmillan Company of India Limited, 1977.

Hoffmann, S.A. *India and the China Crisis.* Berkeley: University of California Press, 1990.

Horowitz, D. *Coup Theories and Officers' Motives: Sri Lanka in a Comparative Perspective.* Princeton: Princeton University Press, 1980.

Hough, R. *Mountbatten: Hero of Our Time.* London: Weidenfield & Nicolson, 1980.

Huntington, S. *Political Order in Changing Societies.* New Haven: Yale University Press, 1968.

Huntington, S. *The Soldier and the State: The Theory and Politics of Civil-Military Relations.* Cambridge: Harvard University Press, 1957.

Huntington, S., ed. *Changing Patterns of Military Politics.* New York: The Free Press of Glencoe, Inc., 1962.

Ingall, F. *The Last of the Bengal Lancers.* London: Leo Cooper, 1988.

Jacob, Lt. Gen. J.F.R. *Surrender at Dacca: Birth of a Nation.* New Delhi: Manohar, 1997.

Jalal, Ayesha. *Democracy and Authoritarianism in South Asia: A Comparative and Historical Perspective.* Pbk ed. Cambridge: Cambridge University Press, 1995.

Janowitz, M. *Military Conflict: Essays in the Institutional Analysis of War and Peace.* Beverly Hills: Sage Publications, 1975.

Janowitz, M. *The Military in the Political Development of New Nations: An Essay in Comparative Analysis.* Chicago: University of Chicago Press, 1964.

Janowitz, M., ed. *Civil-Military Relations: Regional Perspectives.* Beverly Hills: Sage Publications, 1981.

Janowitz, M., ed. *The New Military: Changing Patterns of Organization.* New York: Russell Sage Foundation, 1964.

Janowitz, M. and J. van Doorn, eds. *On Military Intervention.* Rotterdam: Rotterdam University Press, 1971.

Jeffery, R., ed. *People, Princes and Paramount Power: Society and Politics in the Indian Princely States.* Delhi: Oxford University Press, 1978.

Johnson, J.J., ed. *The Role of the Military in Underdeveloped Countries.* Princeton: Princeton University Press, 1962.

Johri, S.R. *Chinese Invasion of Ladakh.* Lucknow: Himalaya Publications, 1969.

Joshi, G.N. *The Constitution of India.* London: Macmillan & Co. Ltd., 1954.

Kadian, R. *India and its Army.* New Delhi: Vision Books, 1990.

Kapur, R.A. *Sikh Separatism: The Politics of Faith.* Pbk. ed. New Delhi: Vikas Publishing House Pvt Ltd, 1987. First published London: Allen & Unwin; n.d.

Katari, Admiral K.D. *A Sailor Remembers.* New Delhi: Vikas Publishing House Pvt. Ltd., 1982.

Kaul, Lt. General B.M. *The Untold Story.* Bombay: Allied Publishers, 1967.

Kaul, T.N. *Reminiscences Discreet and Indiscreet.* New Delhi: Lancers Publishers, 1982.

Kavic, L.J. *India's Quest for Security: Defence Policies, 1947-1965.* Berkeley: University of California Press, 1967.

Khan, M.A. *Friends Not Masters: A Political Autobiography.* London: Oxford University Press, 1967.

Khan, A.M. *Leader by Merit: A study of the career and character of Sardar Patel, as well as his ideas and ideals, including all his important speeches from 1921 to 1946.* Lahore: Indian Printing Works, 1946.

Khan, Lt. Gen. G.H. *Memoirs of Lt. Gen. Gul Hassan Khan (The Last Commander-in-Chief of the Pakistan Army).* Karachi: Oxford University Press, 1993.

Khanduri, Brig. C.B. *Field Marshal KM Cariappa: His Life and Times.* New Delhi: Lancers Publishers Pvt. Ltd., 1995.

Khera, S.S. *India's Defence Problem.* Bombay: Orient Longmans, 1968.

Kohli, A., *Democracy and Discontent: India's Growing Crisis of Governability.* Cambridge: Cambridge University Press, 1991.

Kohli, A., ed. *India's Democracy: An Analysis of Changing State-Society Relations.* Princeton: Princeton University Press, 1988.

Kukreja, V. *Civil-Military Relations in South Asia: Pakistan, Bangladesh and India.* New Delhi: Sage Publications, 1991.

Kumar, P. *Polluting Sacred Faith: A Study of Communalism and Violence in India.* New Delhi: Ajanta Books International, 1991.

Lakshmi, Y. *Trends in India's Defence Expenditure.* New Delhi: ABC Publishing House, 1988.

Lal, K. *Emergency: Its Needs and Gains*, Hittashi Publishers, 1976.

Lal, Air Chief Marshal P.C. *My Years with the IAF.* Ela Lal, ed. New Delhi: Lancer International, 1986.

Lang, K. *Military Institutions and the Sociology of War: A Review of the Literature with Annotated Bibliography.* Beverly Hills: Sage Publications, 1972.

Larus, J. *Culture and Political-Military Behaviour: The Hindus in Pre-Modern India.* Calcutta: Minerva Associates (Publications) Pvt. Ltd., 1979.

Lee, J.M. *African Armies and Civil Order*. New York: Praeger Press, 1969.

LeFever, E.W. *Spear and Sceptre: Army, Police, and Politics in Tropical Africa*. Washington, DC: The Brookings Institution, 1970.

Leys, C., ed. *Politics and Change in Developing Countries: Studies in the Theory and Practice of Development*. Cambridge: Cambridge University Press, 1969.

Lieuwen, E. *Arms and Politics in Latin America*. New York: Praeger, 1960.

Longer, V.I. *The Defence and Foreign Policies of India*. London: Oriental University Press, 1988.

Longer, V.I. *Red Coats to Olive Green: A History of the Indian Army 1600-1974*. Bombay: Allied Publishers, 1974.

Lowenthal, A.F., ed. *Armies and Politics in Latin America*. New York: Holmes and Meier, 1976.

Lunt, L., ed. *From Sepoy to Subedar: Being the Life and Adventures of Subedar Sita Ram, a Native Officer of the Bengal Army written and related by himself*. London: Routledge & Kegan Paul, 1970. Translated and first published by Lieutenant-Colonel Norgate, Lahore, 1873.

MacMunn, Lieut.-General Sir G. *The Indian States and Princes*. London: Jarrolds, 1936.

MacMunn, Lieut.-General Sir G. *Vignettes From Indian Wars*. London: Sampson Low, Marston & Co. Ltd., 1932.

MacMunn, Major G.F. *The Armies of India*. Bristol: Crecy Books, 1984. First published A & C Black, 1911.

MacMunn, Major G.F. *The Martial Races of India*. London: Sampson Low, Marston & Co., Ltd., 1933.

Majumdar, R.C. *The Sepoy Mutiny and the Revolt of 1857*. Calcutta: Firma K.L. Mukhopadhyay, 1963. First published 1957.

Martin, M.L. and E.S. McCrate, eds. *The Military, Militarism, and the Polity: Essays in Honour of Morris Janowitz*. New York: The Free Press, 1984.

Mankekar, D.R. & K. Mankekar, *Decline and Fall of Indira Gandhi: 19 Months of Emergency*. Pbk. New Delhi: Orient Paperbacks, 1977.

Mason, P. *A Matter of Honour: An Account of the Indian Army, Its Officers and Men*. Pbk. ed. London: Macmillan Publishers Limited, 1986. First published London: Jonathan Cape Limited, 1974.

Mason, P. *A Shaft of Sunlight: Memories of a Varied Life*. London: Andre Deutsch, 1978.

Mason, P. *The Men Who Ruled India*. London: Pan Books in association with Jonathan Cape Limited, 1985. First published in two volumes as *The Founders* (1953) and *The Guardians* (1954).

Masters, J. *Bugles and a Tiger*. London: Michael Joseph, 1956.

Masters, J. *The Road Past Mandalay*. London: Michael Joseph, 1961.

Maxwell, N. *India's China War*. New York: Pantheon Books, 1970.

Moon, P. *The British Conquest and Dominion of India*. London: Duckworth, 1989.

Moorhouse, G. *India Britannica*. Pbk. ed. London: Paladin Books, 1984. First published n.p.: Harvill Press, 1983.

Moraes, F. *Jawaharlal Nehru: A Biography*. New York: The Macmillan Company, 1956.

Mullik, B.N. *My Years with Nehru: Kashmir*. Bombay: Allied Publishers, 1971.

Mullik, B.N. *My Years with Nehru: 1948-1964*. Bombay: Allied Publishers, 1972.

Mullik, B.N. *My Years with Nehru: The Chinese Betrayal*. Bombay: Allied Publishers, 1971.

Musa, General M. *Jawan to General: Recollections of a Pakistani Soldier*. New Delhi: ABC Publishing House, 1985.

Muthanna, I.M. *General Cariappa: The First Indian Commander-in-Chief*. Mysore City: Usha Press, 1964.

N.a. *The Supercession: Spotlight on Lt. General S.K. Sinha*. Foreword by D.P. Singh. Patna: Parijat Prakashan, 1984.

Nanda, B.R., ed. *Indian Foreign Policy: The Nehru Years*. New Delhi: Sangam Books, 1990.

Navarone, V. *The Uniform and I (Reminiscences of an Army Wife)*. New Delhi: Army Educational Stores, n.d.

Nayar, K. *The Judgement: Inside Story of the Emergency in India*. Pbk. New Delhi: Bell Books, 1978.

Nayar, K. and K. Singh. *Tragedy of Punjab: Operation Bluestar & After*. Pbk. ed. New Delhi: Vision Books Pvt Ltd. incorporating Orient Paperbacks, 1984.

Nehru, J. *Jawaharlal Nehru: An Autobiography*. New Delhi: Oxford University Press, 1980. First published London: John Lane, The Bodley Head Ltd., 1936.

Nehru, J. *Toward Freedom*. Pbk. ed. Boston: Beacon Paperback, 1958.

Nkrumah, K. *Dark Days in Ghana*. London: Panaf, 1968.

Nordlinger, E.A. *Soldiers in Politics: Military Coups and Governments*. Englewood Cliffs, New Jersey: Prentice-Hall, 1977.

Ocran, A.K. *A Myth is Broken: An Account of the Ghana Coup d'État*. London: Longmans, Green and Co. Ltd., 1968.

Ocran, A.K. *Politics of the Sword: A Personal Memoir on Military Involvement in Ghana and of Problems of Military Government*. London: Rex Collings, 1977.

O'Kane, R.H.T. *The Likelihood of Coups*. Aldershot: Avebury, 1987.

Owen, F. *The Campaign for Burma*. New Delhi: The English Book Store, 1967.

Pal, D. *Traditions of the Indian Army*. 3rd ed., 1978. First published New Delhi: National Book Trust, 1961.

Palit, D.K. *War in High Himalaya: The Indian Army in Crisis, 1962*. London: C. Hurst, 1991.

Palmer, J.A.B. *The Mutiny Outbreak at Meerut in 1857*. Cambridge: at the University Press, 1966.

Palta, K.R. *My Adventures with the I.N.A.* Lahore: Lion Press, 1946.

Panikkar, K.M. *Problems of Indian Defence.* London: Asia Publishing House, 1960.

Percival, J. *For Valour: The Victoria Cross: Courage in Action.* London: Methuen London Ltd., 1985.

Perlmutter, A. *The Military and Politics in Modern Times.* New Haven: Yale University Press, 1977.

Perlmutter, A. and V.P. Bennet. *The Political Influence of the Military: A Comparative Reader.* New Haven: Yale University Press, 1980.

J.J.M. Pettigrew, *The Sikhs of the Punjab: Unheard Voices of State and Guerrilla Violence.* Pbk. ed. London: Zed Books, 1995.

Potter, D.C. *India's Political Administrators, 1919-1983.* Oxford: Clarendon, 1986.

Praval, K.C. *Indian Army After Independence.* New Delhi: Lancer International, 1987.

Ram, Moti, ed. *Two Historic Trials in Red Fort: An Authentic Account of the Trial of captain Shah Nawaz Khan, Captain P.K. Sahgal and Lt. G.S. Dhillon and the Trial by a European Military Commission of Emperor Bahadur Shah.* N.p.: Moti Ram, n.d.

Range, W. *Jawaharlal Nehru's World View: A Theory of International Relations.* Athens, Georgia: University of Georgia Press, 1961.

Reid, E. *Envoy to Nehru.* Delhi: Oxford University Press, 1981.

Rikhye, R. *The Militarization of Mother India.* New Delhi: Chanakya Publications, 1990.

Rikhye, R. *The War That Never Was.* Pbk. ed. New Delhi: PRISM India Paperbacks, 1989. First published New Delhi: Chanakya Publications, 1988.

Robinson, Francis, ed. *The Cambridge Encyclopedia of India, Pakistan, Bangladesh, Sri Lanka, Nepal, Bhutan and the Maldives.* Cambridge: Cambridge University Press, 1989.

Rosen, S.P. *Societies and Military Power: India and its Armies.* Ithaca: Cornell University Press, 1996.

Royle, T. *The Last Days of the Raj.* London: Michael Joseph, 1989.

Rudolph, S.H. and L.I. Rudolph. *Gandhi: The Traditional Roots of Charisma.* Pbk. ed., 1983. First published Chicago: University of Chicago Press, 1967.

Seervani, H.M. *Partition of India: Legend and Reality.* Bombay: Emmenem Publications, 1989.

Sen, Lt. Gen. L.P. *Slender was the Thread.* New Delhi: Sangam Books, 1973. First published Orient Longmans, 1969.

Sharma, V.D. *Through Two Systems: Encounters and Experiences of an I.A.S. Officer.* New Delhi: Associated Publishing House, 1982.

Sidhu, K.S. *The Role of Navy in India's Defence.* New Delhi: Harnam Publications, 1983.

Sikka, R.P. *The Civil Service in India: Europeanisation and Indianisation Under the East India Company—(1765-1865).* New Delhi: Uppal Publishing House, 1984.

Singh, Lt. General Harbakhsh. *War Dispatches: Indo-Pak Conflict 1965.* New Delhi: Lancer International, 1991.

Singh, Air Vice Marshal Harjinder. *Birth of An Air Force: The Memoirs of Air Vice Marshal Harjinder Singh.* Air Commodore A.L. Saigal, ed. New Delhi: Palit & Palit, 1977.

Singh, Major M.P. *Indian Army Under the East India Company.* New Delhi: Sterling Publishers Pvt. Ltd., 1976.

Singh, General Mohan. *Leaves From My Diary.* Lahore: Free-World Publications, 1946.

Singh, Brigadier Rajendra. *Soldier and Soldiering in India.* 3rd ed., 1964. New Delhi: Army Educational Stores, 1964.

Singh, Brigadier Sukhwant. *Three Decades of Indian Army Life.* Delhi: Sterling Publishers, 1967.

Sinha, Lt. Gen. S.K. *Of Matters Military.* New Delhi: Vision Books, 1980.

Sinha, Lt. Gen. S.K. *A Soldier Recalls.* New Delhi: Lancer International, 1992.

Sinha, Major-General S.K. *Operation Rescue: Military Operations in Jammu & Kashmir 1947-49.* New Delhi: Vision Books, 1977.

Sisson, R. and L.E. Rose. *War and Secession: Pakistan, India and the Creation of Bangladesh.* Berkeley: University of California Press, 1990.

Slim, Field-Marshal Sir W. *Unofficial History.* London: Cassell, 1959.

Smith, D.E. *Nehru and Democracy: The Political Thoughts of an Asian Diplomat.* Bombay: Orient Longmans, 1958.

Smyth, J. *Sandhurst The History of the Royal Military Academy, Woolwich, the Royal Military College, Sandhurst, and the Royal Military Academy, Sandhurst 1741-1961.* London: Weidenfeld, 1961.

Spear, P. *A History of India: Volume Two.* Pbk. ed., 1984. First published Harmondsworth: Penguin Books, 1965.

Stevens, Lieut.-Colonel G.R. *Fourth Indian Division.* Toronto: McLaren and Son Limited, n.d.

Subrahmanyam, K. *Indian Security Perspectives.* Rpt. ed., 1983. First published New Delhi: ABC Publishing House, 1982.

Tahmankar, D.V. *Sardar Patel.* London: Allen & Unwin, 1970.

TePaske, J. J. and S. N. Fisher, eds. *Explosive Forces in Latin America.* N.p.: Ohio State University Press, 1964.

Thapar, Lieut.-General D.R. *The Morale Builders: Forty Years with the Military Medical Services of India.* Bombay: Asia Publishing House, 1965.

Thapar, R. *A History of India: Volume One.* Pbk. ed., 1986. First published Harmondsworth: Penguin Books, 1966.

Thomas, Lt. Gen. M. T. and J. Mansingh. *Lt. Gen. P.S. Bhagat, PVSM, VC.* New Delhi: Lancer International, 1994.

Thompson, W.R. *The Grievances of Military Coup-Makers.* Beverly Hills: Sage Publications, 1973.

Thorat, Lieut.-General S.P.P. *From Reveille To Retreat.* New Delhi: Allied Publishers Private Limited, 1986.

Trench, C.C. *The Frontier Scouts.* Pbk. ed., 1986. First published Oxford: Oxford University Press, 1985.

Trench, C.C. *The Indian Army and the King's Enemies, 1900-1947.* London: Thames and Hudson, 1988.

Tuker, Lieut.-General Sir Francis. *While Memory Serves.* London: Cassell and Company, Ltd., 1950.

Tully, M. and Z. Mansani. *From Raj to Rajiv: 40 Years of Indian Independence.* 3rd Indian rpt., 1989. New Delhi: Universal Book Stall, 1988.

Tully, M. and S. Jacob, *Amritsar: Mrs. Gandhi's Last Battle.* Pbk. ed. Calcutta: Rupa & Co. by arrangement with Pan Books Ltd., London, 1985.

Van Doorn, J., ed. *Armed Forces and Society Sociological Essays.* The Hague: Mouton & Co. N.V., 1968.

Vas, Lt. Gen. E.A. *Fools and Infantrymen: One View of History (1923-1993).* Meerut: Kartikeya Publications, 1995.

Veliz, C., ed. *The Politics of Conformity in Latin America.* New York: Oxford University Press, 1967.

Verma, Lieut.-General S.D. *To Serve with Honour: My Memoirs.* Dehradun: Natraj Publishers, 1988.

Vira, D. *Memories of a Civil Servant.* Delhi: Vikas Publishing House Pvt. Ltd., 1975.

Welch Jr., C.E. *Soldier and State in Africa: A Comparative Analysis of Military Intervention and Political Change.* Evanston: Northwestern University Press, 1970.

Welch Jr., C.E., ed. *Civilian Control of the Military: Theory and Cases from Developing Countries.* Albany: State University of New York Press, 1976.

Welch Jr., C.E. and A.K. Smith. *Military Role and Rule: Perspectives on Civil-Military Relations.* North Scituate: Duxbury Press, 1974.

Woolacott, J.E. *India: The Truth.* London: Philip Allan & Co. Ltd., 1930.

Yardley, M. *Sandhurst: A Documentary.* London: Harrup, 1987.

Yeats-Brown, F. *Bengal Lancer.* Pbk. ed., 1984. First published London: Anthony Mott Limited, 1930.

Younger, P. *From Ashoka to Rajiv: An Analysis of Indian Political Culture.* Bombay: Popular Prakashan, 1987.

Ziegler, P. *Mountbatten.* Pbk. ed., 1986. First published New York: Perennial Library Harper & Row, 1985.

Internet Resources: Email Mailing Lists

Pakistan News Service <pakistan@netcom.com>
IndiaWorld Headlines <listserv@indiaworld.co>
Southern Asia Internet Forum <kkhoja@stimson.org>

Official Publications

Chand, Tara. *History of the Freedom Movement in India.* Government of India Ministry of Information and Broadcasting, 1961.

Council of Ministers 1947-1984: Names and Portfolios of the Members of the Union Council of Ministers. From August 15, 1947 to December 30, 1984). New Delhi: Lok Sabha Secretariat, 1985.

Demarcation of Responsibilities: Subjects for Which Different Ministries and Departments of Government in India are Responsible. New Delhi: Lok Sabha Secretariat, 1986.

Hutton, J.H. Census of India, 1931 Vol. I-India Part I-Report. Delhi: Manager of Publications, 1933.

India: A Reference Annual. Ed. and comp. by Government of India Ministry of Information and Broadcasting, n.d.

Padmanabha, P. *Census of India 1981: Series-1 India: Paper 1 of 1982: Final Population Tables.* Registrar General & Census Commissioner for India, n.d.

Sen, S.N. *Eighteen Fifty Seven.* Government of India Ministry of Information and Broadcasting, 1958.

The Military Year Book 1974-. Government of India Ministry of Information and Broadcasting, 1974-.

The Tiger Triumphs: The Story of Three Great Divisions in Italy. HMSO for the Government of India, 1946.

Venkateswaran, A.L. *Defence Organisation in India: A Study of Major Developments in Organisation and Administration since Independence.* Government of India Ministry of Information and Broadcasting, 1967.

Pamphlets

Chibber, Lt. Gen. M.L. *Leadership in the Indian Army During Eighties and Nineties.* USI Papers (Number Eight). New Delhi: United Services Institution of India, n.d.

Chibber, Lt. Gen. M.L. *Para Military Forces.* USI Papers (Number Four). New Delhi: United Services Institution of India, 1979.

Commonwealth War Graves Commission. *Commemoration of the War Dead of Undivided India.* Maidenhead, England: Commonwealth War Graves Commission, n.d.

Rao, P.V.R. *India's Defence Policy and Organisation Since Independence.* USI National Security Lectures. New Delhi: The United Services Institution of India, 1977.

Review of the Organisational Pattern of the Indian Army. USI Seminars (Number Seven). New Delhi: United Services Institution of India, n.d.

Rustomji, K.F. *Aid to Civil Authority.* USI Seminar (Number Twelve). New Delhi: United Service Institution of India, 1986.

Sinha, Lt. General S.K. *Higher Defence Organisation in India.* USI Papers (Number Seven). New Delhi: United Services Institution of India, 1980.

Periodicals

Baranwal, S.P. ed. and comp. *Military Yearbook.* New Delhi: Guide Publications, 1965-.

India and Pakistan Year Book Including Who's Who, 1948-1953. Bombay: The Times of India, 1948-1953.

India Who's Who. New Delhi: Infa Publications, 1969-.

Indian Year Book And Who's Who, 1931-1947. Bombay: The Times of India, 1931-1947.

Sarkar, S, ed. *Hindustan Year Book and Who's Who, 1992.* Calcutta: M.C. Sarkar & Sons Private Ltd., 1992

Singh, Jaswant, ed. and comp. *Indian Armed Forces Yearbook.* Bombay: n.p., 1964-.

The Times of India Directory and Year Book Including Who's Who, 1954-. Bombay: The Times of India, 1954-.

Unpublished Materials

Heathcote, T.A. 'A Nominal Roll of Indian Gentlemen Cadets Attending the Royal Military College at Sandhurst Between 1 January 1919 and 31 December 1927'; 'Seniority Roll of Indian Gentlemen Cadets Attending the Royal Military College at Sandhurst Between 1 January 1919 and 31 December 1927'; and 'Summary of India Gentlemen Cadets at the RMC Between January 1919 and December 1927'. Unpublished documents compiled from the *Registrar of Gentleman Cadets of the Royal Military College from 1919 to 1927* by the curator, the Royal Military Academy Sandhurst Collection, and sent to me in correspondence, 1990.

Lodhi, M. 'Bhutto, The Pakistan People's Party and Political Development in Pakistan, 1967-1977'. London School of Economics and Political Science PhD thesis, November 1980.

Omissi, D. 'The Sepoy and the Raj: The Indian Army 1860-1940'. Manuscript. Later published as *The Sepoy and the Raj: The Indian Army 1860-1940.* Basingstoke: Macmillan Press in association with King's College, 1994.

INDEX